PENGUIN BOOKS

A VOICE FROM THE ATTIC

Robertson Davies has written more than two dozen books, among which are the celebrated novels that make up "The Deptford Trilogy": *Fifth Business*, *The Manticore*, and *World of Wonders*.

Mr. Davies was born in 1913 in Ontario and was educated in Canada and at Oxford. A much-produced playwright in Canada, he once studied acting at the Old Vic, where he was Sir Tyrone Guthrie's literary assistant and where he met his wife, Brenda. He was for twenty years the editor of the *Peterborough Examiner*, during which time he wrote a number of novels and books of criticism, and also served as the principal book reviewer for the *Weekly Saturday Night*.

Mr. Davies and his wife now divide their time between homes in Toronto (where he was a professor and Master of Massey College at the University of Toronto until his retirement in 1981) and in Caledon, Ontario.

ROBERTSON DAVIES

A Voice from the Attic

Essays on the Art of Reading

Revised Edition

PENGUIN BOOKS

PENGUIN BOOKS
Published by the Penguin Group
Viking Penguin, a division of Penguin Books USA Inc.,
375 Hudson Street, New York, New York 10014, U.S.A.
Penguin Books Ltd, 27 Wrights Lane,
London W8 5TZ, England
Penguin Books Australia Ltd, Ringwood,
Victoria, Australia
Penguin Books Canada Ltd, 2801 John Street,
Markham, Ontario, Canada L3R 1B4
Penguin Books (N.Z.) Ltd, 182–190 Wairau Road,
Auckland 10, New Zealand

Penguin Books Ltd, Registered Offices:
Harmondsworth, Middlesex, England

First published in the United States of America by Alfred A. Knopf, Inc., 1960
Published with a new preface in a Viking Compass Edition 1972
This revised edition published in Penguin Books 1990

1 3 5 7 9 10 8 6 4 2

An abridgment of Chapter I appeared originally as
"Battle Cry for Book Lovers" in *The Saturday Evening Post.*

LIBRARY OF CONGRESS CATALOGING IN PUBLICATION DATA
Davies, Robertson.
A voice from the attic/Robertson Davies.
p. cm.
ISBN 0 14 01.2081 5
1. Books—Reviews. 2. Books and reading. I. Title.
PR9199.3.D3V6 1990
028.1—dc20 90-6803

Printed in the United States of America
Set in Sabon

A book is a mirror. When a monkey looks in, no apostle can look out.

Georg Christoph Lichtenberg

Contents

II. *Enjoying and Enduring*, 38

III. *Ovid Is Not Their Master*, 73

IV. *From the Well of the Past*, 107

V. *Making the Best of Second Best*, 147

VI. *The Hue and Cry after a Good Laugh*, 190

VII. *In Pursuit of Pornography*, 240

VIII. *Spelunking on Parnassus*, 273

Preface

This book was first published in 1960 and reprinted in 1971; I do not think that much in it needs bringing up to date, excepting the comments on pornography. The past quarter century has seen a revolution in this sort of publishing, and writers now enjoy a freedom that would have roused the astonishment and envy of some of the greatest Victorians, and perhaps of Joyce and Lawrence. Whether the arts of the novel and the play have been correspondingly enlarged we cannot yet know, but it is plain that pornography as a genre in itself has entered on a new life. If I were to rewrite Chapter VII, I do not think I would strike anything out; rather, I should add some additional comment, but as I make no claim to being an expert in this realm, and write of pornography rather as an area for the collector than as a genre in itself, the reader will be just as well off without any extension of my opinions. There are references, also, to writers who were *avant-garde* when the book was written and who are so no longer, though I do not think their work has lost much in value for that reason. Books of the *avant-garde* either establish themselves as books of lasting value, or they slip from the rear guard into the discard, and I believe the writers I mentioned have not proven trivial. This is, after all, a book about reading, and the kind of reader I am addressing does not care primarily about being in fashion.

ROBERTSON DAVIES

A VOICE FROM THE ATTIC

Prologue

A voice, certainly—any book is a voice—but why from the Attic?

In this book I want to comment and digress on some aspects of the world of books today, by no means always seriously and certainly not with any desire to impose my taste on anyone; rather, I expose my taste hoping that it may provide diversion for the reader. I do this as one who, for twenty years, reviewed books for a living (or part of a living, for I never found that it provided a whole one) and as one who has given hard knocks as a reviewer and taken them as an author. Because I am a Canadian, my outlook may possess some novelty for readers in the United States, for my country sees not only the greater part of the books produced in yours, but those published in Great Britain as well—not to speak of our own books. Canada is, I believe, the only country so blessed.

Statesmen are fond of stressing Canada's role as a mediator between the United States and Great Britain. Sometimes for us in Canada it seems as though the United States and the United Kingdom were cup and saucer, and Canada the spoon, for we are in and out of both with the greatest freedom, and we are given most recognition when we are most a nuisance. If, in these reflections, I seem not to be committed to either side, it is because I am a Canadian, and of Canada one of our poets, Patrick Anderson, has said:

> . . . I am one and none, pin and pine, snow and slow,
> America's attic . . .

—and that is why this is A Voice from the Attic.

·I·

A Call to the Clerisy

Layman is a word which has gained a new and disquieting currency in our language. For much of the five hundred years or so that it has been in use it meant simply one who worshipped, as opposed to a priest, who had knowledge of the sacred mysteries. Then, by extension, it came to mean the client or the patient, in his relation to the lawyer and the physician. But nowadays the word is used loosely for anybody who does not happen to know something, however trivial, which somebody else knows, or thinks he knows. The meat-eater is a layman to the butcher, and the seeker for illumination is a layman to the candlestickmaker. Most reprehensibly, the word is used among people who should meet as equals in education and general knowledge, within wide bounds. The layman is the nonexpert, the outsider; the implication is still that the layman's opposite has not merely special knowledge, but a secret and priestlike vocation.

It is particularly displeasing to hear professional critics using the term "layman" to describe people who are amateurs and patrons of those arts with which they are themselves professionally concerned. The fact that the critic gets money for knowing something, and giving public expression to his opinion, does not entitle him to consider the amateur, who may be as well informed and as sensitive as himself, an outsider. Admitting that there are triflers hanging to the skirts of the arts it is generally true that we are all, critics and amateurs alike, members of a group which meets on a reasonably equal footing. The critics have their special tastes and firm opinions and are, in some cases, more experienced and sensitive than any but the most devoted of amateurs. But they should never assume that it is so; they, of all people, should know the humility which art imposes and avoid the harlotry of a cheap professionalism.

That is why I address this book, which is about reading and writing, to the clerisy, knowing that many in that large body will be my superiors, but not, for that reason, contemptuous of me, any more than I presume to dismiss those who are not so widely read, or so particular in their tastes, as I am.

Defining the Clerisy

WHO ARE THE CLERISY? They are people who like to read books.

Are they trained in universities? Not necessarily so, for the day has long passed when a university degree was a guarantee of experience in the humanities, or of literacy beyond its barest meaning of being able, after a fashion, to read and write.

Are the clerisy critics and scholars, professionally engaged in judging the merit of books? By no means, for there are critics and scholars who are untouched by books, except as raw material for their own purposes.

Then does the clerisy mean all of the great body of people

who read? No; the name can only be applied with justice to those within that body who read for pleasure and with some pretension to taste.

The use of a word so unusual, so out of fashion, can only be excused on the ground that it has no familiar synonym. The word is little known because what it describes has disappeared, though I do not believe that it has gone forever. The clerisy are those who read for pleasure, but not for idleness; who read for pastime but not to kill time; who love books, but do not live by books. As lately as a century ago the clerisy had the power to decide the success or failure of a book, and it could do so now. But the clerisy has been persuaded to abdicate its power by several groups, not themselves malign or consciously unfriendly to literature, which are part of the social and business organization of our time. These groups, though entrenched, are not impregnable; if the clerisy would arouse itself, it could regain its sovereignty in the world of letters. For it is to the clerisy, even yet, that the authors, the publishers, and the booksellers make their principal appeal.

Has this group any sense of unity? It had, once, and this book is written in the hope that it may regain it. This is a call to the clerisy to wake up and assert itself.

Reading a Private Art

Let me repeat, this is a call, not a roar; it is an attempt to arouse the clerisy, but not to incite it to violence or rancorous controversy. Anything of the sort would be bound to fail, for by its very nature the clerisy is not susceptible of such appeals. Moral causes, good and bad, may shout in the ears of men; aesthetic causes have lost the fight as soon as they begin to be strident. Reading is my theme, and reading is a private, interpretative art. Let us have no printed shrieks about reading.

In 1944 a book by B. H. Haggin was published, called *Music for the Man Who Enjoys Hamlet*; some parts at least of this book might be called *Reading for the Man Who Enjoys Music,* for I want to write about the actual business of reading—the interpretative act of getting the words off the page and into your head in the most effective way. It is not the quickest way of reading, and for those who think that speed is the greatest good, there are plenty of manuals on how to read a book which profess to tell how to strip off the husk and guzzle the milk, like a chimp attacking a coconut. There are remedial reading courses for adults who are dissatisfied with their speed, which show you how to snatch up clumps of words with your eyes, and how to bolt paragraphs at a glance, so that a determined zealot can flip through *War and Peace* in five hours, and, like a boa constrictor, gobble up all Plato in a week. But if you read for pleasure, such gormandizing will not appeal to you. What musician would hastily scan the pages of a sonata, and say that he had experienced it? If he did so, he would be laughed at by the others. Who among the clerisy would whisk through a poem, eyes a-flicker, and say that he had read it?

The answer to that last question must unfortunately be: far too many. For reading is not respected as the art it is.

Reading and Time

Perhaps it would be more just to say that most people, the clerisy included, are impatient of any pace of reading except their fastest, and have small faith in their interpretative powers. They do not think of themselves as artists. But unless they make some effort to match their interpretative powers to the quality of what they would read, they are abusing their faculty of appreciation. And if they do not mean to make the most of their faculty of appreciation, why are they reading? To kill time? But it is not time they are killing; it is themselves.

What is time? Let the philosophers and the physicists say what they will, time for most of us is the fleeting instant we call Now. Any enjoyment or profit we get from life, we get Now; to kill Now is to abridge our own lives.

Yet how many people there are who read as though some prize awaited them when they turned the last page! They do not wish to *read* a book; they want *to have read* it—no matter how. The prize they seek is to have done with the book in hand. And so, as they read, they are always straining forward toward the goal of completion. Is it astonishing that they experience so little on the way, and that while they may be "great readers" quantitatively they are wretchedly poor readers qualitatively, and that they reveal by the poverty of their minds how ill-read they truly are?

Ends and Means

DOUBTLESS there are philosophical terms for this attitude of mind, of which hasty reading is one manifestation, but here let us call it "end-gaining," for such people put *ends* before *means;* they value, not reading, but having read. In this, as in so many things, the end-gainers make mischief and spoil all they do; end-gaining is one of the curses of our nervously tense, intellectually flabby civilization. In reading, as in all arts, it is the means, and not the end, which gives delight and brings the true reward. We laugh at tourists who dash through the Uffizi, to say that they have "done" it; we know that if they have any serious feeling for pictures, fifteen minutes with one masterpiece would far outweigh the pleasure of such dashes. But do we not dash through books, to say that we have "done" them?

The Decorums of Stupidity

NOT ALL RAPID READING is to be condemned. Much that is badly written and grossly padded must be read rapidly and nothing is lost thereby. Much of the reading that has to be done in the way of business should be done as fast as it can be understood. The ideal business document is an auditor's report; a good one is finely edited. But the memoranda, the public-relations pieces, the business magazines, need not detain us. Every kind of prose has its own speed, and the experienced reader knows it as a musician knows Adagio from Allegro. All of us have to read a great deal of stuff which gives us no pleasure and little information, but which we cannot wholly neglect; such reading belongs in that department of life which Goldsmith called "the decorums of stupidity." Books as works of art are no part of this duty-reading.

Books as works of art? Certainly; it is thus that their writers intend them. But how are these works of art used?

Suppose you hear of a piece of recorded music which you think you might like. Let us say it is an opera of Benjamin Britten's—*The Turn of the Screw*. You buy it, and after dinner you put it on your record player. The scene is one of bustling domesticity: your wife is writing to her mother, on the typewriter, and from time to time she appeals to you for the spelling of a word; the older children are chattering happily over a game, and the baby is building, and toppling, towers of blocks. The records are long-playing ones, designed for 33 revolutions of the turntable per minute; ah, but you have taken a course in rapid listening, and you pride yourself on the speed with which you can hear, so you adjust your machine to play at 78 revolutions a minute. And when you find your attention wandering from the music, you skip the sound arm rapidly from groove to groove until you come to a bit that appeals to you. But look—it is eight o'clock, and if you are to get to your meeting on time, Britten must be choked off. So you speed him up until a musical pause arrives, and then you stop the machine, marking the place so that you can continue your appreciation of *The Turn of the Screw* when next you can spare a few minutes for it.

Ridiculous? Of course, but can you say that you have never read a book in that fashion?

One of the advantages of reading is that it can be done in short spurts and under imperfect conditions. But how often do we read in conditions which are merely decent, not to speak of perfection? How often do we give a book a fair chance to make its effect with us?

Fiction and Feeling

Some magazine editors say the public no longer enjoys fiction; it demands "informative" articles. But informative writing requires less effort to assimilate than does fiction, because good fiction asks the reader to feel. There is no reason to suppose that people today feel less than their grandfathers, but there is good reason to think that they are less able to read in a way which makes them feel. It is natural for them to blame books rather than themselves, and to demand fiction which is highly peppered, like a glutton whose palate is defective.

The clerisy at least want to feel. They have reached that point of maturity where they know that thought and reason, unless matched by feeling, are empty, delusive things. Foolish people laugh at those readers a century ago who wept over the novels of Dickens. Is it a sign of superior intellect to read anything and everything unmoved, in a gray, unfeeling Limbo? Happy Victorians! Perhaps their tears flowed too readily. But some of Dickens's critics—by no means men of trivial intellect—wept. If this should meet the eye of any modern critic, let me ask: When did you last weep over a book? When did you last give a book a fair chance to make you do so?

Feeling is a condition of appreciation, and there can never have been a time when people were so anxious as they now are to have emotional experiences, or sought them so consciously. On the North American continent today sensual experience is frankly acknowledged as one of the good things of life. The popularity of "mood music" shows how eagerly we seek to deepen the quality of our experience. Any shop which sells phonograph records can supply long-playing discs and tapes to accompany a dozen activities with supposedly appropriate music. There is even one called, simply, *Music For——*, and the picture on the envelope—of female bare feet, toes upward, bracketing a pair of male bare feet, toes downward—makes plain *what* it is music for. Everywhere there is evidence of this anxiety that no shade of sensual enjoyment should be missed; the emphasis, indeed, is on nursing sensual enjoyment to its uttermost power, and advertising of all sorts reveals it. Do great numbers of people feel that they are missing some of the joy of life? Who can doubt it?

Like all anxiety, this is end-gaining, and carries the seeds of its own failure. Not ends, but means must be the concern of those who seek satisfaction in the pleasures as well as the obligations of life.

The Means of Reading

As this is a book about reading, let us consider the means of satisfactory reading. If we look after the means, we may be confident that the ends will take care of themselves.

It is a truism that we shall find nothing in books which has no existence in ourselves.

> Bookes give not wisdom where none was before,
> But where some is, there reading makes it more

says Sir John Harington, Elizabethan epigrammatist (and, blessed be his name, the inventor of the water closet); what is true of wisdom is true also of feeling. We all have slumbering realms of sensibility which can be coaxed into wakefulness by books. Aldous Huxley tells us that "writers influence their readers, preachers their auditors, but always, at bottom, to be more themselves." But do they know what they themselves are? Is not that what they are reading books to find out?

The best of novels are only scenarios, to be completed by the reader's own experience. They do not give us feeling: they draw out such feeling as we have. If fiction is going out of fashion (which is said from time to time but which I do not believe), it is not because fiction is any worse than it was; apart from the pepper and curry fiction already referred to, the general level of it is probably better. But great numbers of people find fault with fiction because they do not give themselves a chance to respond to it.

It is the way they read which is at fault. The great success of Emlyn Williams in reading Dickens and Dylan Thomas to large audiences showed us where the trouble lies. I have seen

Mr. Williams hold a large audience spellbound as he read, in two and a half hours, an abridgment of Dickens's *Bleak House*. He had their undivided attention, and he read with all the resources of a consummate actor. He and his hearers were, for the evening, giving the best of themselves to *Bleak House;* his audience was moved to curiosity, to laughter, to horror, to tears, as audiences are not often moved by plays.

Sir John Gielgud moves audiences similarly by reading Shakespeare. Thomas's *Under Milk Wood* comes to life on phonograph records, and the catalogues of the large recording companies contain many examples of recorded plays and excerpts from books. Ah, you may say, but those are performances by actors. Yes, and if you want the best from reading, you must learn to give the best performances of which you are capable, sitting soundless in your chair, with your book before you. The gifts demanded of a good reader are less those of the critic than of the actor. You must bestir yourself, and above all you must cultivate the inward ear.

An Age of the Eye

WE LIVE IN an age when the eye is feasted and the ear, if not starved, is kept on short rations. Special merit is accorded to the cartoon which makes its effect without a caption. In the theater we expect a higher standard of scenic design, aided by elaborate lighting, than playgoers have ever known. It is not uncommon for a stage setting, at the rise of the curtain, to be greeted with a round of applause. But how long is it since you heard an actor applauded because he had delivered a fine speech particularly well? This calls attention to our comparative indifference to fine speech; it is not altogether lacking, but we do not insist upon it as we insist on the gratification of the eye. But how do the books you read reach your consciousness? By words you hear, or pictures you see?

Unless you have a visualizing type of mind, by words. And how do those words reach you?

Teachers of rapid reading are opposed to an inward vocalizing of the words read, and some of them write about it with the asperity of a Puritan divine condemning lace ruffles. But so far as I can find out, they oppose it only because it decreases reading speed. They say it adds nothing to understanding. That may be, but we are concerned here with something more subtle than simple understanding: we are talking about reading for pleasure, for emotional and intellectual extension, for the exercise of the sensibilities. For these things, some measure of vocalizing is indispensable.

In the Middle Ages readers spoke aloud the words they read, and a temporary hoarseness or loss of voice was a sufficient reason for a scholar to suspend his studies. In monasteries it was the custom for someone to read aloud during meals, and this practice persists in many religious houses. In universities a principal means of instruction was the lecture—literally "a reading aloud"—in which the master read to the undergraduates from a work of his own composition: the custom persists still, though many lectures are, in effect, speeches and exhibitions of personality—not necessarily the worse for that. Holy Writ was read aloud in churches, and a point which was greatly emphasized during the Reformation was that it should be read in a language known to all the hearers and not only to the clerisy. The reason for all this vocalizing of what was read was that it might strike inward not only through the eye but through the ear; even the most learned did not trust to the eye alone, simply because they could read. "It is voicing things that makes them real," said Miss Ivy Compton-Burnett; it is a psychological truth neglected in our day.

Neglected by readers, but not therefore unknown. Television advertisers do not scorn the medieval aids of repetition and rhyme, assonance and rhythm, in selling their goods. Whatever the content of their compositions, their techniques derive from the anonymous composer of *Beowulf,* the unknown makers of folk song, and the originators of such mnemonics as:

> Thirty days hath September
> April, June and November.

Our emphasis on the eye as the high road to the intellect is a new thing, and we all use our ears readily when we are asked to do so. Even when we do not desire it (as with advertising jingles), what enters our consciousness through the ear is likely to stick.

The Inward Voice

CERTAINLY it is not my purpose to suggest that we should return to all this reading aloud, creating in every library a hubbub like that which one hears when walking through the corridors of a conservatory of music. But are we not foolish to give up that inward voice in which books can speak to us? And in the pursuit of speed, of all things! What has speed to do with literary appreciation? Speed, unless some real, defensible good is achieved by it, is nothing but end-gaining, which is the death of all enjoyment of the arts. Not *ends,* but *means* bring delight and fulfillment to the reader, and his means of reading is listening to the inward, reading voice.

What is that voice like? Its quality depends on your ear. If you have a good ear and some talent for mimicry, you can read to yourself in any voice, or as many voices as you please. You have seen Sir Laurence Olivier's film of *Richard III?*

Very well, can you hear him again when you read the play? If you can, and if you are a playgoer and a filmgoer, you should be able to find voices for all the characters in the books you read. James Agate, the English theater critic, amused himself by casting the novels of Dickens, in which he delighted, with the actors whom it was his professional duty to watch; his favorite Mr. Dombey was Sir John Gielgud.

This is a game, and a very good game, but it asks for a good ear, and makes heavy imaginative demands upon the reader. You may not be able to play it; perhaps you have no desire to do so; it is not for all temperaments. Your taste may be more austere. Besides, it only works with novels and plays. What about reading history or poetry?

The inner voice is of your own choosing, of your own development. It may differ greatly from the voice in which you speak. To read Trollope in the tones of Kansas, or Joyce in the cadences of Alabama, is as barbarous as to read *Huck Finn* with a Yorkshire accent, or Edith Wharton in the voice of Glasgow. One of the most dismaying experiences of my college days was to hear the whole of *Hamlet* read by a professor whose voice was strongly nasal, and whose vocal range was well within one octave. Did he, I wondered, read to himself in that voice? Or did he hear, inside himself, a full, rich, copious, nobly modulated sound unlike the dispirited drone which came out of his mouth? There are, one presumes, utterly tone-deaf readers.

Authors As Readers

BUT WHAT DOES literature mean to them? Good writing sets its own tune, insists on its own cadence. Joyce presents a particularly interesting example. Nothing of his, and *Finnegans Wake* least of all, can be read comfortably except in the

Joycean mode. There exists a phonograph record which illustrates that mode, with Joyce himself reading, but thousands of readers have found it, or some part of it, without the record: the mode arises from the page.

The examples of authors are not always so happy. Recordings of another Irish author, Sean O'Casey, also exist; few could endure to hear a whole book in the O'Casey voice, as exemplified there. But Joyce, a singer, was also a great reader, and the musical allusions and echoes which abound in his work (so strangely missed by those of his critics who do not know the queer, second-rate nineteenth-century repertoire in which he delighted) give not only a special comic or sardonic flavor to it, but dictate the rhythms of some of his most expressive passages.

Talk of the rhythms of prose may alarm some readers who have trouble enough with the rhythms of poetry. But poetic rhythm is the rhythm of song, whereas prose rhythm is the rhythm of speech. Not always the speech of the streets or of conversation, but speech rising to nobility, to prophecy, to denunciation. It was Thomas Mann who contrasted the rhythms of verse with "the finer and much less obvious rhythmical laws of prose." Less obvious, but still to be captured by the attentive inward ear, and when so captured, to give a new and splendid dimension to the pleasure of reading.

To some of my readers it may seem that I am advising them to conjure up within themselves a host of dialect comedians, and that I want them to read with the embarrassing vehemence of old-fashioned elocutionists. Nothing could be farther from my intention, and I know that many readers are happiest with a low-keyed and antitheatrical approach to their pleasure. But I do urge them to approach reading in a less passive and more interpretative spirit.

Reader As Interpreter

INTERPRETATIVE, you will observe: not creative. The word "creative" is used now so carelessly that its real meaning is being rubbed away. The reader cannot create; that has been done for him by the author. The reader can only interpret, giving the author a fair chance to make his impression. As Lord David Cecil makes plain in his essay *The Fine Art of Reading*, the reader allows the writer to act upon him. "Every reader is a Lady of Shalott, who, secluded in his secret chamber, forgets the hours, as he sits watching the endless procession of human thought and passion and action, as it passes, motley and tumultuous, across the gleaming mirror of literature." This cannot be done if the reader, in his secret chamber, hears what he reads declaimed at the speed and in the tones of a tobacco auctioneer.

We would not dream of judging a piece of music which we heard performed on an untuned and neglected piano by a player not up to the work, long out of practice and ill-taught. But we treat a piece of literature, too often, in a comparable fashion. Good reading is the only test of good writing. Can you read this at high speed, without inward vocalizing, and make anything of it?

> Rest not in an Ovation, but a Triumph over thy Passions. Let Anger walk hanging down the head; Let Malice go Manicled, and Envy fetter'd after thee. Behold within thee the long train of thy Trophies not without thee. Make the quarreling Lapithytes sleep, and Centaurs within lye quiet. Chain up the unruly Legion of thy breast. Lead thine own captivity captive, and be *Caesar* within thyself.

You have no desire to read Sir Thomas Browne, and do not care what he has to say? Well, what about Mark Twain?

> It was a real bully circus. It was the splendidest sight that ever was when they all come riding in, two and two, and gentleman and lady, side by side, the men just in their drawers and undershirts, and no shoes nor stirrups, and resting their hands on their thighs easy and comfortable—there must 'a' been twenty of them—and every lady with a lovely complexion, and perfectly beautiful, and looking just like a gang of real sure-enough queens, and dressed in clothes that cost millions of dollars, and just littered with diamonds. It was a powerful fine sight; I never see anything so lovely. And then one by one they got up and stood, and went a-weaving around the ring so gentle and wavy and graceful, the men looking ever so tall and airy and straight, with their heads bobbing and skimming along, away up there under the tent-roof, and every lady's rose-leafy dress flapping soft and silky around her hips, and she looked like the most loveliest parasol.

A Critical Instrument

THE SECOND of these passages is undoubtedly easier than the first, but neither can be taken at a gallop. The difficult Browne yields his secret, and his exquisite savor, when his pace and tone have been discovered—so does Huck Finn. The reader who has cultivated his appreciation of pace and tone has at his command one of the most powerful of critical instruments, and he will not be content with "those hopelessly banal and enormous novels which are typed out by the thumbs of tense mediocrities and called 'powerful' and 'stark' by the reviewing hack"—to quote Vladimir Nabokov, a novelist himself remarkable for the individuality of his pace and tone. Attentive, appreciative reading quickly sorts good writing from bad; to the book-gobbler no such discrimination is possible, for he reads so quickly that he has no time in which to discover what is not worth reading.

This is not another evangelistic book, officiously seeking to insure the literary salvation of its readers by exhorting them to read nothing save "the best." The best, as every true reader knows, is not always what one wants; there are times when one does not feel equal to the demands of the best. Indeed, one may without shame confess that for the time being one is tired of the best. Very often one wants no more than "a good read," to shut out the world while those bruises heal which the world has given. But there are degrees in all things, and degree is vastly more important in those realms which are not quite first rate than on the level of "the best."

Critical Heresy

Nor is the exercise of judgment in reading to be confused with the attitude of the journalistic or academic critic. His special heresy is that his trade makes him an explainer, rather than an experiencer, of literature. In this heresy he is followed by many of those intellectuals who are not quite intellectual enough, and who would rather be modish than individual in their taste. All too often, to this type of mind, explaining a thing robs it of value. Having discovered what makes the clock go, it is no longer a matter of interest to them that the clock can tell time.

It is not necessary, in rejecting the critical-intellectual heresy, to rush to another extreme. Nobody can say nowadays, as Thomas à Kempis said in the fifteenth century: "Take thou a book into thine hands as Simon the Just took the child Jesus into his arms to carry Him and kiss Him. And when thou hast finished reading, close the book and give thanks for every word out of the mouth of God; because in the Lord's field thou hast found a hidden treasure." But a decent book is in some measure a work of art and deserves to be treated as one. The reader should submit himself to it until it shows itself worthy of further submission or of rejection. Readers should not be, as Yeats complained, "sciolists and opinionated bitches." They should read as, were they authors, they would wish to be read.

Thomas à Kempis wrote as he did because in his day printed books were rarities; most books were still copied by hand, and the production of a single volume was too great a labor to be undertaken except in the case of works of proven value. (The books he knew were likely to be works of edification, clothed in individual beauty, which ensured them of a regard not wholly dependent on an objective critical estimate of their contents.) The ability to read, also, was restricted to a clerkly minority. In our day books appear by the score, every day; there is no limit to the number of copies which can be made, and everybody can read them; the analphabet is a rarity in our time.

The Great Experiment

THIS UNCONTROLLED proliferation of books is one of the consequences of an astounding experiment which has been in progress in the English-speaking world for about a century and a quarter—nothing less than an attempt to create a complete literacy. The experiment was undertaken as part of the democratic-philanthropic enthusiasm which goes with modern idealism. There is plenty of evidence that the early advocates of the experiment supposed that if everybody *could* read, everybody *would* read, and would furthermore read the best books they could lay their hands on.

Most English-speaking people today can read and write. Great Britain asserts that inability to do so is negligible within her confines; in the United States the latest available figure shows a 2.7 illiteracy, and in Canada the figure is 3.79; in Australia it is 4.7, and in South Africa it is 2.34 among the white population. The illiterates are said to be among the older people, and presumably the time is in sight when illiteracy will have no statistical existence in the English-speaking world. But although they can read, millions of these heirs of eighteenth-century idealism do not read, and of those who read, there are great numbers whose choice of books would make the injunction of Thomas à Kempis (supposing they were to act upon it) a gross blasphemy.

Its Present State

We need not despair because so many people, having been taught—with what staggering cost in time and money, with what wholesale creation of teachers and building of schools! —to read, read nothing at all, or read trash. The experiment is perhaps the most revolutionary in the history of mankind, and far from being done, it is hardly begun. We have reached the point where English-speaking adults can all read, after a fashion; that is a cause for triumph. Only mad romantics can ever have expected them all to read in the same fashion.

There is no democracy in the world of intellect, and no democracy of taste. Great efforts have been made to pretend that this is not so, but they have failed. The spread of literacy has emphasized what was apparent before. Teach everybody to read, and they will read what appeals to them, what accords with their experience and ideal of life. Their wealth or poverty have little to do with the matter; the man of means who reads rubbish, and the poor man who exhausts the classics in his public library, are still among us. But in the latter throes of the great experiment the clerisy, as an entity to be reckoned with in the population, has disappeared. It is due for revival, because it is needed if the future stages of the great experiment are to go in the right direction.

The Clerisy As It Was

A CENTURY AND A HALF AGO the reading population was much smaller than it is today, and the clerisy was still a recognizable and important element in it. The education of the clerisy was on a plan which stressed study of the Greek and Latin classics almost to the exclusion of everything else; such an education was narrow in matter, but very wide in scope; it developed taste and encouraged independent thought in minds with any aptitude for such things. It had its ridiculous side, and it developed certain snobberies. Dickens's Dr. Blimber was one kind of Victorian schoolmaster, and Mr. Curdle, who defined the dramatic unities as "a kind of universal dove-tailedness with regard to place and time," typifies Dr. Blimber's duller pupils. But that classical culture—even on the Curdle level—gave a coherence to the reading public.

Classical culture was not the only one; there was a widespread Biblical culture also, and it was a powerful shaper of thought and expression. The Bible is a classical literature of history, poetry, drama, legend, and prophecy, which used to be reasonably familiar to all educated people in the great

King James version. What if it were not understood completely, as modern scholarship reckons completeness? What if it were uncritically reverenced? It was understood at least as well, and reverenced little more, than Homer or Virgil. And it is characteristic of classics that their influence is not dependent so much on critical understanding as on love and familiarity. The Biblical culture of the nineteenth century had its ridiculous side, as did the classical culture, but both provided touchstones of taste to which a writer could appeal, and which he could depend upon in his audience.

The last gasps of these cultures were to be heard within the experience of living North Americans. School reading books, sixty years ago, contained sinewy passages from Shakespeare, Ben Jonson ("It is not growing like a tree, In bulk, doth make man better be"), Sir Walter Scott, Addison (well do I recall grappling with *The Vision of Mirzah* at the age of eleven), Sheridan, R. L. Stevenson, Thomas Campbell (readers in the United States probably missed this poet of British military might, but Canadian children knew him well), and of course Emerson, Longfellow, Whittier, and their New England congeners. There was much rubbish in these "readers," too, but nineteenth-century standards still set the tone for them, and set it high.

But what sets the tone now? It is not my intention to denounce modern education. If it is bad, it may be said that all education is bad which is not self-education, and quite a lot of self-education is going on today—some of it in our schools, under the very noses of the teachers! The classical culture has shrunk so that it has no appreciable influence: the Biblical culture scarcely exists, and the writer or speaker who draws a parallel or a quotation from the Bible today will not be understood by any more people than if he made his allusion to something in Homer. Nothing has replaced this culture rooted in Greek, Latin, and Hebrew classics. The kind of education which could formerly be expected in the clerisy has gone, and it is not likely to return.

The Coherent Audience

THIS IS TRUE of the North American continent in a greater degree than it is true of England. Though great changes are at work in education there, the process is slower than it is with us. Geography has some part in preserving the high standard of literacy, and the coherence and self-consciousness of the clerisy, in the British Isles. Population is dense and the land area small; no educated man is far from someone else of much his own standard of education—a comfort so completely forgotten by hundreds of thousands of people in North America that it is hard to conceive what it must mean. The tradition of a clerisy still exists in Britain. In 1958 the distinguished novelist C. P. Snow, writing in the *New Statesman*, could say this:

> It is the variety of experience of the (English) audience that gives it its authority, and so strengthens the writer's confidence. For example, Mr. Macmillan, Mr. Butler, Mr. Gaitskell are all deeply read men, interested in contemporary work; so are a good sprinkling of other members of the House. That would also be true of a surprisingly high proportion of civil servants and miscellaneous administrative bosses.
>
> So our audience scatters itself through society, quite wide and quite deep. . . . In England, the society is so compact that we realize this is happening; we know, almost in a personal sense, whom we are writing for. An American writer can't; he feels much more lost. Do

American politicians, civil servants, school teachers read as ours do? If they do, the writers do not feel their response. That, I think, is the one great creative stimulus we have, which is denied to them.

The result is that on this continent "the writers don't really know whom they are writing for—apart from their fellow writing scholars."

Reviewers and Critics

THEIR fellow writing scholars—damnable tribe! Yet it is true that the place of the clerisy as the desired audience of the writer has been taken by critics and reviewers, whose power, without being absolute, is great, and whose influence on writing is pernicious.

Lambasting critics is easy but profitless entertainment. They exist in great numbers because books drop from the presses in great numbers, and some portion of this monstrous birth must be weighed and valued. Reading reviews is an accepted way of keeping up with what is happening in the world of books. Reviewers gain reputation less by the justness of their criticism than by their own ability to write well and entertainingly, and though this may sometimes cause hardship to authors, it is inevitable. Reviewers themselves live and work under special strain. If they praise much they appear to be simple fellows, too readily pleased, for it is a widespread belief that a truly critical mind exists in a constant state of high-toned irascibility. But blame always looks well. The eighteenth-century playwright knew his business who made his critic say:

> Panegyric and praise! And what will that do with the publick? Why who the devil will give money to be told that Mr. Such-a-one is a wiser or better man than himself? No, no; 'tis quite and clean out of nature. A good sousing satire, now, well powder'd with personal pepper, and season'd with the spirit of party; that demolishes a conspicuous character, and sinks him below our own level; there, there we are pleas'd; there we chuckle and grin and toss the half-crowns on the counter.

The reviewer who does not heed this popular view of his work may find himself reproached, as Arnold Bennett was in his last years, with discovering a new genius every week. The consequence is that reviewers often fall into a state of mind which can be summed up in the phrase "but on the other hand," doling out cautious praise tempered with cautious blame, proving their impartiality to author, publisher, and public alike. They have no time to be appreciators or experiencers. Like most of us, they are end-gainers, reading a book not for itself but as article-fodder, and their own neat phrases pop into their heads as they scan another man's prose. Most of them are too good-natured for sousing satire, well powder'd with personal pepper; most of them are too well balanced to shoot cannon at sparrows; but in most of them the razor edge of appreciation has been hacked and dulled by too much exercise on the firewood which is, inevitably, what comes to them in most abundance.

I am not clamoring for a revision of the reviewing system. I do not see how, under present conditions, it can be revised. I ask for a revival of the clerisy; the existence of a more intelligently self-conscious and literate group in the vast reading public would greatly ease and elevate the reviewers' task. The clerisy would also effectively review the reviewers.

Sciolists and Opinionated Bitches

BEYOND AND ABOVE the daily, weekly, and monthly reviewers lie the university critics, who concern themselves not with the daily black flux of the presses, but with trends, with niceties not understanded of the base, and with all that area of literature which Victorians called "Poesy and Buzzem"—though Buzzem has come to be much more like Brain, of a particularly juiceless and gritty sort.

Their productions are varied in nature and value. At best they are themselves contributions to literature, works which can be read with delight, because in them minds of one rare kind shed light upon minds of another rare kind. But in their second-best rank, books of this academic sort are, of all books, the easiest to write. They chew over what has already been well chewed; they grapple with other scholars, seeking to bear them down into the academic ooze; they explore the vast caverns of the creator's spirit with no illumination save the smoky and fitful rushlight of their own critical intelligence.

The great sin of English writing of this kind is that it feigns sensibility where sensibility plainly does not exist, and pretends (often with remarkable skill) to knowledge which it does not possess. How often we hear the hum (high and fine, like the voice of a gnat) of the "survey" in such writing. How easily come the judgments of these men and women who have not read whole libraries of books, but have "examined" (*i.e.*, leafed over) and read about them! Nobody can have read everything, but to pretend to have read what one has, at best, skimmed, is a nasty dishonesty.

The American fault in these academic works of the lesser sort is more often simple ignorance. The writer knows his subject, but he knows little else; he has no base of general cultivation on which his expert knowledge may rest. He may painstakingly bone up on the historical background of his literary quarry, but he never gets the *feel* of his period, except in the clumsiest and most obvious fashion. Not long ago an American scholar wrote a worthy but juiceless book about Goldsmith in which he set forth all that goodwill and dogged toil could assemble; but he knew so little of eighteenth-century England that he seemed baffled by the term "a pair of stairs." In eighteenth- and nineteenth-century England stairs came in pairs, like scissors and trousers; the "two-pair back" was the room at the rear, two flights up; and a "three-pair back," so often mentioned with shame as the abode of a ruined heroine or a distressed author, was directly below the servants' quarters. How can a man have any light to throw on Goldsmith who has so little of the feel of Goldsmith's age and Goldsmith's vocabulary? To these writers they are themselves the measure of all things, and with honesty and goodwill they reshape great men in their own image. They do not know enough to know that they lack humility.

The Doll's House

THOUGH THIS academic criticism is little read by people who are not themselves, in some way or another, of the literary world, it exerts a strong influence at second hand. It sets the style. It says which authors in the past are most worthy of the notice of the present, and while this is legitimate and necessary within reason, we sometimes feel like adults overhearing a quarrel among children as to which dolls are to have places in the doll's house. No, Tennyson is *not* to have a chair in the best room! His stuffing has been leaking out for years. And George Eliot is *too* ugly—though perhaps she need not still be hidden in the old dolls' box, where she has been for so long. Browning? With his horrid red face and loud, aggressive squeaker? Never! But the Dickens doll is back in favor, and seems to be made of better stuff than we supposed. And the Thackeray doll is tolerable once again. But if we are to keep the Virginia Woolf doll, we mustn't let the Arnold Bennett doll have any affection at all. Thus the doll game is played.

There is an endless rummaging in the doll box, for the need of the scholars for new or neglected material is unappeasable. But how badly the dolls wear! Of course the Shakespeare doll and the Johnson doll will stand up to any amount of rough play, but few of the others are really durable. A. E. Housman, for instance, once such a popular doll, was suddenly banished to the depths of the box, and when he was fished up recently, for another look, it was discovered that he had cherished a lifelong affection of an intense sort for his university friend Moses Jackson. And this, for reasons not wholly apparent to those not in the doll game, so invalidated his poetry that he has gone back into the box, perhaps forever. Yet other dolls with a similar idiosyncrasy, like the Wilde doll, are much cherished.

The scholar's doll game influences the literary world in some unexpected places. *The New Yorker*, in 1958, contained this:

> *Jane Eyre* was written in 1841 by a spinster whose sophistication was largely the product of the parsonage in which she grew up. Her book was a success (Thackeray could hardly restrain his enthusiasm for it), but by depraved modern standards it is not a very good novel.

It is not necessary in writing of this kind to explain why a doll must be refused a place in the doll's house, and must lie in the darkness of the dolls' box. That has been done by the academic critics. The writer in more popular pages has only to pity, and reject, and readers who have no firm opinions of their own will acquiesce, lest their own sophistication and modernity be called in question. Thus the taste of past years is rebuked, and the great dead are snubbed across the Void.

Dwindling Leisure

Not all readers are prepared, at all times, to make independent judgments. But the failure of modern education to equip them to do so even when they have the inclination creates a serious gap in modern culture. The enormously increased production of books, and the appearance of an academic and journalistic junta of criticism, have robbed the reading public of most of its ability to form its own opinions.

This robbery is not the result of a plot. No cabal of professors and reviewers, meeting in secret, have vowed to cheat the reading public of its rights. The reading public has itself connived at the deprivation, and has helped to shove the junta into power. The temper of the time is unfriendly to independent literary judgment. We all lack leisure, for we tend to work longer hours than any but the proletarians of the past. And when we are not working at our jobs, the modern craze for good causes threatens our dwindling leisure; the once sweet voice of charity has risen to an imperious bellow. We pander to the ideal of Work as few Victorians did; university students are eager for holiday jobs, and few of them seem to know that in the beginning, university vacations were made long so that students could spend them in reading which would augment their formal studies. Long toil and small leisure are part of the heavy price we pay for our North American standard of living. It is reputed to be the highest in the world, and so it should be, for it is bought at an inordinate price.

Part of that price has been the resignation of literary taste, by the intelligent reading public, into the hands of professionals, of experts, of an intelligentsia. I have no complaint against the existence of an intelligentsia; on the contrary, I favor it. But I do not favor a small, professional intelligentsia because the very nature of an intelligentsia is that it should be nonprofessional; belonging to it is not something at which anybody works.

Ignoring the Highbrows

NEVERTHELESS, we have a professional intelligentsia now, and it has lost touch with most of the public. Not that determinedly anti-intellectual public which decries one presidential candidate because he is unmistakably literate, and worries about the chances of another because he has a modest skill in playing the piano. The anti-intellectual pose is one of the unforeseen results of our great experiment in complete literacy. Everybody can be made to read and write, but not everybody is going to like it. No, the public with which the intelligentsia has so unhappily lost touch is itself composed of intelligent humanists—a humanist being, by E. M. Forster's definition, a person possessed of curiosity, a free mind, a belief in good taste, and a belief in the human race. The intelligentsia has lost touch with the clerisy. As C. S. Lewis wrote in 1958 (in, curiously enough, a comic magazine, *Punch*), "the Intelligentsia (scientists apart) are losing all touch with, and all influence over, nearly the whole human race. Our most esteemed poets and critics are read by our most esteemed critics and poets (who don't usually like them much) and nobody else takes any notice. An increasing number of highly literate people simply ignore what the 'Highbrows' are doing. It says nothing to them. The Highbrows in return ignore and insult them."

What is to be done? My proposal is a revival of the clerisy. And surely those who have read thus far will know by now of what the clerisy consists.

If it is to become a more vocal and coherent body on the North American continent, the people who comprise it must do a very difficult thing—a thing from which they now shrink. They must accept the fact of their clerisy, and be ready to assert it and defend it with good manners when the need arises. This will expose them to some measure of dislike, and probably a good deal of ridicule. They will find among their ranks many people in whose company they can take no joy—the contentious, the cranks, the ax grinders, the meanly ambitious—those pests who turn up in all large groups, and who seem determined to bring shame upon the cause they espouse. The clerisy must expect to be called "intellectuals," a word which has been given both a comic and a sinister connotation of late years.

The Shame of Brains

WHAT IS SO DREADFUL about being an intellectual? A friend of mine, a European, was engaged by a very important United States company for an important job. He suited all the bosses who interviewed him, and was at last passed on to the high priest of personnel, for a final check. This grandee elicited from my friend that he was keenly interested in music, pictures, theater, but knew nothing of sports; he played no games, but he liked to go for walks, alone; he read much, in English, French, and German; asked about his hobby, he said "Entertaining." What did he do when he entertained his friends? They talked. The personnel genius was by now somewhat hostile and derisive. "I guess you're what would be called an intellectual," said he. "Oh, no," said my friend. "I would not make any such claim for myself; let us say, rather, that an intellectual is what I aspire to be." This naked avowal was more than the personnel man could cope with, and the interview ended.

Why are so many people ashamed of having intelligence and using it? There is nothing democratic about such an attitude. To pretend to be less intelligent than one is deceives nobody and begets dislike, for intelligence cannot be hidden; like a cough, it will out, stifle it how you may. No man has ever won commendation for standing at less than his full height, either physically, morally, or intellectually. If you are an intellectual, your best course is to relax and enjoy it.

This book is about literature (a few odd nooks and corners of it), and it is only in matters relating to literature that I may fittingly exhort my readers to assert themselves in this particular way. My advice as to how they should do so must take the form, chiefly, of prohibitions. No societies, no clubs, associations, or gangs; no buttons, grips, or other means of identification are possible or necessary. Curiosity, the free mind, belief in good taste, and belief in the human race are the marks of the clerisy, allied with a genuine love of literature, not as a manifestation of fashion, not as a substitute for life, but as one of the greatest of the arts, existing for the delight of mankind.

The Cozy Bookman

"Love of Literature"—I know how these words may be misunderstood. The "bookman," sunk deep in his leather chair before the fire, his feet in old and comfortable slippers, his friendly briar filled with the fragrant Nostalgia Mixture, and a cherished volume (for "bookmen" are great cherishers of volumes and never seem to read one which is not "well worn") rises sickeningly before the eye. A pox, yea, a gleety imposthume upon all these bookmen and their snug rituals! They make the whole idea of reading nauseous to thousands of decent people. They love literature only as a kind of intellectual Turkish bath, to caress and lull them. They are the narcissists of the reading world, and their cult belongs in literary clubs dedicated to the Higher Jackassery.

But truly to love literature, to regard it as one of the necessary and occasionally noble aspects of a civilization, is not to be a cozy bookman. It is to belong to the clerisy.

What that means has already been set out in the first few pages of this chapter. It only remains to say how the clerisy can recapture the position in society and the world of letters which it has lost.

An Awakened Clerisy

OBVIOUSLY A REVIVED or awakened clerisy is not going to be the one which fell asleep in the middle of the nineteenth century. We are the spiritual great-great-grandchildren of those people. Their world is not ours, nor have we their classical education or their Biblical culture; we do not live in a society so frankly class-conscious as theirs. Where they had one new book to read, we have a thousand. Where they had a splendid certainty of their own taste and learning—one recalls the Victorian clergyman who replied to a young lady who observed that his pronunciation of a particular word did not agree with the dictionary: "My dear, dictionaries exist to record the pronunciations of people of education, like myself"—we defer to the opinions of journalistic critics who are, in their turn, reflections of academic critics. We live in a world where bulk is often equated with quality, and though we know that the best-seller is not therefore the best book, we can be awed by impressive sales. Nevertheless, we of the clerisy exist; we are not fools; we can make our existence felt by authors, publishers, and critics simply by recognizing that we exist as a class which cuts across all classes, and by making our opinions better known, verbally, in public, by correspondence, and by the other means which present themselves in the course of daily life. We are people to be reckoned with. Courteously but firmly we must refuse the outsider role, the layman label, which we have allowed the world of publishers and critics to foist upon us. By our own sheepishness we incurred this loss of our right; by our intelligence we shall reclaim it. We are not ashamed to reverse the words of Nathaniel in *Love's Labour's Lost:* we *have* fed of the dainties that are bred in a book; we *have* eat paper and drunk ink; our intellect is replenished.

· II ·
Enjoying and Enduring

Doctor Johnson said that books were trash unless they helped their readers "better to enjoy life or better to endure it." He obviously had no prophetic vision of the number and variety of books which our age would produce devoted to these twin aims of enjoying and enduring.

Were he with us now, the Doctor might have been asked to provide an endorsement for Vernon Howard's *Word Power: Talk Your Way to Life Leadership*, a work which "presents a program for becoming the kind of person you want to be—by speaking like that person." Mr. Howard assures us that "habits of speech do much toward making us timid or courageous, energetic or tired, successful or unsuccessful." Boswell occasionally tried to make himself like Johnson by speaking like Johnson, but something appears to have been lacking. Possibly it was Mr. Howard's book.

Certainly there has never been a time before the present when it was possible to buy or borrow a book which would offer advice on virtually every problem of enjoying or enduring with which life can confront puzzled humankind. Because they rarely receive attention from critics of literature in general (being recommended in the main by specialists in the matter concerned), it may be illuminating to look at some of them here. Anything in the nature of a comprehensive study would fill a larger book than this, and would be quite outside my ability, but a selection may be attempted.

The question is, where to begin? A glance in a single bookshop window shows the vastness of the field. Here is *Finding and Using Your Magic Emotion Power*, and beside it *Live at Peace with Your Nerves*; at the back, on a little lectern, is *Emotional Problems of Living* (*Avoiding the Neurotic Pattern*), and in front are *The Art of Living without Tension*, and *Heart Attack*, *New Hope*, *New Knowledge*, *New Life*. To complete the display, there is a book with the provocative title *On Shame and the Search for Identity*. These are stirring times for the ambitious, the hypochondriac, and the unsure. But a beginning must be made somewhere, and the historical approach offers its usual common-sense assistance.

Smiles on Self-help

Let us begin with Samuel Smiles, whose book *Self-Help, with Illustrations of Character and Conduct* sold 258,000 copies in English between its publication in 1859 and the author's death in 1904. This was a great sale for that period, and Smiles's book may be called the father of the manifold guides to enjoying and enduring which have followed. As well as its English and American success, it was translated into Dutch, German, Danish, Swedish, Spanish, Italian, Turkish, Arabic, Japanese, and (the *Dictionary of National Biography* adds with vague splendor) "the native tongues of India." After the book had outlived its early popularity, it was regarded as a joke, but principally by people who had not read it. It was no joke.

Smiles was a successful man, whom Fortune seemed to caress, but she laid upon him one ironical handicap. Is any of us so completely just, or merely so sober-sided, that he can take the name "Samuel Smiles" quite seriously? Especially when it is attached to a book called *Self-Help*? It is a name which Dickens might have given to an idiot optimist, like Mark Tapley, or one of his buoyant philanthropists, like the Cheeryble Brothers. Sturdy Scot that he was, Smiles rose triumphant above his name while he lived, and probably he found nothing amusing in it. But it is a drawback now for the very few who look into his book.

Smiles was trained as a physician, gave up that profession to be an editor, became a railway official, and, after the success of *Self-Help,* spent his time chiefly in social reform and particularly in schemes for the education of working men. It was in an address to a "mutual improvement society" at Leeds in 1845 that the germ of *Self-Help* showed itself. Smiles was inspired by the careers of men who had risen from humble beginnings to great estate through their own efforts; his highest admiration was for engineers and inventors, but success of any honorable sort won his commendation:

> From the barber's shop came Jeremy Taylor, the most poetical of divines; Sir Richard Arkwright the inventor of the spinning jenny and founder of cotton manufacture; Lord Tenderden, one of the most distinguished of Lord Chief Justices: and Turner the greatest among landscape painters, while among distinguished carpenters we find the names of Inigo Jones the architect, Romney and Opie, the painters . . . Masons and bricklayers can boast of Ben Jonson, who worked at the building of Lincoln's Inn with a trowel in his hand and a book in his pocket.

The tone is familiar to anyone who has, in childhood, "sat under" a Scottish Presbyterian minister; these muster rolls of great names, resoundingly uttered without too searching an examination of the real characters of the men or the real nature of their achievement, are a favorite pulpit trick. All those named rose from poverty and obscurity to favored positions in the eyes of men, and that is what matters to Smiles.

Not that Smiles is a vulgar worshipper of vulgar success. Character is what he admires, and it is the struggle rather than the achievement which thrills him. Means, not ends, is his concern. And the means he adjures his readers (whom he doubtless pictured as worthy artisans, puzzling out his book with a little difficulty by their cottage fires) to embrace are perseverance and the strictest honesty. "Work," he writes—and we can almost see the sweep of the Geneva gown as the preacher's finger is upraised—"work is the appointed calling of man on earth; the end for which his various faculties were given; the element in which his nature is ordained to develop itself, and in which his progressive advance towards heaven is to lie." He practiced what he preached, and suffered a stroke of paralysis, owing to overwork, when he was fifty-nine; true to his own principles and courage, he recovered and continued to work, at a somewhat slower pace, until his death at the age of ninety-two. Work; save; be unfailingly honest; respect yourself and other men; success will follow. That is the teaching of Samuel Smiles, and hundreds of thousands of ambitious Englishmen and Americans (not to speak of the Dutch, German, Danish, Swedish, Spanish, Italian, Turkish, Arabian, Japanese, and Indian readers already alluded to) seized upon it eagerly. Not all of them rose to positions of honor, accompanied by a handsome competence. There is doubtless some law, economic or perhaps psychological, which restricts the amount of success possible in any one community in a given time. But what Smiles offered was certainly not fairy gold; do what he says and your lot cannot help but improve, even if the great prizes go to other men.

Bennett's Crowded Hours

BY SMILES'S DEATH in 1904 his book had almost run its course, but in 1908 Arnold Bennett published *How to Live on Twenty-four Hours a Day*, which gained immense popularity. It is in the Smiles vein of exhortation, but its purpose is different: the Victorian book sought to help its readers to get ahead in the world of affairs, of money-making, of social prestige, but the Edwardian book urged ambitious young men to make the most of their leisure time. Bennett assumed—and was rebuked for assuming—that a lot of people are bored by their jobs, and he tried to tell them how to make the sixteen hours away from the job as interesting as possible. His own temperament was that of an artist, allied to a remarkable industry and the canniness of the English Midlands. (He was also an insomniac, which may have had more bearing on his suggested program of life than he was willing to admit.) He counseled young men to read, to listen to music, to look at pictures. He was scornful of rest. "One of the chief things which my typical man has to learn is that the mental faculties are capable of continuous hard activity," he wrote: "they do not tire like an arm or a leg. All they want is change—not rest, except in sleep."

Henry Ford told Bennett that he had bought five hundred copies of *How to Live,* to be distributed among his managers. The book had the same appeal for industrialists as Elbert Hubbard's *A Message to Garcia.* These shrewd men knew that he who slaves at his pleasure will not relax when he is at his work. "Keep going, day in, day out," urged Bennett, and his *Journals* prove that he tried to take his own medicine. Waste no time. Dominate your mind. Force it to concentrate in the morning on the chapter of Epictetus you read last night. Read seriously. Most people sleep themselves stupid. Weariness is an illusion, and disinclination is the tempting of the fiend. It is all very inspiring and much of it is true, even if it is not the whole truth.

Doubtless thousands of people attempted, for a time, to live in the strenuous fashion Bennett outlines. Has anyone ever kept it up for a lifetime? Bennett could not do so, industrious and intellectually sinewy though he was. He died, very tired indeed, at the comparatively early age of sixty-four, and his *Journals* tell us how far short he had fallen of this forced pace for many years before that time. Perhaps that is beside the point. His book was an inspiration to hundreds of thousands of ambitious and discontented young men, for it suggested a concrete program which would help them to become better than they found themselves.

Thinking for Everybody

LET US NOT delay too long over these early examples of a genre which has reached its greatest proliferation since 1945; but before we go on, it is interesting to glance briefly at the first of these self-improvement books which was directed at least in part toward female readers. It is *The Art of Thinking* by Ernest Dimnet, which appeared in 1929. The writer paid women the compliment of assuming that they would like to think better than they did. They responded enthusiastically, and his book sold well.

It is a very good book, vastly more understanding of what humanity is really like than Smiles's or Bennett's. Its tone is quiet, and it recognizes fatigue and frailty not as trivialities, but as the Hydras they are. It is a popular book in the best sense; it offers its wisdom to anybody who can read, but it promises no easy results. Furthermore, its tone is aristocratic. How, then, did it achieve so great a success?

Its author was a Frenchman, which is a very strong recommendation with English-speaking readers. Furthermore, he was a cleric, which is always reassuring; to be taught thinking by a priest could hardly lead to any of those mental enormities with which the thought of lay philosophers so reprehensibly abounds. But its greatest draw, I am inclined to believe, is its title, which is a creation of genius. The art of thinking! Is it, then, an art? We had always been inclined to think of it as work. Art is, of course, elegant pastime. The appeal of that title is enormous. A million clubwomen saw themselves as a million Madame de Staëls, ridding their minds of the trivialities the Abbé so sternly dismisses, seeing deeper into life, writing distinguished letters, diaries, *pensées*—in fact, thinking. The novelty of the idea made the book a sensation; if persistence and a superior understanding could have been given away with each copy, the world might have been revolutionized.

For the Hypochondriac

THIS IS NOT the sort of essay in which we want to pursue the history of books about self-improvement, and the three examples given are enough to show that such books can be of real value, written in sincerity by men of ability and good literary repute. The sincerity of the writers of the books of this character which now flood the market cannot be called in question (because sincerity in this context means simply believing what you say, and there is no limit to what people can believe), but their literary repute does not exist. This is of significance because the crudity with which they are written would make these books unendurable to a public which looked for literary quality. But the public for such books is not drawn from the clerisy. It consists of a very large part of the population which may never read any other sort of book, and which wants to be given answers to two questions: How can I achieve better health? and How can I achieve success?

The health books appeal to the Eternal Hypochondriac, and to the urge which burns in so many of us to play the quack, if only to ourselves. In an age when public health has never been better provided for, and medical men enjoy a respect formerly reserved for the aristocracy and the clergy, millions of people are unwell, or merely feel unwell, or are in dread lest at some future time they may become unwell. It would be interesting to know how many people who read *Heart Attack*, *New Hope*, *New Knowledge*, *New Life* have never had a heart attack. How many people who have diabetes and are under the care of a competent physician nevertheless read books about how to live with diabetes? Every piece of news about cancer research is eagerly read by millions who have no cancer and probably never will have it. Doubtless there is a good side to this preoccupation with health, but it is with health books that we are concerned at the moment, and our concern is literary. Why not? Is it too much to expect that a popular book about health should be written with some regard for literary decency? Great physicians—the name of Sir William Osler comes to mind, and a score of others could be added to it—have not thought a good style incompatible with good medicine. But Sir William regarded his membership in the clerisy as part of his armory as a great physician and a great teacher, for it raised him above the level of a technician. A scientist, as a biologist friend of mine says, is all the better for being an educated person.

Obesity Is Sin

AGAIN AND AGAIN we are assured on the authority of the insurance companies that fat is a killer, and perhaps a third of the population of North America is struggling to get its fat down. Books telling how this may be done are popular, because the person who wants to reduce finds them a comfort; to read a new antifat book gives new hope; we rise from the experience feeling a few pounds lighter. Ninety-two popular books on dieting are in print at the time of writing. A theologian, or merely a literary critic, reading many of these books quickly discovers their secret, which is an evangelistic one; they first of all bring about a powerful conviction of Sin, and then they offer Salvation.

Sin is fat. Perhaps it is Original Sin, to which you are born, because your mother, who was unable to love you as much as she thought she should, crammed you with food as an Affection Surrogate. Perhaps it is your own Sin, springing from an unregenerate nature which expresses itself in greed. You are insecure, and so you eat; you meet emotional stress by stuffing yourself. And what a Hell awaits you! Early death because of an overtaxed heart; or a lingering, joyless existence, a prey to a degenerative disease. Deliverance seems possible only at a frightful price. To offset the evil wrought upon you by a single piece of pie, you must walk thirty-five miles! To consume the energy provided by a jelly sandwich, you must run at top speed for an hour! Almost weeping, you admit that you are a slob without will, a glutton, a bad insurance risk, a creature found unworthy of God's goodness.

But now—Salvation! By means of little pictures of a gnome called Mr. Fat-Prone, or whatever other name appeals to the roguish fancy of the writer, your digestive mechanism is explained to you, and the caloric theory of weight reduction is set forth (unless the book happens to favor another form of metabolic magic, and makes you eat some kind of fat-burning diet). Do thus, says your savior, and infallibly you will lose weight. You must. You cannot help it. If you fail, you must be cheating. You snatch eagerly at the Salvation which is offered, not precisely free but at the seemingly trivial cost of eating what the expert calls an ample and satisfying diet. Some books offer recipes created and tested by the expert himself—recipes which are far, far from the poems of the *haute cuisine*. We understand why the expert has no fat problem; his notions of food would seem frugal to Robinson Crusoe. *It Pays to Be Healthy*, says Dr. Robert Collier Page—in what coin, one wonders, looking over the diet sheet.

Length of Days

HOW PAT the answer comes from another group of books in the same category; the payment is in a lengthened life span. *Live Longer and Enjoy It!* shouts Dr. Peter Steincrohn in one of his books, and *Stop Killing Yourself!* in another. Dr. Steincrohn has also written books explaining how to keep fit without exercise, and how to master fear. He is not a man to give way to doubt himself. "This book can be your first positive step toward a happier, fuller, longer life," he says, at the opening of the first-named of his works, and proceeds to reduce the method of gaining these blessings to a simple and easily remembered formula. This is A.L.E. = H. & H.—which, being interpreted, is "Awareness of your Life Expectancy brings you the greatest promise of enjoying Health and Happiness." Like Dr. Walter Alvarez, another tireless writer about health, he makes us privy to many of the confidences of the consulting room. We are impressed by the high quality of their patients. Dr. Alvarez is happy indeed in the moral beauty of the people who make up his practice, for it is rarely that he has a patient whom he does not describe as "fine," and the worse their physical plight, the finer they are likely to be. The patients of Dr. Steincrohn, on the other hand, are distinguished by their pithy directness of speech. "All I do is belch," says a tormented woman, characteristic of a score of others. The doctor, in his vehement and hortatory style, is similarly direct in dealing with her.

As well as the books for those whose health is already impaired, and the books for those who merely fear that this may be their lot, there is the large class of books for those whose anxiety is about old age. Medical science is credited with having added twenty years to our life expectancy since the beginning of this century. Twenty more years to worry about! Characteristic of many of the books designed for the aging is *The Best Years of Your Life* by Marie Beynon Ray. Septuagenarians who have been looking forward to a few years of sitting quietly in a chair will not need it, but those who fear age may wish to follow her advice and involve themselves in a number of "activities"; the word is in quotation marks because it is one of the witch-words of our time. It seems to signify a variety of arts and skills, serious in themselves, when they are approached in a spirit which is not serious. An "activity" is not really a hobby, for a hobby may be something to which you have been drawn by strong personal inclination. No, an "activity" is something you would never have dreamed of doing until—in old age, for instance—you fall into the hands of some zealot who makes you do it for its supposed therapeutic value.

It does not occur to Mrs. Ray that an elderly person might like to rest after a life of work. No, no, she cries; let them paint, write, play instruments, take photographs, and collect things, including languages. Indomitably cheerful, she goads the beldam and the grandsire on to unremitting activity—no matter what, so long as they drag their old bones out of the chimney corner and make a stir in the world.

Her best point is that education and mental development need not come to a halt as age approaches; we can always learn. But she makes no serious mention of the serenity and peace of age, and many who are now tossing on the heavy seas of middle life may tremble at the thought of a seniority in which they will be compelled to collect orchids or learn to play the trombone.

As a white candle
  In a holy place,
So is the beauty
  Of an aged face.

Thus writes the poet. But Mrs. Ray does not concur; she wants the aged face to blaze with the charmless frenzy of a naked electric bulb. The human predicament, under such circumstances, must conclude not in a fading splendor, but with a fizzle and a pop.

It is not suggested that these books have no value. Their coarse, fibrous prose, and their punching, driving style are devoted to advice which ranges from the harmless to the good and the valuable. There are fastidious readers who cannot accept counsel which is pressed upon them in this graceless fashion, but there are millions of others who gobble it up. What sort of people must they be?

They are people who believe in the Power of the Word. They share with a great part of literate mankind the dream of the Wondrous Book, the invaluable Vade Mecum, in which the answer to their special question is to be found. The rise of elementary literacy, discussed in our first chapter, has put them in possession of the power to read, and has had a part in sophisticating them to the point where they no longer regard the Holy Bible as the one Miraculous Book, as their parents and grandparents may have done. Their problems have no kinship with those of Abraham and Jacob, but are rooted in a world where all ills and discontents are supposedly curable, and where there *must* be a way of beating arthritis, or heart disease, or simply old age. There must be an anodyne for their Hydra-headed Anxiety. And so they seek these books, and the books appear for a time to fulfill their need. The sad part is that the books are so bad, considered as pieces of writing and thinking, and that those who ask for bread are given a few ounces of wood pulp.

Right Thinking Means Success

It is when we leave the realm of physical health and look at the books which promise mental health—invariably equated with success—that pity changes to disgust. The best in this kind belong to that category of writing which is not philosophy, or psychology, or religion, but a watery draught in which the flavor of all three may be faintly discerned. It used to be called Uplift; perhaps we might call it Soulmanship. It is vaguely Emersonian in manner, but has no more than a whiff of Emerson's good sense. A characteristic example is *The Mind Alive,* by Harry and Bonaro Overstreet, with the subtitle "How to keep our Mental and Emotional Level High: How to Live so that Life has Meaning." It offers some advice which is good, but it takes a man already wise to learn further wisdom from a book. People in distress, or merely unhappy, need spiritual directors or psychiatrists to cope with them. They want a human contact, and they want to hear advice in a human voice. They need praise and scoldings from someone whom they respect. What are they to make of *The Mind*

Alive, with its chilly goodwill and watered-down New England stoicism?

We must pity the hungriness of heart which clamors for reassurance and wisdom, but which shrinks from religion and philosophy, either of which might, in different ways, fill their need and soothe their sorrow. Our age has robbed millions of the simplicity of ignorance, and has so far failed to lift them to the simplicity of wisdom. Roaming the broad purgatorial plains between these two states, they seize upon books of mild inspiration. "Deeply and persistently, we have come to realize, the individual seeks himself in and through others," say the Overstreets in another of their books, *The Mind Goes Forth*. This is a half-truth, but for those to whom it applies, inspirational books are of no use; they need living teachers, whom they can hear and touch, and who can keep them on what is, for them, the right track.

Wishes in Overalls

THE TEACHING of such writers as the Overstreets seems almost inspired when we drop to such works as *Best Wishes* by Brownie Wise. The message of this writer (whose chief recommendation seems to be that she was chosen by the National Sales Executives as "Business Woman of 1957") is simply that you can have whatever you wish for; if you don't get it, obviously it was not a "worthwhile wish"; if you follow her technique, your wishes will "don overalls and go to work for you." "Wishing with a purpose works a magic all its own," she writes, in the rhythmic prose which is her special gift. Something of its flavor is to be found in this brief excerpt:

> Six hundred and twenty years before the birth of Christ, a man named Aesop set a goal and began to share his

> imagination with his fellow man. Today, a man named Disney is continuing the ageless art of fantasy, sharpening the tools of inspiration of still another generation. . . . And we, the living one and all, share the wealth of inspiring dividends. Of course there was a lot of fantasy in the tales they told. Yet can you recall a single fairytale without a moral, one in which the treasure was not actually earned, in which some single character was not better off for what he learned? A child without faith in fantasy, finds it difficult to believe as a man.

Brownie Wise says naïvely that wishing will make it so. Countless other writers repeat her assertion, but the naïveté is gone. They cloak their magic in the robes of pseudo science. Dr. Hornell Hart, of Duke University, has devised a system which he describes in *Autoconditioning: The New Way to a Successful Life*; his book is sold complete with a device called a Mood-Meter, which is "a simple, scientific way for measuring the degree of your happiness or unhappiness." Autoconditioning is self-hypnosis, or autosuggestion, and when you have mastered its technique, you will experience "induced intuition," also called "getting-hunches-to-order." With autoconditioning you will get rid of tension, and "release almost unlimited reserves of energy."

The yearning to give this sort of voodoo the prestige of science leads Dr. Norman Vincent Peale (a clergyman) and Dr. Smiley Blanton (a psychiatrist) to assert, in *The Art of Real Happiness*, that "the pulpit behind which the pastor stands is a sacred desk but it is also a laboratory table," and the benefits they promise are rooted in "spiritual laws as specific as the laws of physics and chemistry." Their special advice is contained in some words attributed to Captain Eddie Rickenbacker—"Think positively and masterfully, with confidence and faith, and life becomes more secure, more fraught with action, richer in achievement and experience. This is the sure way to win victories over inner defeat. It is the way a humble man meets life or death."

Scientific Weather Control

SUCH A COMBINATION of the humble with the masterful is encountered also in *Faith Is Power* by the Reverend Dr. Daniel A. Poling, editor of *The Christian Guardian*. General Patton displayed it when he prayed for, and got, "battle weather" for his Third Army on the Rhine. The General ordered his Senior Chaplain to address a polite but firm request to Almighty God to stop the rain which halted his advance. The result, written by Colonel James O'Neil, goes right to the point. God is asked to "restrain these immoderate rains with which we have had to contend." (It is to be supposed that the Divine Ear turned a little red at the criticism implied in "immoderate" and "contend.") "Grant us fair weather for battle," the prayer continued, so that "we may advance from victory to victory and crush the opposition and wickedness of our enemies. . . ." Could Joshua or any other conqueror of the Old Testament have put it up to God more sternly? This was masterful, positive thinking indeed, and it was humble, as well, for General Patton knew that he could not stop the rain unaided. It is interesting to recall that the rain stopped. There will be those who have prayed for or against rain, however, who will have to decide whether their cause did not meet Brownie Wise's test of being "worthwhile," or whether the laws of prayer are a little less specific in their action than Drs. Peale and Blanton say they are.

Lifemanship and Wifemanship

COMPARED with the religious approach, the frankness of Dale Carnegie is refreshing. When he is dealing in magic he calls it magic; his "magic formula to stop worrying situations" (also called "eight words that can transform your life" in *How to Stop Worrying and Start Living*) is a quotation from Marcus Aurelius—"Our life is what our thoughts make it." This is admirable, until we discover what Mr. Carnegie thinks we want to make of life. Over and over again he stresses the magic of thought, but the kind of thought he suggests can bring no satisfaction to any but the narrow egoist, the go-getter, the me-first. Nobody can find fault with legitimate ambition, but when the wealth of the spiritual and intellectual life is reduced to a formula for overcoming sales resistance, we protest.

The Carnegie world outlook has been extended by Mrs. Carnegie in a book called *How to Help Your Husband Get Ahead*, which is a manual of Wifemanship. Three ways of making the husband popular are set forth: (a) make him lovable to others by presenting him in contrived situations where his heart will seem great; (b) display his talents by paving the way for his funny stories, or whatever else the poor brute seems to his wife to do well; (c) touch the chords that bring out his best—whatever that may mean. Which of us has not seen deluded women at these pitiable and transparent devices? It is for this that Mrs. Carnegie urges wives to "raise their standard of loving," and lift their EQ (enthusiasm quotient). Respect for the dignity of the human spirit forbids comment on this transcendently disgusting book. It is enough to say that it was not thus that Portia loved Brutus, or Elizabeth Barrett, Robert Browning. Could love long survive the well-intentioned meddling which has its genesis not in passion, respect, or shared interests, but in a calculated inflation of the EQ? Would not some compensating disillusion inevitably follow?

Whether religious or secular in vocabulary, the lesson is always the same. The clerical writers express a coarse, strong, somewhat unspiritual, getting-ahead kind of religion. They seem quite content with the world as it is, desiring a generalized decency rather than spirituality. Their religion is a means of getting on in the world, and the reader sometimes feels that if moderation and honesty worked against success, moderation and honesty would get short shrift. But of course honesty is the best policy; it is a spiritual law as fixed as the laws of chemistry, and a score of anecdotes can be adduced to prove it. It is astonishing to read again and again in these books by parsons phrases which suggest that religious faith is a type of investment. They insist that it "pays dividends."

The secular books say the same things, and not in a strikingly different way. Great emphasis is laid on getting people to like you, and this is not mentioned as a possible consequence of good conduct, but as an end in itself. Being liked is important because it is a way of achieving success. A secret of gaining popularity, suggested seriously in one of these manuals, was that of the man who repeatedly asked for help in these words: "You're a lot smarter than I am, so I come to you." We are told that this "made friends fast," and the progress of the petitioner was rapid. Presumably the discovery of such a valuable secret entitled this man to be called "creative," which is a favorite word of the inspirational writers. Everybody must *create*, but when the word is examined in the context in which they use it, it seems to mean nothing more than being ordinarily competent on the job. Had the creator in question no sense of becoming a hypocrite as his material success grew?

Secrets of success are many, and it is interesting that silence is frequently recommended as one of them. Sit in silence for as little as fifteen minutes a day, and splendid inspirations will surely come to you. Henry Ford, it appears, thought well of silence, and if we aspire to success, what better model can we find than he whom no less a seer than Ralph Waldo Trine called "inventor, poet and prophet"?

The emphasis is always on "success" in its meaning of prosperity and good fortune, and the lesson of all these books is that success can be compelled. Follow the directions and it *must* come. There would be nothing very harmful about this if success were not so often equated with virtue, and if success were not so nakedly touted as the best gift of God. But that is the message of a majority of these books: success is from God, and God can be cajoled or compelled to give it to you. One need not be of a profoundly religious nature to find this shocking.

The Power of Dr. Peale

LET US EXAMINE in some detail the self-confessed "great inspirational best-seller of our time," *The Power of Positive Thinking* by the Reverend Dr. Norman Vincent Peale. *The Episcopal Review* says that "Dr. Peale combines the deep strength of Christian faith with the insights of modern science to produce a most helpful book for radiant living." Well, let us see.

Dr. Peale says of his book that "it makes no pretence to literary excellence nor does it seek to demonstrate any unusual scholarship on my part." We may assume that Dr. Peale has small regard for these qualities, for by the infallible technique of success which he demonstrates, they could surely be easily acquired. Nevertheless, there is an occasional squib of scholarship in the book, as when he says that the word "pastor" derives from a word meaning "a cure of souls"; those of us who thought it derived from the Latin word for a shepherd will not be so cranky as to dismiss all of the doctor's scholarship because of a slip that any busy, successful man might overlook. And when he tells us of the old lady who said to him "How daily life is!" we wish that we knew such witty old ladies, for we have to read Jules Laforgue to be told the same thing. But when he outlines his "prayer formula" as (1) Prayerize (2) Picturize (3) Actualize, we begin to ask if a certain reasonable fastidiousness about the debauching of English may not also be among God's gifts, and we wonder uneasily if the style may not be, all too revealingly, the man himself.

Is it stupid and unfair to deny value to the book solely because we do not like the way in which it is written? Or is the repulsion we feel in fact a valid and critical response? "This merriment of parsons is mighty offensive," said Dr. Johnson, who was under no compulsion to be consistent for, in his day, guides to enjoying and enduring life were few, and were rarely the work of the clergy. If Dr. Peale wishes to direct his female readers to "God's beauty parlour" (which is his way of saying that a quiet spirit improves the looks), must we not let him know best how to appeal to his audience? Are we justified in our cynicism about that marvelous store of anecdotes which he holds in common with so many of his calling; may it not be characteristic of the successful, positive thinker that the experience of many men, and even of men long dead, is subsumed and reborn in himself?

Strong faith is notoriously tonic in its effect. Dr. Peale urges his readers to affirm ten times every day "I can do all things through Christ which strengtheneth me." It would be astonishing if such a belief, worked into the grain of a man, did not give him more than ordinary self-confidence. If Christ is with him (and he knows that this is so), who dares be against him? Any of us who have had to oppose men and women who are so armed with faith know how quickly their astonishment gives place to indignation. Those who truly believe that Christ is with them are subject to a particularly distressing form of mistaken identity. There must be times, in the world of business, when two Peale-powered personalities find themselves in opposition. Number One is determined to achieve success by selling Number Two a great gross of non-molting dust mops; Number Two is equally determined not to have the mops. Both have affirmed an equal number of times that he can do all things through Christ which strengtheneth him. What happens? Theologians will scratch their heads over this, and Immensity itself may feel a tremor.

But Dr. Peale has no misgiving. Hear his words:

> Where is the old-fashioned businessman who says that religion is theoretical and has no place in business? Today any successful and competent businessman will employ the latest and best-tested methods in production, distribution and administration, and many are discovering that one of the greatest of all efficiency methods is prayer power.

Prayer power is not always used for a narrow, personal advantage, of course. Dr. Peale is greatly attracted by the technique of his colleague in spiritual science, Dr. Frank Laubach, who uses "flash prayers" which he "shoots" at people in public places; often the people thus shot turn toward him and smile. Says Dr. Peale, admiringly: "Dr. Laubach believes that he has often changed the entire atmosphere of a car or bus full of people by the process of 'swishing love and prayers all around the place.' "

Who Approves Peale?

To whom does spiritual help on this level make its appeal? To troubled people who find their lives or their circumstances unsatisfactory, we assume. But such people vary greatly, and to answer the question more carefully, we turn to *Social Class and Mental Illness* by August B. Hollingshead and Frederick C. Redlich, where we find the people of a supposedly typical United States community divided into five classes, according to education, income, and prestige. According to these researchers only 1 per cent of the psychiatric patients from their community come from Class One; 7 per cent come from Class Two; 13.7 per cent from Class Three; 40.1 per cent from Class Four; and 38.2 per cent from Class Five. Though as this last and lowest class comprises only 17.7 per cent of the total population, it will be seen that it provides by far the greatest number of psychiatric cases numerically. The first three classes contain virtually all of the neurotics, who do not require psychiatric treatment but who are "disturbed personalities," and as the two lowest classes are made up of people who read very little, and who do not seek help from the printed word, we may assume that self-help books are read by the upper three classes. Of these it is probably Class Three which is most impressed by autoconditioning, wishes in overalls, positive thinking, and other marvelous and easy ways to mental health, and of course success.

Self-help by Self-examination

It will not be amiss at this point to consider the comparatively small but valuable class of books which exist for those whose aim is self-knowledge and self-exploration, rather than magical formulas and monetary betterment. The desire of these readers is not to bend the external world to their will, but to live on better terms with themselves, and they have no illusions about their ability to bribe Fate, or to involve Christ in their struggle for worldly advancement.

Three books must suffice, all of which deal in a different way with the problem of self-analysis. The first is *A Practical Method of Self-Analysis* by E. Pickworth Farrow. The author's history is of interest; he was trained as a biologist and has achieved distinction in the field of ecology. Following the first Great War, he was troubled by neurosis, and undertook psychoanalysis with two physicians, eventually quarreling with both of them. Being of a determined nature, he decided to analyze himself, which he did to his own satisfaction. Perhaps more significantly, he did so to the satisfaction of Dr. Sigmund Freud, who consented to write a Foreword to his book. It is worth quoting in full, because of the light it throws both on Farrow and on Freud:

> The author of this book is known to me as a man of strong and independent intelligence who, probably on account of a certain wilfulness of character, could not get on well with the two analysts with whom he experimented. He then had recourse to a consistent application of the process of self-analysis which I had once used myself in order to analyse my own dreams. His results deserve notice, especially because of his special individual technique.

A less guarded recommendation from Freud comes by way Professor A. G. Tansley of Cambridge, who reports that when he discussed Farrow's technique of free-association with the founder of psychoanalysis, he commented: *"Ja, tadellos"* ("Yes, beyond reproach").

Freud's caution in his Foreword is understandable. He was willing to admit that he had analyzed himself, but he was not prepared to suggest that anyone else attempt such a feat, nor was he optimistic about the outcome of such an experiment. When we read, in Dr. Ernest Jones's great biography, of the struggle and agony which self-analysis cost Freud, we understand his reluctance. He knew what was involved, and he knew how uncommon were Farrow's sturdiness of intellect and determination.

These qualities of Farrow's appear on every page of his book. He says frankly that he had little use for introspection of any kind until a war neurosis drove him to seek relief by what he believed to be the best method; having set out on psychoanalysis, not even the despair of the analysts with whom he quarreled would turn him from it. His triumph as he tracks down each part of his trouble has the quality of a man who has chased a burglar and given him a sound thrashing. His industry is awesome. He records that after four hundred and fifty solitary hours of self-analysis, he succeeded in recalling a memory which he was able to confirm went back to an incident in his sixth month of life.

Those who are daunted by the strenuosity of Farrow will find a gentler and more reassuring book in *Self-Analysis* by the late Dr. Karen Horney. Herself a distinguished analyst, she has not the sense of triumphing over that profession which is observable in Farrow, and from her professional experience she knows how few people have Farrow's persistence. Her belief in the possibility of self-analysis arose from her observation that those of her patients who were separated from her for a time returned to treatment with insights and improvements which made it clear that they had been carrying on the analytical work by themselves, whether fully aware of it or not. If this were possible, what degree of analysis lay within the power of the solitary worker?

Dr. Horney has no easy optimism on this point. Success depends upon the character of each worker, and on the problems they have to solve. She does not think that self-analysis lies within everybody's power, because one of its first requirements is a degree of honesty in examining one's own recollections and processes of thought—an ability which is not given to everybody and which varies widely in power where it exists at all. Where it does exist, the slow and strenuous work involved in a self-analysis creates another hazard; intellectual honesty and industry need not go hand in hand. Her conclusion on the matter is this:

> On theoretical grounds, then, I see no stringent reason why self-analysis should not be feasible. Granted that many people are too deeply entangled in their own problems to be able to analyze themselves; granted that self-analysis can never approximate the speed and accuracy of analytical treatment by an expert; granted that there are certain resistances that can be surmounted only with outside help—still, all of this is no proof that in principle the job cannot be done.

The spirit which informs this book is one of enviable wisdom and cultivation. The benefits it assumes the reader is seeking from self-analysis are intellectual and spiritual ones; the values which lie at its foundation are worthy of our admiration. The reader feels that Dr. Horney has qualities which he would greatly like to develop in himself. It is this that marks the book off from the works of Dr. Peale and the other advocates of easy self-improvement.

Farrow, independent as his approach was, worked along strict Freudian lines. Dr. Horney was also Freudian, although some modifications of Freud's doctrines are observable in *Self-Analysis*, as in her other works. For the troubled or the neurotic, their manuals may be best, but for those who are intent on deepening their self-knowledge, but who have no specific distress they wish to allay, the Jungian approach to self-analysis could be more congenial. It is worth noting also that Dr. Jung's approach to the obscure places of the mind by means of depth-psychology seems to work better for people who have passed the age of forty than the uncompromising Freudian method.

A personal approach to self-knowledge by Dr. Jung's path is described at length in *Experiment in Depth* by P. W. Martin. The process is no less long or difficult, but it is different in method. The end that is sought is the same—an integrated personality—but it is achieved by what Martin (taking a phrase from Arnold Toynbee) calls "the withdrawal-and-return." The withdrawal is from the outer world to the inner world of the psyche; the return is from that realm, where a new way of life has been found.

Like so much that is associated with Jung, this book is written in terms which some people will dismiss as "mystical," and those who have no taste for the mystical, or who fear it, had better leave Martin's book alone. The warning he utters is even sterner than that given by Dr. Horney:

> The experiment in depth concerns everyone, but it is not for everyone to undertake. The way is dangerous. It demands of a man that he obey the injunction "Become what thou art"; and to this end leads him to his own encounter. What he will find there, no one can know in advance. This much, though, is reasonably certain. Wholeness has to proceed against the heaviest of odds: the values, habit patterns, attitudes, laid down by earlier conditioning in a society where the creative contact has

been to a great extent lost. Individuation does not begin with a *tabula rasa,* but with a personality more or less malformed.

Beyond lies the deep unconscious. Here, all is at the hazard. As Jung has said, there are those who go digging for an artesian well and come instead upon a volcano. Cumulated upon this uncertainty is the harsh fact that our knowledge of the other side of consciousness is still, for the most part, in the earliest stages of hypothesis. Much of it may be wide of the mark, some completely mistaken. It is not only that the beaten way does not as yet exist. Such track as there is may be deceptive. A man takes it at his peril. In making the experiment in depth there are bound to be casualties, casualties that could not reasonably be foreseen. It is well to realize that one's own name may figure among them.

Whether he wishes to try the experiment in depth on himself or not, the reader of Martin's book will be grateful for a sympathetic but not uncritical exposition of Jung's depth-psychology, which as a fascinating excursion into the vast compost heap of myth and legend is surely one of the great adventures in the history of the human mind. For those who seek to understand literature (and perhaps through literature, themselves) it is a rich feeding ground. Martin himself has indicated the bearing Jungian investigation has on the works of T. S. Eliot and Arnold Toynbee. J. B. Priestley and Laurens Van der Post have acknowledged their indebtedness to Jung. The literary investigator, unlike the psychiatrist, is not obliged to consider whether Jung's depth-psychology is as complete and as "true" as Freud's psychoanalysis; if it sets him off on new paths of exploration and reflection, that is enough; the truth which engages his mind is not the truth that the physician seeks. Literature owes much to books and systems of thought which are not true in the most modern and scientific sense. Poetic truth must also have its due, and in that realm Burton's *Anatomy of Melancholy* has served literature at least as well as the publications of the Psychoanalytical Society. As Thomas Mann has pointed out, many of Freud's discoveries gave clinical validity to insights which had been common to poets for centuries.

Freud Misunderstood and Misused

To digress briefly, we may wonder whether the preoccupation with Freudian psychoanalysis which has so greatly influenced fiction and poetry during the past forty years has not robbed literature of as much as it has given. This is not to question the valuc of Freud's discoveries and the theories he evolved from them; that would be impertinence. Not only has psychoanalysis taken its place as a therapeutic method, but its influence has been felt in virtually every part of modern life, and particularly in the arts. As a critical approach to works of art, it has been productive of much that is interesting and revealing, though it is by no means a substitute for a cultured mind, or for delicate sensibility and intuition, as some critics have supposed. Psychoanalysis is no bigger than the man who is using it, even when he has a good understanding of its theory and practice. Unfortunately it is applied, in nine cases out of ten, by critics who have not been analyzed and who have not otherwise troubled to equip themselves for what they attempt.

As for the creators, the writers, too many of them seem to have read a little psychoanalytical literature, but have not given the time and thought to the subject which it imperiously demands. Anyone who has read what Sigmund Freud and his principal followers actually wrote, and who has tried to understand it, must marvel at the opinions attributed to these men by critics and writers who plainly have not troubled to inform themselves, and by the deductions they make about the work of others. They have sought to make a half-baked notion of Freudianism serve them in the place of the observation and insight without which a writer is worthless. How much better is the method of Frank O'Connor, who, well knowing what psychoanalysis has to offer, sets it aside and works from his own point of view, relying on what he has seen and felt, rather than on what he has read. He has grasped what Mann has so finely expressed—that psychoanalysis corroborates and fills in what the artist knows in his own way—or else he is no artist. For instance, in his fine story *My Oedipus Complex*, Mr. O'Connor brings to a small boy in a poor district of Cork the problem which, in Freud, appears in terms of myth and theory. O'Connor throws fully as much light on Freud as Freud does on O'Connor, and the great concept, far from being diminished, gains force from the humorous reality of the tale. Except in his title, O'Connor gives no hint that he has ever heard of Freud, and the child's plight has the fresh and personal quality which common experiences have when we meet them directly, and not through the minds of others. To O'Connor the Oedipus complex is an archetype; to lesser writers it is all too often a stereotype.

Critics and writers who try to make some measure of Freudian psychology do service for personal insight narrow their range and inhibit whatever talent and imagination they may possess. Freud's writings, like psychoanalysis itself, tend to emphasize and confirm whatever a man truly is; but partly read and much misunderstood, they beget a barren pessimism which is not a true, philosophic pessimism, and which is good for nothing at all. It smears and effaces all moral values, whereas a fuller knowledge of psychoanalysis tends toward a deeper understanding and an enlargement of moral values.

The novels and poems which proceed from writers in the grip of this barren pessimism are of the kind which make narrow moralists fume, and use words like "decadence"; the writers rejoice, because making narrow moralists (who are usually frightened people) hop with rage is a sign that they have hit a mark, and they do not understand how poor and easy a mark it is. But when one sort of fool vexes another sort of fool, the result is not necessarily a literary triumph, and need not signify that anybody on either side has been saying anything of the least consequence. Such controversies belong to the Higher Jackassery, and should not be confused with the development of literature or the human spirit.

The matter of the influence of psychoanalysis in modern literature will certainly come up again in later chapters, but for the moment we must return to our books about enjoying and enduring.

The Industrious Apprentice Rejected

THEY HARP insistently upon success, and success is clearly defined as getting ahead in business, including the parson business. We may wonder if they are not written to satisfy a need among readers which is little heeded by writers of fiction. There are few books written nowadays about the Industrious Apprentice who works hard and faithfully, marries his master's daughter, and lives a contented life. Nevertheless, the Industrious Apprentice still holds his place in the human heart. If fiction shows him to be a rascal, who gets his fortune by tricky means, or a dull oaf whose soul is content with money-grubbing, or a favorite of fortune who rides on the crest of an economic wave, so much the worse for fiction. Readers who want the Industrious Apprentice will look elsewhere.

Success, insofar as it appears in modern fiction, is given a wry turn. A whole school of American writers, of whom John P. Marquand was a distinguished example, have shown that success is as much dust and ashes as inherited social and economic position. The Angry Young Men of England thought poorly of it; John Wain, in *The Contenders*, goes to some pains to show that in business and the arts it is bought at an inordinate price, and one of the great charms of Kingsley Amis's *Lucky Jim* is that the success of the hero is utterly undeserved. In the novels of Jack Kerouac the "success" is the hipster, whose aim in life is "getting his kicks" and who regards conventional success as richly funny. Samuel Smiles, if he were to return to earth today, would look in vain for fiction which would support his own firm notions of the goodness of success founded on desert.

We cannot suppose that Smiles would approve of the self-help books which offer success founded on religion, for he would instantly spot them for what they are—delusive offerers of success founded on craft. Get God on your side and success is yours. God is not the rewarder of virtue, but the Genie in the Bottle, who comes when you utter the magic formula. We must deny that this is religion in any high sense.

God Not the Only Listener to Prayer

PERHAPS WE MAY deny that it is religion at all. Mystics have often warned against powers which may be set at work by means of prayer and which are not related to God, but rather to the Devil. To speak of the Devil in our time is to invite mockery; he is not in fashion. Therefore let us say that there are powers which may be called to one's aid which are not powers of the highest good, and that these powers can be cajoled or bullied into giving us our own way. If worldly success appears to a man to be the highest good, rather than one among many pleasing and comfortable things which belong to the second order of benefits, he is likely to think that anything which gives him what he so earnestly desires must needs be God. After all, has not St. Thomas Aquinas said that it is legitimate to pray for anything it is legitimate to desire? And if Dr. Peale can show us how to pray for these things in a way which delivers the goods, are we not ungrateful to say that the imitation of Peale is not necessarily the Imitation of Christ?

Yet if we look a little more carefully than the greedy man who cannot conceive of a benefit greater than worldly success, we find not a flaw but a vast chasm in any such argument. Prayer is petition, intercession, adoration, and contemplation; great saints and mystics have agreed on this definition. To stop short at petition is to pray only in a crippled fashion. Further, such prayer encourages one of the faults which is most reprehended by spiritual instructors—turning to God without turning from Self. When that happens, the experts in these matters warn us, we should know that God is not the only answerer of petitions. Where do the other answers come from? The answer is an unfashionable one.

If this seems to be hitting too hard at a class of books which most people consider harmless, let me call attention to the style in which the books themselves are written. The name of God is very freely used, and therefore the grounds of argument have been chosen by the writers. But when God comes into an argument, we are able to call upon the authority of men and women whose intuitions and experience have won the admiration of deeply serious people for many centuries, and they are not in agreement with these apostles of God as a way to Success. That God may grant worldly success is possible, they say; that He may approve of it is also possible; but that He can be compelled to give it by means of infallible formulas they utterly deny.

The writers who offer God as an assistant in business are in tune—no, not even with the Infinite as understood by Ralph Waldo Trine—with an intensely materialistic concept of religion which is common in our day. Whereas once it was assumed that happiness and salvation were to be sought, not in our environment, but in our attitude toward our environment, it is now assumed that the environment is of primary importance. Insofar as the individual's state of mind is important, it is important as a means of influencing his surroundings, and this comes close to magic. If a man wishes to resort to magic in order to obtain the treasures of this world, that is his own affair; but let him not be deluded that what he is doing is necessarily pleasing to God or that the rewards he gets are evidences of God's grace.

Let him be very well aware that what he is dealing with is the Kingdom of this World, and that although his Positive Thinking, or whatever it may be, will doubtless develop some of his powers which have hitherto been quiescent, he is not engaged in a quest for God. Nor is he seeking to be subsumed in anything greater than himself, which is the usual desire of those who undertake a spiritual quest. If he wants success (and there seems, on the face of it, to be little harm in wanting to be solvent and comfortable), let him be well and truly aware of it. It is not self-help, as defined by Smiles and his like, which disgusts; it is making a religion of it, and equating success with virtue.

This book has no pretension to being a work of theology, and if some passages immediately foregoing appear to have a theological flavor, it is because such a study as this demands that the works under examination be related to others of vastly greater value. Our purpose here is literary criticism.

These books of enjoying and enduring call for consideration because they are so numerous and so popular, and because they represent one element of what people in general are reading, as opposed to what literary critics and literary enthusiasts are reading. If they have been condemned harshly, it is because they cheat and bamboozle their readers; they seem to offer gold, but it is fool's gold.

The Literary Test

HOW CAN WE be so sure? By one literary test, at least. It may be stated as a law of criticism that any book which has anything of worth to say will impress a receptive reader by the style in which it is written. This is not to say that it will be written in a great style, or an easy and accomplished style, but that it will be written in a style which compels attention and impresses by its aptness. The quality of what is said inevitably influences the way in which it is said, however inexperienced the writer. It is the critic's task to be sensitive to such writing, even when it at first repels by a superficial ineptitude. If you seek examples, read the outpourings of some of the great religious enthusiasts of the Quaker persuasion; they have no art, but the worth of what they say can be plainly felt, and gives dignity to their writing.

Most of the books which fall into the class dealt with in this chapter fail in this test: Smiles and Dimnet are the rare exceptions among them; even Bennett has the air of a man seeking to persuade others to believe something he wishes, rather than believes, to be true.

If this rule of criticism seems arbitrary as it stands, it may be related to the elementary dictum of philosophy that "the thing known is in the knower according to the mode of the knower"—which is a grand way of saying that you cannot pour more than a pint out of a pint pot. Nor, conversely, can you pour more than a pint into the same pot when it is empty. The pint-size writer finds pint-size readers. These books of self-help can all be boiled down to the old Latin maxim *Volentem ducit, nolentem trahit,* which is as much as to say that success will come to those who want it most, and will avoid those who, for whatever reason, stand in their own way.

As for the striking numbers of books about enjoying and enduring which are published now, and the great success of some of them, they may be explained by recalling the reply of King Charles the Second to one who asked him the reason why vast crowds gathered to hear a certain preacher: "I suppose his nonsense agrees with their nonsense," said the Merry Monarch.

· III ·
Ovid Is Not Their Master

How many people are there who can honestly say that they have no interest in love? How many have not enjoyed some dream of success in love? One of the effects of increasing literacy has been to give love an importance it never enjoyed before in human history. "Love is only one of many passions . . . it has no great influence on the sum of life," said Dr. Johnson; if he were alive today, he could not be so certain. The vastly extended realm of psychology, as well as popular belief, would be against him. It is not surprising that in an age when we have come to believe that virtually everything can be learned from books, there should be so many books which offer, not merely general advice, but plans and techniques by which love may be won and held.

The earliest of such books in the Western World, and one which is still of great interest to those who read it understandingly, is the *Ars amatoria*, or *Art of Love*, by the Roman poet Publius Ovidius Naso; he wrote it, so far as we know, about the year 2 B.C. Dr. S. G. Owen, in the *Encyclopaedia Britannica*, calls it "perhaps the most immoral work ever written by a man of genius." Considered by modern standards of morality, this sharp judgment may be defended; Ovid has no place in his poem for that warm reciprocal admiration which moralists today consider to be a necessary accompaniment of a satisfactory sexual union; nor does he assume, as moralists are apt to do, that a love affair should be approached as though it were to last a lifetime. He wrote his poem to tell men and women how to attract, how to please, and how to hold their lovers until they wanted a change. The word "*ars*" in his title means "art," but in the sense of "technical instruction."

He wrote very much as a man of the world and as a man of taste. His work is as free of underbred leering and nudging as it is of moralizing; he wrote a poem and a textbook, but not a work of pornography or edification. When he has to speak of delicate matters, he writes frankly but sparely. The tone of the poem is brilliant and witty, but it is not heartless, and it does not lack passages of beauty and tenderness. The second and third books of the poem end with virtually the same words: "emulate my precepts and write upon the trophies of your conquests, *Ovid was my master*."

As we read the books which are written for the guidance of lovers in our time, we find that they have little to say which Ovid did not say before them, and thus far he is indeed their master. But we may wish that he had been their master in style, as well. It is not only his genius as a poet, but his lack of vulgarity in thought and expression which distinguishes Ovid from all but a few of those who, since the attempt to establish general literacy, have gone over the same ground.

Fowler the Phrenologist

TRACING the earliest of these books which may be called "modern" is a task for the research scholar. It will be enough for us here to look at one which enjoyed a very wide popularity between its publication in 1870, and 1910. The name on the cover is, discreetly, *Science of Life,* but on the title page the author is more specific, thus:

CREATIVE
AND
SEXUAL SCIENCE
OR
MANHOOD, WOMANHOOD, AND THEIR MUTUAL INTERRELATIONS
LOVE, ITS LAWS, POWER, ETC.

Selection, or Mutual adaptation; Courtship, Married Life and Perfect Children
Generation, Endowment, Paternity, Maternity, Bearing, Nursing and Rearing; Together with Puberty, Boyhood, Girlhood, etc., Sexual Impairments Restored, Male Vigor and Female Health and Beauty Perpetuated And Augmented, Etc.

As Taught By
PHRENOLOGY AND PHYSIOLOGY
BY PROF. O. S. FOWLER

Practical Phrenologist and Lecturer; Founder of Fowler and Wells; Author of "Human Science," "Sexual Science," "Self-Culture," "Love and Parentage," "Matrimony," "Offspring and Their Hereditary Endowment," "Maternity," "Amativeness," Etc. Etc.

Comprehensive as this title page seems to be, it neglects a few of the valuable contents of the book, including instructions as to how to build a good rain-water cistern at a total cost of $26.20. There are ten hundred and fifty-two pages in all, and most of them are entertaining.

The author, Orson Squire Fowler, was well known in his day as a lecturer on phrenology. He was born in Cohocton, N.Y., in 1809, graduated from Amherst in 1834. Presumably it was at Amherst that his lifelong zeal for phrenology was aroused, for he began practicing that species of divination in 1835 in New York City, and continued in it until his death in 1887. Phrenology has passed out of favor, and is laughed at by people who are not at all sure of what it was. But in its time it was as seriously regarded as vocational guidance is today, and many eminent people were among its supporters. It may be assumed that it suited the tone of the time, and by examining the Professor's book, we can learn much of what that tone was.

Anyone who undertakes to read Fowler's book must accustom himself to the Professor's heaving, pulsing—perhaps I may say tumescent—prose. It is impossible to give any notion of this style without quoting, though it rebukes the quoter, for nothing less than a few thousand words is adequate. Here, however, is a flourish from the Preface:

> NATURE'S CREATIVE ordinances thus become the all-important subject of human inquiry. To learn just *what parental* conditions confer superior and what inferior bodies and minds, what the most and best talents and virtues, and what particular *kinds,* as well as what preclude and what promote physical diseases and sinful proclivities, should be the paramount study of all prospective parents, all students of Nature, and of man. Though all know that all parents transmit all their specialties, dis-

eases included, to their issue, yet who has ever shown precisely *what* parental conditions entail longevity or consumption, these constitutional excesses and those defects? And yet these *ante*-natal causes affect all they say, do, and are a thousand-fold more than all *post*-natal influences combined.

ASTOUNDING that sensible marital candidates ignore, even taboo, this only *rationale* of marriage! How cruelly recreant to self-interest and progenital welfare!

MUST HUMANITY FOREVER IGNORE a subject thus infinitely eventful to all parents and children, communities and the race!

No, thunders out this volume.

The Professor tells his readers that he writes under an IMPERIOUS MANDAMUS issued from the Supreme Court of Truth, and has no patience with fopperies of composition and the delights of rhetoric. Describing his own style, he says: "Catering little to epicurean literary fastidiousness, it presents its thoughts, principles, arguments, and facts as clearly and forcibly, yet succinctly, as possible, seeking mainly to be fully understood, reach the head, probe the heart, and improve the *life* of every reader, and adopts a plain, straightforward, business-like style which exactly expresses the meaning intended."

An odd echo of Ovid, whom the Professor otherwise ignores, occurs in this trumpetlike preface. "Its beneficiaries," he says of his book, "remember your *benefactor*."

A Pioneer in Sex Instruction

WHAT ARE the benefactions bestowed by this book? It may be said that for all its oddity and phrenological bias, it was the nearest thing that most of its readers encountered to a scientific explanation of sex. The Professor was a pioneer in sexual instruction. In a footnote he tells us: "In 1841, I paid in advance for the lecture-room of Rutger's Seminary, N.Y., for a lecture on marriage, and on entering was forewarned that if I applied my subject to the production of fine children, its gaslights would be turned off, and I imprisoned. I *dared* them, and have continued to dare their kindred till to-day, as this book attests." Rhetorically haranguing somebody called Sweet Sixteen, the Professor demands why she incurs "toilet expenditures" in her "half-crazy efforts to get married" but will not hear the lessons of eugenics? Sweet Sixteen, who is just as accomplished a word-spinner as the Professor, replies: "Because it is improper, immodest, impure, corrupting, and prematurely provokes those passions which should slumber till marriage." Quaint though this attitude seems now, it was unquestionably the prevalent one in the nineteenth century, and it would be over-bold to say that it will never return to favour, for the range of human folly is infinite.

It is necessary to remind oneself continually when reading Fowler that he was a pioneer, at grips with ignorance and prejudice on a scale now hard to imagine. His bumptious egotism sets us against him, and wherever time has deflated him, we are pleased. His ancestry led him to believe, on phrenological grounds, that he would live to a great age, and he records that "at over 68" he was "sprightly, works harder than can well be told, and writes and reads this *without glasses*." He died at a mere seventy-eight, which must have surprised him. He makes wild assertions, such as: "Dwarfiness is hereditary. The exhibition of Tom Thumb, Commodore Nutt and their wives, and like diminutives, before pregnant women, has produced many dwarfs." No field of speculation is closed to him, and he drops such comments as "Irishmen are irate, and perhaps were so named because their irritable, excitable, impulsive ancestors were so ireish." Brigham Young he regards as "very near being a premium male," and Daniel Webster is "the highest type of manhood," a distinction he shares with George Washington, Thomas Jefferson, and John Hancock.

Female Beauty Defined

Fowler's notions of female beauty are those of his time, but he has his own way of describing his ideal. "A Prominent Mons Veneris Desirable" is the heading of subsection 562, and in 563 he tells us that "ovarian or groin fulness is very beautifying." Like other right-thinkers of his time, he condemns tight-lacing and roars against mothers who urge their daughters into extreme corsets, but he asserts that a small waist—which in his day meant a very small waist indeed—is natural, and a sign of health. Pads for the hips he rebukes thus:

> Paniers Are a Toilet Abomination.
>
> Besides making a great postal bag, which shakes around with every quick motion, it bunglingly imitates the form of her seat, the cleaving of the back at the bottom of the spine, the bulging out on each side of the seat, and—Sha, sha, fashionable ladies. You outrage taste to nausea. For shame!

But "men admire large female limbs with small feet," and beauty at its highest is revealed in his countryman, Hiram Powers's statue called "The Greek Slave." This piece, now in the Corcoran Gallery in Washington, D.C., was one of the wonders of the American Section at the Great Exhibition of

1851, and was thus described by a contemporary observer: "During the early Greek revolutions the captives were exposed for sale in the Turkish Bazaar, under the name of 'slaves.' The artist has delineated a young girl, deprived of her clothing, standing before the licentious gaze of a wealthy Eastern barbarian. Her face expresses shame and disgust at her ignominious position, while about her lip hovers that contemptuous scorn which a woman can so well show for her unmanly oppressor." This opinion is repeated because the modern beholder may well miss any such look on the ovine face of the Slave. She was much employed to throw shame on tight-lacers, or merely those whom Nature had denied a good figure. Says Fowler: "To see at Presidential and other receptions ladies arrayed in the height of style, showing their pipe-stem arms and deficient breasts, looks utterly pitiable and mean. Go home, girls, and cultivate arm-muscle, and work with them bare. Your washing-maids are your superiors. Help them Beaux, just see how much better the arms of Una, Menken, and Powers's Greek Slave, than those of Emily Regal." (Miss Regal, an actress of the day, is shown in a bad line drawing as an example of "The Faun, or Slim Female Figure," though to modern eyes she seems positively strapping.)

Another type of femininity condemned by Fowler is "Miss Woman's Rights," pictured as a creature of minatory expression, whose pernicious opinions "antagonize the sexes and hinder offspring."

Platonic Love Man's Normal State

THE EXTREME freedom with which Fowler expresses opinions on matters far from his professed subject, and his busybody airs, seem to have been characteristic of social reformers in his day, and may have been expected. His ideas about sexual behavior and marriage are those of North America in his time. To love was to propose marriage; any other course was dishonorable. Flirting imposed dangerous strains on the nervous system. The mating period ordained by Nature lay between the ages of nineteen and twenty-three. The vigilance of a good mother over her daughters was "lynx-like." Verbal proposals were permissible, but a letter was much to be preferred because it could be kept for future reference. Platonic love, even in marriage, was "man's normal state," and such love did not involve physical desire because it created no semen in the male. Continence, except to beget children, must be the rule of marriage, for "manifesting passion begets a mutual commonness, a letting down in each other's eyes."

On the matter of continence Fowler seems to have been in some confusion, for he insists that it is a necessary course not only for purity, but because without it the world would "get full"; nevertheless, he is agonized by the frequency of "fashionable small families" among the wealthy.

He believed, and passed on, the medieval notion that spermatozoa contain all the human organs in miniature. He condemned the marriage of cousins. He passes on a method of controlling the sex of children, which he attributes to a French veterinary, Professor Thury of Geneva; if a girl is desired, conception must take place within three days of the close of menstruation, but if it is delayed until the week following the seventh day after the close of menstruation, the child will be a boy. *The Lancet* is quoted in support of this theory. On the questions of birthmarks and prenatal influences, his attitude can only be called superstitious.

In Search of the Angel Child

FOWLER SPEAKS for his age in his highly colored and cruel condemnations of masturbation; the nineteenth century seems to have had a maggot on this subject. The acne of adolescence is attributed to it, and so is adolescent self-consciousness, manifesting itself in "a mawkish, shamed, repellent look." All faults of complexion aroused suspicion, and so did a bad breath. Prostitutes and men of evil life could be distinguished by their disgusting smell. But the masturbator was of all sexual offenders the most wretched. Fowler quotes with approval from Adam Clarke's *Commentary on Onan*: "The muscles become flaccid and feeble, the tone and natural action of the nerves relaxed and impeded, the understanding confused, the memory oblivious, the judgement perverted, the will indeterminate and wholly without energy to resist; the eyes appear languishing and without expression, and the countenance vacant; *appetite ceases,* for the stomach is incapable of performing its proper office; *nutrition fails;* tremors, fears and terrors are generated; and thus the wretched victim drags out a miserable existence, till, *superannuated,* even before he had time to arrive at *man's estate,* with a mind often debilitated even to a state of idiotism, his worthless body tumbles into the grave, and his guilty soul (guilty of self-murder) is hurried into the awful presence of its Judge!" The book's anti-intellectual bias reveals itself in the comment that self-pollution is particularly rife in the universities, and that "literary institutions" are its hotbeds.

Fowler's rule for sexual intercourse may be quoted as embodying a widely held and admired nineteenth-century ideal: "CONDUCT EVERY SEXUAL REPAST throughout precisely as if it were to originate an angel child for both to love and nurture."

Is there anything of value in Fowler's book? Yes, there is enough to assure him of some stature as a pioneer of sexual enlightenment. He describes the act of coition scientifically, which was daring in a book intended for the general reader, and he says that women like it and receive benefit from it, which is extremely daring for 1870. The idea was widely held then that women submitted themselves to the act of procreation submissively, but with some disgust, and that they could find no pleasure in it. A woman who did so was a wanton, and it is observable that in the literature of the time the character of the Good Prostitute always protests that she hates her trade. Women endured sex in order that they might have children. It was as mothers, not as lovers, that decent women fulfilled themselves. If Fowler's admission that women enjoy coitus in marriage seems to contradict his certainty about Platonic Love, it is not the only contradiction in his thousand-odd pages.

The conventional nineteenth-century attitude cannot be reconciled with the stock comic figure of the amorous Old Maid in the fiction and drama of the time. Unmarried women were coarsely and cruelly taunted with their supposed eagerness to get a man—any sort of man. Presumably they wanted him for Platonic Love. There is no logic in such popular attitudes. But most of the books to be considered in this chapter make it clear that whatever our society professes to believe about sex, an earthy knowledge of what it involves and how it works lies beneath the professions, and is at odds with them.

Dr. Chevasse and Associates

FOWLER'S BOOK appeared in 1870. It is instructive to look at a popular book which came out in the United States in 1880, but which was not of American authorship. It was, in the main, the work of an English physician, Pye Henry Chevasse, with "notes and additions by an eminent American author," and certain passages from French and German writers. It is called *Man's Strength and Woman's Beauty*, and as a scientific work it is a considerable advance on Fowler. It has a sane discussion of the marriage of blood relatives; it denies that the sex of a child can be determined by any method; it suggests, gingerly, that masturbation need not bring about madness and death; it is dubious about the value to health and the spirit of complete continence within marriage; it is sensible in the regimen it prescribes for pregnant women. But it is a book of its time, declaring on the first page of its preface that it is not written "to feed the prurient fancies of a vulgar mind"—which seems to exclude any suggestion that sex is something other than a burdensome religious duty.

Dr. Chevasse and his unnamed collaborators warn continually against the dangers of a fashionable life, for it hastens puberty, and greatly increases the perils of the menopause. It leads to light and trashy reading, which, as night follows day, brings about menstrual disorders and a nasty ailment called Leucorrhea, and may lead to "secret bad habits." But true love makes a woman "almost an angel" and will assist her to fulfill her destiny. "For man, love is an end; for woman, but a means of becoming a mother, for the young mother exists already in the heart of the young maiden; to her eyes a sexual union is less the satisfaction of a desire than the origin of a hope; for woman loves, long before its birth, the infant within her breast."

How to Control Desire

IF SEXUAL DESIRE should, by some mischance, exist in both parties, its remedy is set forth in an anecdote of a physician named Zimmerman. One of his patients, a prince (ah, fashionable life!), complained: "I am worn out with exhaustion from too frequent indulgence. Such is the transport of our mutual love that we are gradually led to its consummation on every occasion of our meeting. How can I exercise greater self-control?" "Very easily," replied the physician: "simply by repeating the Lord's Prayer before your dalliance is commenced."

When sexual intercourse is regarded in such a light, and is surrounded with so many restrictions, readers of a psychological turn of mind may not be surprised to find Dr. Chevasse enthusiastic in another direction. "No family ought to be without a *good* enema apparatus, to fly to in any emergency." The cold-water enema is recommended as "bracing and strengthening." No restriction or prayerful deterrent is placed on the number of enemas except, presumably, that imposed by satiety, which governs this pleasure, as all others.

The works of Fowler and Chevasse have been given detailed attention here because they illustrate how timidly the new literacy of the nineteenth century approached a subject which was taboo. Fowler showed some courage, but he was not a man who doubted current opinion in large matters, and he was innocent of scientific training. His chief concern was with his bump-feeling, and his interest in sex stemmed from it, for he wanted to get the right skulls together to breed a superior race of Americans; his notion of superiority, if we judge by his book, would be in terms of more and more maidenly girls, unlaced, full-groined, big-limbed, and small-footed, uniting with youths of the Daniel Webster type in a matrimony of Platonic abstinence, enlivened by very occasional devout attempts to lure an angel out of heaven and into the cradle. Dr. Chevasse was a scientist in the sense that most medical men are scientists, which is to say that his deeper prejudices about moral matters had been given the reinforcement of a conventionally scientific training. Neither Fowler nor Chevasse had the slightest notion of how to approach sexual matters in a truly scientific spirit, or any desire to do so. Sexual deviation or idiosyncrasy was either unknown to them or, more likely, considered too horrible for discussion.

Havelock Ellis a Man of Letters

It is against this background that we must understand the sensation caused in 1897 when Havelock Ellis published the first volume of his *Studies in the Psychology of Sex*, which dealt with sexual inversion. Ellis was not prosecuted himself, but a bookseller who sold his book was defendant in *Regina vs. Bedborough*, and Ellis left England for a time. The continuation of his great work was assured by arrangement with F. A. Davis of Philadelphia, a reputable medical publisher who had brought out Krafft-Ebing, to publish the subsequent five volumes in the U.S. It is interesting that in matters relating to supposedly scandalous publication, Britain and the United States are often at odds, each offering consolation to authors from the other land who have been roughly used at home. There is no discernible principle of free expression in these exchanges, and what will excite the prosecutors in either country continues to be a mystery.

Ellis was the first man of letters, and the first person with the outlook and instincts of a gentleman, to write a book about sex in English. He had the additional qualification of a scientific training, for he had studied medicine for eight years, not with a view to practice (he never practiced), but to satisfy his boundless and ever fresh curiosity about mankind. Scientists of sex were many, and some of them had great reputations, but their writings reveal an ignorance of life, a conventionality of outlook, and an inability to see what was under their noses; when a man has become a great figure in society as a physician, we must not be surprised if he regards the laws of society as the laws of Nature—but we need not respect him for it.

Good Breeding Means Passivity

SUCH a sexual scientist was Dr. Richard von Krafft-Ebing, professor of psychiatry and nervous diseases at the University of Vienna. His *Psychopathia Sexualis* was a great pioneer work, though he made it clear in his preface that he wished to "exclude the lay reader" and had thus written some of his book in Latin. (There is a charming simplicity in his supposition that only doctors know Latin.) But it was a book of sexual pathology; as Ellis points out, it gives scant attention to normal sexuality, and of what it has to say on that subject, much is wrong. Consider these key passages from the relevant chapter. "Woman . . . if physically and mentally normal, and properly educated, has but little sensual desire" . . . "Woman is wooed for her favour. She remains passive. Her sexual organization demands it, and the dictates of good breeding come to her aid" . . . "Man primarily loves woman as his wife, and then as the mother of his children; the first place in woman's heart belongs to the father of her child, the second to him as husband" . . . "The wife accepts marital intercourse not so much as a sensual gratification than as a proof of her husband's affection." This is not much better than Fowler or Chevasse, yet it is the considered view of a nineteenth-century physician of the highest repute, expressed in defiance of all that literature and his practice might have taught him. For Krafft-Ebing, normality was the set of beliefs according to which upper-class Vienna imagined itself to live. This was indeed that "sleep of the world" which Sigmund Freud said he gave mortal offense by disturbing.

Ellis had neither a reputation nor a medical practice to consider when he decided to make an investigation of sexual behavior the chief work of his life. He was seventeen, attempting to earn his living as a schoolmaster at Sparkes Creek, in the Australian bush, and his decision arose because of the perplexities his own sexual development brought him. That was in 1879, and the first volume of the *Studies* did not appear until 1896. Through no doing of his, it was the volume dealing with Sexual Inversion, and it was described legally as "a wicked, bawdy and scandalous and obscene book," intending "to vitiate and corrupt the morals of the liege subjects of our Lady the Queen, to debauch and poison the minds of divers of the liege subjects of our said Lady the Queen, and to raise and create in them lustful desires, and to bring the liege subjects into a state of wickedness, lewdness and debauchery." It is no wonder that the essentially pure-minded Ellis needed a holiday after a trial in which Bedborough pleaded guilty, and was bound over after a fearsome moral lecture from the judge, Sir Charles Hall.

Queens, Elephants, and Clergymen

THE *Studies* were revolutionary because they marshaled a vast amount of evidence from literature, books of travel, folklore, and anthropology, and personal communication, showed how it all held together, and put it forth without moral judgments. Thus the behavior of a mythic Irish Queen was adduced to throw light on the curious Saturday-afternoon micturition contests of girls in an upper-class English school in the nineteenth century; thus homosexuality—which has always cherished its intellectual and *avant-garde* trappings—was discussed in terms of sailors and American hobos, as well as in terms of Leonardo and Michelangelo, and was shown to be common among such diverse creatures as doves and elephants, as well as men; even the rooted notion that women—except of the depraved sort—shrank from sexual experience was questioned. Perhaps the most alarming of all Ellis's ideas was his insistence on the play element in sexual relationships. Sex for fun! The idea which underlay three quarters of the dirty jokes of the nineteenth century seemed hideously indecent when Ellis propounded it in all sincerity to a society which considered itself, at highest, to be seeking to bring down angels from Heaven.

Much of the scandal of the book attached to the personal communications which Ellis printed. These are autobiographical accounts of sexual development and experience written for him by people who had sought his help, and who consented to their publication, with names suppressed. Some of them are from clergymen, some from officers in the services, some from teachers. Later writers on sexual subjects have complained that taken as a whole, they do not cover a very wide range of society or a very large number of people. But they were the first things of their kind, and they are excellent reading still. They have the ring of truth, and some of them have the dull egotism of the sex fusser in every line. They throw an extraordinary light on Victorian life, and particularly upon the place of servants in the sexual enlightenment of the middle and upper classes in England. It was a great part of Ellis's genius that he was able to call forth such documents. I have been told by friends who knew him that his honesty and cleanness of heart were so apparent, his understanding and compassion so great, and his advice so admirable, that he won confidence very readily.

A Great Work

SINCE THE APPEARANCE of the *Studies*, books about sex have undergone radical change. Of course the *Studies* were not widely sold, for the firm of F. A. Davis made no attempt to offer them except to medical men, lawyers, large libraries, and the like. But they were very widely read. I first encountered them in the librarian's private room in a Canadian university; they could not be taken away without his approval; yet they were read almost to tatters, for they satisfied a curiosity which is universal.

Furthermore, they satisfy it as no writer between Ovid and Ellis tried to do, and as no writer, to my knowledge, has done since; these are the writings of a man of letters who was, incidentally, a man of science. These are books which can be read with pleasure: most books about sex have to be read for what is in them, while the critical, literary faculty is kept on the chain. But in *Studies in the Psychology of Sex* Havelock Ellis wrote the greatest work of literature which is also a work of science in the English tongue, after Robert Burton's *Anatomy of Melancholy*. Like Ovid, he can write of the most delicate matters without becoming mawkish or sly; his dissertation on the play element in love-making is masterly in its avoidance of those earth-bound ecstasies, those asthmatic raptures which mar, for instance, even so valuable a book as Van de Velde's *Ideal Marriage*. And always there is the astonishment of his remarkable erudition. However his successors may nibble at his conclusions, they will not destroy him unless they can write like him. His strengths are those of Ovid: he loved truth better than the morality of his day, he had the instincts of a gentleman and a man of cultivation, and he wrote as an artist.

After Ellis

NOTHING IS TO BE gained from individual consideration of the great number of books about sex and making love which are now offered to the public. They sell steadily, and they are great favorites with borrowers from public libraries. Upon the whole, this may be considered one of the victories of our general literacy. Ellis said: "The largest part of the troubles of marriage and of the perils of sex is due merely to ignorance and superstition." There are now many books suited to every level of intelligence which will dispel ignorance and superstition. If our age is not distinguished for a greatly increased number of happy marriages and a more intelligent approach to the problems of sex, we may surely assert that *some* forms of misery in the sexual realm are less widespread than they used to be; and of the many people who are unhappy, thousands have some idea of what lies at the root of their unhappiness, and thus far they are better off than their forefathers, who had none, or attributed their distress to sin.

"America appears to be the only country where love is a national problem," wrote a French traveler, Raoul de Roussy de Sales, in the *Atlantic* in 1938. It might be nearer the truth to say that America is the only country sufficiently lacking in self-consciousness to admit it; the writings of psychiatrists and social workers make it clear that love is a problem everywhere. But the United States tackles the problem with characteristic zeal, discussing it in thousands of books and magazine articles, some of them by people who know what they are talking about. But it is clear that frank discussion is not enough.

One of the most interesting aspects of the studies of the late Dr. Kinsey and his associates is the material they bring forward to show that sexual habits vary greatly among people of different standards of education—that it is, in fact, related to class. This is something many people knew already, but most people are apt to deny. "Love levels all ranks," says the Captain of the *Pinafore* when he has suffered a sharp demotion. "It does to a considerable extent, but it does not level them as much as that," says the First Lord of the Admiralty. In our day, statistics relating to levels of education and levels of income are on the side of the First Lord. This is not, of course, to say that the mating of two millionaire Ph.D.'s necessarily results in bliss, whereas two loving share-croppers cannot hope for it. It does not even mean that if a millionaire Ph.D. chooses a beggar maid for his bride they may not be happy. The permutations and combinations of human misery are too complex for any such rules. But it seems clear that as a general thing, people marry most happily with their own kind. The trouble lies in the fact that people usually marry at an age where they do not really know what their own kind is.

In the resulting welter the marriage counselor appears as a new figure in our complex society, and marriage counselors often write books. I have read many of them, and though I am perhaps too squeamish in such matters, I should not like to take their advice, because they offer it in such nasty prose. Not only do they like to reduce emotional problems to terms of charts and graphs, pictographs and tables, but when they are forced to use language, they show a regrettable fondness for such phrases as "overly meticulous" and "laughter—the best of all possible teen-tonics"; they are likely to call marriage "a great, thrilling, creative adventure"; they declare their intention to "make vivid the appeal of marriage at its best." And if I am rebuked for confusing tasteless expression with the quality of the advice offered, I had better say here and now that I do not trust any advice which is given in bad prose, and I think that matters relating to sex demand taste above all things in their discussion. Most of these books are badly written, and affect a seriousness of tone which, because it is so obviously pompous and false, arouses ribaldry in the reader. When a marriage counselor says of a woman who is behaving badly that "the deep fountains of her nature have never been unsealed," I do not see why I should take such writing any more seriously than I would if I met with it in a bad novel.

Bliss with a Chemical Engineer

THAT SOME of the advice in these books is useful, and that it is based on wide experience, is not denied. If people need a book to tell them that in marriage kindness and forbearance are necessary, and that the sexual act is happier when it is undertaken to give pleasure as well as to receive it, these books are what they want. Possibly people so lacking in understanding of themselves and others do not mind being addressed in the coarse, grainy prose of the marriage counselor. For others, there is much innocent joy to be derived from such books.

Consider, for instance, the "Happiness Rating According to Husband's Occupation," which Richard O. Lang includes in his *Predicting Success or Failure in Marriage*. What girl is not pleased to be warned against the dangers of marriage with barbers, laborers, traveling salesmen (those amorists of legend!), musicians, and plumbers? What prudent girl will not take heed and, dropping her fiddler or barber, encourage the approach of some electrical engineer, educational administrator, athletic coach, college professor, or clergyman? Perhaps, if she is a lucky girl indeed, she may land the very best risk of all—a chemical engineer! Why chemical engineers have this strange power to give happiness beyond other men is not explained; the fact is recorded, and we are left to ponder on it.

Compared with the marriage counselors, those who simply offer information about sex are better writers, and more in control of their material. Many of them are physicians, and they write in a bustling, consulting-room style which conveys both information and a slight patronage of the patient. Only rarely do they follow Fowler or Chevasse by giving moral lectures; they are content to tell what they know, and that is a combination of modern science with practical experience. The differences among their books are differences of style, for the facts of sex do not allow of much individual interpretation in their elementary form. The same unpleasing charts of the sexual organs (the male, like plans for a gravity water system; the female like the skull of an elk, with vastly branching antlers), the same cycle of puberty, maturity, and decline (with reassuring notes on the menopause and the prostate), the same brief description of procreation (without a word to hint that it could be a pleasure), of gestation, and of parturition (with ample assurance that it need not be a pain)—these are their inevitable contents. There is so little variety here that if our concern is literary, we may yearn for the spacious days of Fowler, and his high-minded yearning to play the pimp between Daniel Webster and Powers's Greek Slave. Fowler was a phrenologist and an ignoramus, but he had gusto; his book does not reek, as these do, of iodoform.

From this useful but undistinguished mass a few books rise as being of special merit. Simply as a presentation of fact, *A Marriage Manual* by Drs. Hannah and Abraham Stone manages to be at once comprehensive and brief, because of its question-and-answer form. Another work of deserved popularity is *Ideal Marriage* by Dr. T. H. Van de Velde, which has appeared in twenty-three languages. Its success lies in the fact that it is written, in the words of Dr. Johnson Abraham's preface to the English edition, "soberly, scientifically, completely, without a scintilla of eroticism, and yet with a sustained note of high idealism." The idealism is certainly there, and it is welcome; the flat, no-nonsense approach of the consulting room is not for Dr. Van de Velde; it is impossible to judge his style in an English translation, but it quite often aims—not always successfully—at lyricism. I cannot quite agree with Dr. Abraham that there is no "scintilla of eroticism" in what Van de Velde writes, for to write of sexual union at its highest levels without eroticism is to falsify one's subject and cheat the reader—and that is what Van de Velde does not do. Precisely for this reason he succeeds where most others fail. Where they are afraid of eroticism, he accepts it as an integral part of the kind of union he seeks to encourage because it is good. Those writers who have set themselves the task of writing about sex without eroticism are like dieticians who write about food without once suggesting that eating is, among other things, a pleasure.

The Era of the Erotic Novel

IF OUR WRITERS of books of sex instruction are fearful of eroticism, our novelists are not. Nor is their eroticism colored by the nobility of emotion which impels Van de Velde. Chevasse warned against fiction which might arouse passion by describing it; Fowler linked novel reading with liquor and tobacco in its ability to "inflame the Propensities." It is amusing, but beside the point, to speculate on what they would have thought about our age, when virtually every novel, good and bad, deals with sex in some degree, and the reader is often compelled to blunt his understanding if his Propensities are not to exist in a perpetual state of incandescence. We live in the era of the Erotic Novel, and it is part of our inheritance from the nineteenth century.

The depth-psychologies of Freud, Jung, and Adler had their beginnings in the latter part of the last century, though they did not achieve their present wide acceptance until after the First World War. How wide that acceptance is we cannot understand unless we are continually alert to the echoes, faint and distorted though these often are, which reach us in the advertising and social gabble of our time, as well as in every kind of writing. Much of the effect of this great revolution is good, for it has compelled us to take note of the huge place which love and sex occupy in the inner lives of men, women, and children. We are still unable to realize how great an emancipation it has been, for the work of the depth-psychologist has but begun, and is continually being extended and modified. But the brief survey of Fowler and Chevasse at the beginning of this chapter recalls a little of the immense blanket of humbug which has been lifted from the human mind.

Not that all our forbears were deluded. As Thomas Mann made clear in the great speech he gave on Freud's eightieth birthday in 1936, the depth-psychologists have discovered little that is new; they have but given a scientific form to what artists and poets have known for ages; they have codified and made coherent a vast store of poetic insight. The novelists who were contemporary with Fowler knew how many beans made five, but they were not free to say so plainly, for fear of offending "the young person" about whom Mr. Podsnap was so deeply concerned; her Propensities must not, under any circumstances, be inflamed. Dickens and Thackeray both regretted this attitude, but they bowed to it. Certain Victorian novelists—Surtees is a remarkable example—got away with a surprising amount of suggestion in their work. Trollope managed to say a good deal about the sexual side of the lives of the young men about town who appear in his novels.

Victorian Psychologists

THESE NOVELISTS were admirable psychologists, so far as public opinion and the dictation of the lending libraries would permit. Trollope, who stands for Victorian insipidity and dullness only in the minds of those who have not read him, was in some respects the greatest of them all. His study of a sluggish and unwilling middle-aged passion in the character of Nicholas Broune, the editor in *The Way We Live Now*, and of love in old age in the character of Sir Peregrine Orme, in *Orley Farm*, are of a brilliance which remains undimmed when we compare them with anything written since. The sense of obligation which makes Broune attempt to begin an affair with Lady Carbury, the chivalry which makes Sir Peregrine offer the shelter of his reputation to Lady Mason, are sexual in a sense not comprehended by our novelists of the grunt-and-puff school, but they are sexual all the same. And Trollope was not alone, though he is remarkable, in the possession of insight into sexual complexities. An examination of *Middlemarch* in this light is instructive; does anyone pretend that George Eliot did not know how much sexual incompatibility had to do with dividing Dorothea Brooke from Casaubon, or how much sexual passion served to bind Tertius Lydgate to Rosamond Vincy? By no means all of the Victorians were Fowlers, but they had to breathe the same air as Fowler, and that makes a greater difference than most of us can understand without some reflection.

The Victorian novelists, at their best, triumphed astonishingly over the restraints which were laid on them because they knew people and expected some answering knowledge in their readers: many modern novelists write as though they knew no one but Sigmund Freud—and that imperfectly—and expected their readers to know nothing at all.

Depth-psychology and Reason

THE RESPONSIBILITY for this state of affairs cannot be laid on the depth-psychologists. Freud and Jung have repeatedly made it clear that the purpose of their investigations is to strengthen the dominance of reason over human behavior by disciplining those hidden and ill-understood mental energies which defy or pervert reason. They have revolutionized our notion of how the mind works, and they have turned up fascinating material which no intelligent writer could be expected to resist. They have been grossly misunderstood and misinterpreted by the literary world. They have cast new light on every phase of human behavior and emotion, and in that light some acts and emotions have lost the prestige which formerly attached to them; but they have never, to my knowledge, denied the validity of reason as the greatest civilizing influence in human life; in order that reason may function at its best, a vast amount of material which is contrary to reason and frequently inimical to it must be examined and understood.

Modern fiction has entered into this task of examination with enthusiasm, but has usually shirked the hard task of pressing onward to understanding. The modern writer is too often a Theseus so enamored of the grotesque appearance and strange cavortings of the Minotaur that he has decided to make his permanent abode in the Labyrinth, and to accept the Minotaur's laws as his own.

Novels which lay the discoveries of the depth-psychologists under tribute and make a disciplined use of their material are among the finest written in our time. A notable example is Thomas Mann's *Felix Krull,* a novel of decidedly erotic character in which the insights of psychology are controlled by the reason and artistic discretion of the writer. A very different work, but produced by the same union of insight and reason, is *À la Recherche du Temps Perdu,* of Marcel Proust. Yet another example, superficially different from these but one with them in genesis, is Joyce's *Ulysses.* The list could be extended many times, but these three books serve as examples of works which could hardly have been written without the discoveries of the new depth-psychology, but which make those discoveries subordinate to the insight and artistic control of the writers.

Freud, Jung, and Adler continually stress the necessity to be as intelligent as possible in all departments of living, and their work is designed to support and strengthen intelligence and reason where they exist. But great numbers of writers who are gifted—sometimes greatly gifted—in their ability to express themselves appear to be mistrustful of intelligence and reason as guides in art. They are so proud of their ability to feel (or perhaps merely to simulate) the hot pulsings of emotion and unreason that they have no wish to go further, to make a synthesis of this material or to relate it to a background of intelligence and reason.

To do so would be to make their work, not moralistic, but moral. To use such a word today is to court mockery, for we are in revolt against so many false and cruel moralities, that great numbers of people rashly assume that there is no true morality. I am not a philosopher, and if I go too far into this water I shall certainly drown. But I am a critic of writing, and I feel that what is wrong with scores of modern novels which show literary quality, but which are repellent and depressing to the spirit, is not that their writers have rejected a morality, but that they have one which is unexamined, trivial, and lopsided. They have a base concept of life; they bring immense gusto to their portrayals of what is perverse, shabby, and sordid, but they have no very clear notion of what is Evil; the idea of Good is unattractive to them, and when they have to deal with it, they do so in terms of the sentimental, or the merely pathetic. Briefly, some of them write very well, but they write from base minds which have been unimproved by thought or instruction. They feel, but they do not think. And the readers to whom they appeal are the products of our modern universal literacy, whose feeling is confused and muddied by just such reading, and who have been deluded that their mental processes are indeed a kind of thought.

To continue further in this direction would be outside the purpose of this book, but if you wish to pursue the matter, a book by an American critic, Edmund Fuller, called *Man in Modern Fiction*, discusses it fully from the Christian-Judaeo point of view.

Sex in the Modern Novel

IT WOULD BE possible for a shy young man or woman to read twenty modern books of sex instruction without finding out any more than the mechanics of procreation. But twenty novels would suffice to turn a virgin of either sex into an accomplished theoretical amorist. Indeed, we may wonder whether the realities of sex would not seem tame to such a reader. Every feeder cannot be a gourmet; sexual experience will not provide the riot of sensation for everyone which the novels so elaborately describe. As the Welsh proverb says, we must sing with what voices God gave us. Students of our literature in future centuries may be surprised at the extreme value we place on sexual prowess in our time, and may draw the unflattering conclusion that we were both wistful and doubtful about it.

Not only heterosexual love, but homosexuality and aberration appear frequently in modern fiction. And why not? Art must be free to range over the whole of human experience, and if Faulkner writes of a perverted rape, or if Proust, or Mann, or Angus Wilson write of homosexuality, who wishes it otherwise? It is only where the element of art is weak, and where these themes are treated with a sickly romanticism which imagines itself to be realism, that our taste rebels. There can be scant knowledge of a character in fiction when the writer is only slightly acquainted with himself. It is in this writing, which proceeds from writers who know little of themselves and less of other men, that we find the grotesque sexual attitudes, the cult of what Fuller calls the Yahoo Hero. It is significant that many of these books are war books, or books about groups of men under stress, in which we find that there is exaggerated sexual activity with women who are described in terms of the uttermost contempt, whereas the true sentiment, the real love, is reserved for the "buddy," and is plainly homosexual.

Plainly? Perhaps that is putting it too strongly. It does not seem to be plain to the author, who fails to realize that the morality of his Marines, or whatever they may be, is that of the Theban Band. They are tough guys in battle, but they are unfitted for any other kind of life.

The Problem of the Good Woman

WHAT SORT of women do the tough guys encounter, in their unreal world? Good women, sweethearts and wives, who are good at sex; a woman who is not good at sex is certain to be discarded, and she will have other unpleasing characteristics, as well. Bad women, the Good Whores who have hearts of gold, and whose charity puts to shame those virtuous women who lack it. The Good Whores are often rich in motherly qualities and, if they are bawdy-house keepers, have a store of salty, hard-won wisdom. They are stereotypes, quite as romantic as the Good Whores of Victorian fiction, who melodramatically bewail their downfall.

It is, of course, very difficult to draw a portrait of a good and resolute virgin, and in evidence we may produce the dim creatures who serve as heroines in the novels of J. R. R. Tolkien, C. S. Lewis, and Charles Williams—three whom Mr. Fuller praises for their mastery of the demonic element in fiction. Demons these writers may understand: women, no. It is a common complaint against the novels of consciously moral writers—excellent as many of these are in other respects—that their heroines are wooden. Such characters are not women at all, but creatures embodying those qualities their authors would like women to possess, and no others. Their place in the story is that of an Ideal to be defended, and a Prize which may eventually be won. Perhaps the most striking single difference between Malory's *Morte d'Arthur* and Tennyson's *Idylls of the King* is that Malory's women are all human beings, and that Tennyson's are, in greater or less degree, prizes for good conduct. T. H. White, in his fine modern treatment of the Arthurian story, *The Once and Fu-*

ture King, again endows the Arthurian women with recognizably human character.

The Cult of the Meaningless

THE EMPHASIS on sex is probably no greater in modern life than it was a century or more ago, when the Great Experiment in universal literacy was begun. But it is different. Sexual matters are discussed in literature which have never previously been common knowledge. Undoubtedly, in the eighteenth and nineteenth centuries, millions of people lived and died without ever knowing that such a thing as homosexuality existed; such knowledge was confined to the upper classes, whose education was classical, and to the lowest class, whose poverty and ignorance stripped them of every pretense. In a social sense, the present widespread enlightenment about sexual matters has probably done far more good than harm. But in literature it has provided a great number of writers with themes which they use extravagantly, clothing them in a debased romanticism which does duty for thought, for artistic synthesis, and for a reasonably coherent morality.

Whether or not they find their own lives meaningless, they write as though they found life without meaning. Whether their hero is the Angry Young Man of English fiction, or the Holy Goof of Kerouac and the Beat Generation, he lives for the moment. It is not as though "Do what thou wilt shall be the whole of the law" was a precept from which splendid fiction could not be drawn; it is rather that what these small-time rebels choose to do is so trivial, so cheap, and in the end, so dreary.

Which Is Sex?

So we have in our bookshops and libraries two classes of books which deal with sex so differently that it is hard to realize that they are talking about the same thing. The books of instruction are aimed at a world in which everybody seems to want to live a complete and happy sexual life within the framework of conventional morality. The books of fiction seem to be addressed to a public which does not believe this to be possible, or even, perhaps, desirable. The books of instruction are written, in the main, without art, and their authors feel so heavy a weight of moral responsibility toward society that they succeed in taking the erotic element out of sex. They describe it; they recommend it; they *say* that it is a source of pleasure, refreshment, and fulfillment to mankind. But nothing they write supports these assertions. The books of fiction, on the contrary, are often strongly erotic in matter and treatment, and they are written without the sense of moral responsibility which inhibits the instructors. For some of these writers sex seems to be the greatest good in life (insofar as they relate their work to any large concept of life) and a very poor good at that.

The books of instruction are written by men and women who would certainly not acknowledge Ovid as their master, even if they knew about him. The works of fiction are written by novelists to whom Ovid's high-bred hedonism is, for quite different reasons, meaningless. What they seek to evoke is sensation, and Ovid is not a sensational poet. The novelists tacitly declare themselves to be artists, though few of them bring an artist's vision, selection, and distillation of experience to this important aspect of their material.

Yet both classes of books are widely popular. How can we account for it?

Divided Desire

Clearly both of them satisfy a strong desire in the universally literate public of our time. The books of instruction are aimed at the Real, and the novels are aimed at the Ideal. The former appeal to the reason, that self-doubting guide to conduct, and the latter appeal to unreason, the dark forces which the depth-psychologists have uncovered and partly explored. A young couple approaching marriage may, without any real contradiction, find great solace in books of both sorts. They seriously desire to mate happily, hygienically, eugenically, and wisely, meeting all the problems of the honeymoon, the Early Years (including that shrewd budget upon which, as much as upon the marriage bed, the counselors assure them that their happiness rests), Middle Age, the Menopause, Waning Powers, and the Sunset Years, in the prudent, moderate, thin-blooded spirit of the books of instruction. But in their secret hearts they may long for quite a different sort of life; for burning, dangerous passion, for frequent change of partner, for variety of experience even when it includes degradation and moral squalor—for Life in the Large, in fact, with plentiful inflammation of the Propensities. Social man is pretty well tamed by what we call civilization, until a war or a disaster shatters the cellophane wrapping. But as the depth-psychologists tell us, there lies deep within him a memory of other things—not necessarily better things, but wilder things which he may not want in reality, but which he likes to indulge in fantasy. The novelist wakens the memory of those wilder things, and ministers to it. It is not a particularly difficult feat; any competent drummer with a tom-tom can do as much.

Art lies in understanding some part of the dark forces and bringing them under the direction of reason. Great novelists have done it, and so have many whom we do not call great, but to whom we must not deny the name of artist. If we are to quarrel with the writers of erotic novels, it must be with that rather large group who merely beat the tom-tom. They can strike the erotic rhythm, but they cannot bring it into accord with any other. They are not without defense, and when asked why they write of a world which seems to hold nothing but sex and violence, their answers often remind us of Captain Boyle's declaration at the end of *Juno and the Paycock*—"The whole worl's in a terrible state o' chassis!" A sufficiently valid attitude, if we wish to share the Captain's ignorant imperceptiveness and his intellectual degradation. But Ovid knew a chassis quite as overwhelming as any of ours, and he accepted the artist's obligation to find form and meaning even there.

·IV·

From the Well of the Past

There is always something rather absurd about the past. For us, who have fared on, the silhouette of Error is sharp upon the past horizon. As we look back upon any period, its fashions seem grotesque, its ideals shallow, for we know how soon those ideals and those fashions were to perish, and how rightly; nor can we feel a little of the fervour they did inspire." Thus, in 1894, Max Beerbohm wrote of the world of 1880; his opinion is, at best, an elegant half-truth. Of course, if we are looking for the silhouette of Error, we are certain to find it. However, if we really want to recover the flavor of a past age, we must bring not only intelligence, but sympathy and feeling to the task. The sense of absurdity may well remain with us, but in an extended form; not the absurdity of the past only, but of a great part of life itself, will impress itself upon us. But more important than the absurdity may be a sense of kinship with the past.

Not, of course, that nonsense which finds expression in such phrases as "You can't change human nature." You can; you do. It is rather that some attention to the literature of a past age will encourage and teach you to feel in the mode of that age. Such an extension of sympathy has many justifications, but needs no excuse other than that it is pleasant. Some stern critics call it "escape," and their choice of epithet is significant; one seeks to escape from the intolerable, the restrictive, the merely tiresome; however happy our lot, we all at times find contemporaneity a prison and a bore. As Christopher Fry's "holiday in a complete vacuum" is an impossibility, a holiday in the past becomes the next best thing. But what past, and how?

Not the Best, But the Most

THE BEST THAT has been thought and said? Not if it is escape we seek, for the best that has been thought and said has of necessity some quality of modernity. No, if we want to get away, we must look for that which has been thought and said most, and most heeded, in the segment of the past which is our choice. Therefore we shall probably turn to fiction, and not the great fiction, but the popular fiction. In what follows I want to talk about a handful of Victorian books which provide the kind of escape which has no taint of the cultural or the educational about it. They are books which modern critics have, with one exception, ignored. There is no virtue, no prestige, in reading them, unless they happen to amuse you.

They are all English books, and all Victorian. I have chosen them only because I like them, and because the Victorian age is the easiest one for the modern reader to escape into. There are still a few late Victorians walking the earth, and all of them remember parents and earlier forbears who belonged to an age without electricity, without rapid transport, rapid dissemination of news, or general literacy. The Victorians of a century ago were nearer in feeling to the eighteenth, yes, and to the seventeenth century than to our own; to have known them is to hold the key to an even more remote past. An old friend of mine who died recently at a great age was, in infancy, held on the knee of an elderly godmother who had been, in her infancy, held on the knee of yet another godmother who had been held on the knee of Queen Anne, who died in 1714. Viewed unsympathetically, this is nothing, a chance association-by-knees; yet if we cherish life, and are not mere creatures of death and sepulcher, deluded by the notion that only our own experience is real and our demise the end of the world, we see in it a reminder that we are all beads on a string—separate yet part of a unity. The past is only partly irrecoverable. The clerisy should accord it at least as much courtesy as they offer to the future.

Henry Cockton

First is the most popular work of a forgotten novelist, *Valentine Vox the Ventriloquist*, by Henry Cockton, who was born in 1807 and died of consumption in 1853. Little is known about him, though we can make some guesses at his character and the quality of his life from his books. *Valentine Vox* was written when he was thirty-two, and appeared in monthly numbers, the complete book being offered in 1840. It was a great success in its day; *The Times* of London said that it would keep the most melancholy reader in side-shaking fits of laughter. It maintained a sort of life up to the outbreak of the First World War, as a book for boys, though I should be surprised if many boys read it all. It belongs to a genre not quite dead—the book in which a curiously gifted hero passes through a series of adventures in which he scores heavily at the expense of stupid or merely conventional people. Patrick Dennis's Auntie Mame books of our time have a kinship with *Valentine Vox*, for Auntie Mame is surely as prodigious in her zest for life as ever Valentine was in his power of "throwing his voice." As a boy, I remember serials in *Chums* (an English paper for schoolboys which is now extinct) in which a Terrible Trio—comprising a conjuror boy, a ventriloquist boy, and an India-rubber boy—made life intolerable for everybody who was so unfortunate as to come near them. It kept me in side-shaking fits of laughter and stirred me to ill-fated excesses of emulation, which a lack of talent and even of rubberiness quickly subdued.

> The power of an accomplished Ventriloquist is well known to be unlimited. There is no scene in life in which that power is incapable of being developed; it gives its possessor a command over the actions, the feelings, the passions of men, while its efficacy in loading with ridicule every prejudice and every project of which the tendency is pernicious cannot fail to be perceived at a glance. The design of this work, although essentially humorous, is not, however, to excite peals of laughter alone; it has a far higher object in view, namely, that of removing social absurdities and abuses by means the most peculiarly attractive and pleasing.

Thus begins the preface of *Valentine Vox*; it is a good example of Cockton's style, which is ramshackle and ornate, and of Cockton's thought, which is heavily moralistic. I am going to be funny, he says, but only in order to instruct and do good. Let us see how he gets on.

The only other ventriloquist in fiction who touches Valentine in accomplishment is the monster Erik in Leroux's *Phantom of the Opera*. Erik could sing superbly in several voices; Valentine could imitate musical instruments so well that the conductor of an orchestra was deceived. But in the main he confines himself to breaking up public meetings, provoking fist fights, bringing ridicule on people who have offended him, wasting other men's goods and money, causing unnecessary hard work and being a general nuisance. Although he can "throw" his voice anywhere, he cannot think of anything very amusing to say with it, and he depends a great deal on groans (proceeding from locked or inaccessible places) or "telling laughs," which spread dismay among the self-important. He uses his power to be a punisher of petty wrongdoing, and an exposer of pretension, but in spite of Cockton's brave assertion, he is not peculiarly attractive or pleasing. The dull fact is that the fun of ventriloquism, even when stretched well beyond the limits of credibility, is mild, and soon palls.

What, then, gives the novel its interest? Its plot, which is plainly dearer to Cockton's heart than Valentine's antics.

The Private-asylum Abuse

COCKTON was an earnest reformer. His second novel was an attack on the laws relating to bigamy. Another novel, of which we shall hear shortly, was a protest against the laws relating to adultery and divorce. *Valentine Vox* attacks the laws governing the maintenance of private asylums for the insane. When Cockton wrote it, anybody in England could be committed to a private asylum if certified insane by two medical practitioners (which meant physician, surgeon, or apothecary) who might see him either together or separately; anybody could keep such an asylum, and inspection was infrequent and cursory. Consequently, anyone who wanted to get rid of a tiresome relative (perhaps to gain access to his money) had but to bribe a couple of venal apothecaries, and the deed was done; the commissioners who inspected these madhouses had authority only within a seven-mile radius of London, and madhouses beyond that area were literally prisons, where little care and no treatment was given the patients. Extraordinary as it seems, nobody could visit the patients in these places except the persons who had committed them; thus, once in a country asylum, a man or woman was lost to the world, and those who were not mad already quickly became so.

The plot of *Valentine Vox* is built upon this abuse. Valentine goes to London to visit his guardian's eccentric old friend Grimwood Goodman, who has made his fortune in sperm oil, which was the superior machine lubricant of the day. Goodman's brother Walter is fearful that the attractive Valentine may become Grimwood's heir, so he sends two physicians to his brother who enrage him with questions as to whether he does not claim kinship with the Queen, and are then prepared to certify that he is insane and violent. Grimwood Goodman is soon afterward seized in the street, and borne off to Dr. Holdem's private asylum. Here he is ill-used and bullied, so that when an inspector calls, he is unable to protest coherently against his imprisonment.

Meanwhile, Valentine has distinguished himself by rescuing a Mr. Raven and his lovely daughter Louise, who have been so unfortunate as to fall off a pleasure craft in the Thames; he becomes an intimate of their house, falls in love with Louise, and is soon the friend of her cousin Fred Llewellen, a Welshman who adds to the side-shaking nature of the book by speaking in an elaborately transcribed Welsh accent. Mr. Raven is a man of immense wealth, and of a haughty, vaunting disposition.

At last Valentine and his guardian, good Uncle John, discover where Goodman is, and rescue him from the madhouse, with Whitely, a similarly wronged gentleman who has befriended him there. It is then discovered that Whitely had been committed to Dr. Holdem's by none other than Raven, who had coveted his wife, his fortune, and his infant child Louise; further, it proves that Llewellen is not Louise's cousin, but her brother, thus explaining the strong affection, not quite romantic love, which had so long united them. Goodman, exhausted by his misfortunes, dies and leaves everything to Valentine and Louise; Whitely does not long survive their marriage. Raven, stricken with remorse, gives all he has to Valentine and Louise, and tries to crawl back to respectability by proposing marriage to Valentine's mother. But she will not have him, and this, we are told, was "a death-blow," and "he never left the house alive after that." The wicked Walter Goodman goes mad and commits suicide.

So Valentine and Louise are left with wealth and happiness. "I scarcely know that we ought to receive this; and yet, were we to return it, it would perhaps break his heart," says Valentine of Raven's twenty-thousand-pound wedding gift.

> The life and adventures of Valentine as a ventriloquist may be said to have ended with his marriage. He did—for the pure gratification of Louise, whom he continued to love with the most affectionate warmth—indulge occasionally in the development of his power; but as he found that in proportion as the strength of his assumed voice increased, that of his natural voice diminished, he on all other occasions contented himself with a relation of the various scenes which his peculiar faculty had enabled him to produce, and never failed to excite by such relation the most uproarious mirth.

And so we leave him "glorying in acts of benevolence," with all his dear ones about him, including Uncle John, "who was always in a state of rapture," living "in the purest enjoyment of health, wealth, honour and peace."

Victorian Novel and Theater

WHERE DOES the pleasure lie in reading such a book as this? Not in the fun of Valentine's ventriloquism, certainly. Not in the cheap and quickly exhausted pleasure of mocking the past. No, it lies in the state of prolonged and agreeable wonderment that the book provokes; we are held by the vitality which comes through the clumsy writing, and which makes the book live, although it is so unlike anything we recognize as life. This, we must conclude, is how great numbers of people in the first half of the nineteenth century wished life to be. This is the farthest thing possible from realism; rather it is what Carlyle called "phantasmagoria and dream-grotto," which is what hundreds of thousands of readers have always demanded from literature and from the theater.

The theater has put its mark on *Valentine Vox*; these rhetorical speeches, scenes of remorse, scenes of melodramatic confrontation, interspersed with scenes of farce, arise from that vital, vulgar, unliterary theater which so much influenced Dickens. It was an actor's theater, and it is astonishing how many characters in Victorian novels seem to be based upon actors rather than upon people observed at first hand. A creature like Raven is not a man; he is a "heavy" in melodrama, just as his daughter Louise is a "heroine," and Valentine a "light comedian." Uncle John is the Good Old Father of the melodramatic stage (a character which still lives in catalogues of theatrical grease paints, in which a brick shade is named "Ruddy Old Man"). Fred Llewellen is a "dialect comedian," and thus through this book and others of its kind we can assign the roles to the actors who made up such stock companies as that of Vincent Crummles. In Dickens the characters have independent vitality; in Cockton, who might be called Dickens without genius, they seem to be drawn from the stage rather than from life. They are shadows of a shade.

Why? Are we to leap to the shallow conclusion that our forbears of a century ago knew less of human character than we? No, we are only entitled to say that they saw it differently; they saw it in types, in gaudy colors, in what appear to us to be caricatures, in what seems at times to be some framework derived from the Jonsonian comedy of "humors." We see it through spectacles of Freudian depth-psychology which are sometimes like microscopes in their power to reveal the minute and the unsuspected, but which also limit and cloud our vision. What they saw in color, we see in monochrome detail.

Unthinkable without Illustration

WAS THEIR VISION false? Does anyone dare to say so? Let us say rather that when it was at less than its best, it was stagey, just as ours, in any hands but those of a master, is apt to be gloomily clinical. Stagey as they were, Victorian novels nevertheless reflected something their readers accepted as life; in 1840 a different social structure and a different idea of democracy provided obvious variations of character which apparently gave pleasure to the very large number of people who were conscious of them; in our day general education, as much as any other factor, has smoothed out such variations, though they are still there for the keen eye to see.

It is unnecessary to labor this point if we take heed of the illustrations, without which a Victorian novel was unthinkable. *Valentine Vox* appeared in its earliest printings with sixty plates by Thomas Onwhyn. For the modern reader they set the stage, provide the actors and costumes, and give the tone of the book. We may assume that they did so for its earliest readers, or why would they have been provided? No modern publisher would think of giving sixty illustrations with a novel, and no public would want them, for we feel with the characters we read about, but do not appear to visualize them clearly. Indeed, the art of illustration is lost, and modern artists, when they are appealed to for pictures to accompany a book, "decorate" it rather than offer settings and puppets.

Yet we delude ourselves if we think we have gone beyond the age of illustration. We still need pictures for books of an earlier day, and the time is not far off when Scott Fitzgerald, for instance, will have to be offered in illustrated editions if new generations of readers are to understand the tone of his books. Few characters in any novel are so well revealed in the spirit that readers in a later time want no guide to the trappings of his flesh.

The Era of "Crim. Con."

THE CRUSADE against the iniquity of private madhouses, which were, in effect, prisons, provides much of the vitality of *Valentine Vox*. The novel was helpful in calling attention to this condition and arousing indignation against it, but Cockton's reforming zeal was not always so successful. The novel which followed, *Sylvester Sound the Somnambulist*, was cut on the same pattern; Sylvester does not know that he walks in his sleep, rides horses to exhaustion, writes love letters, covers chimney pots with sacks, and walks along a parapet high above the street (so that a policeman is moved to say: "I never saw a man in so perilous a position"); he even makes an effective speech in Parliament while asleep, thus giving Cockton a hook for some of his characteristic angry political satire; but the mainspring of the book is the action for adultery which Sir Charles Julian brings against his wife, from whose chamber he has seen Sylvester (fast asleep) emerging. This action is, in fact, taken for "criminal conversation" (the "crim. con." which is referred to so mysteriously in many Victorian novels), a charge rendered obsolete by the Matrimonial Causes Act of 1857; action on this charge was brought against the wife's paramour for damages. It was an interesting alternative to a duel. Whether the novel had anything to do with the subsequent reform, I have been unable to determine, but as complaint against crim. con. cases was widespread, it would be vain to attribute too much influence to it. Certainly *Sylvester Sound* is a decidedly inferior piece of work to *Valentine Vox*.

Suppers and Somnambulism

NEVERTHELESS, it contains a good deal of matter which is of interest to the reader who seeks escape to the past. The very cause of Sylvester's somnambulism, which was diagnosed as "eating suppers," recalls an era, strange to us, when dinner might be eaten any time between half-past three and seven, and when those who dined early took another meal of game, meat pie, deviled bones, mutton chops, or something of the kind, washed down with champagne and sherry or some other fortified wine, at about midnight. Around such suppers there hung a guilt which we are now at a loss to understand; we see that they might cause somnambulism without knowing why they were reprehensible on moral grounds. Apparently they were associated with fast women; the great courtesans of the time were famous for them, and their custom was copied by fast night-houses; it is at such a supper on a grand scale that Violetta Valéry appears as hostess in the first act of *La Traviata*. Marriage put the closure on Valentine's ventriloquism; marriage finishes Sylvester's suppers and his somnambulism.

London Low Life

In *Sylvester*, even more than in *Valentine*, Cockton shows his extensive knowledge of London's sordid life. Not all of it was criminal, or even especially low; Cockton had a journalist's eye for the variety of mankind.

Much of the interest of Victorian novelists, great and small, lies in their descriptions of low life which, for all their greater freedom of expression and their cult of realism, modern novelists have not bettered. Indeed, except for a greater frankness in giving sexual detail, the moderns have added nothing to it. Contrary to a widely held belief, the Victorians did not hold themselves aloof from the poor and the wretched any more than we do; like us, they got most of their knowledge of social conditions from the press and from novels; unlike us, they often had human wretchedness thrust under their noses by the sight of unhappy creatures in the streets. We do not recognize how much public-health legislation and organized charity have done to sweeten our imaginations.

A Digression on Henry Mayhew

This seems to be the logical point to digress from our discussion of Cockton to take some account of the greatest single source of our knowledge of low life in Cockton's day. It is a four-volume work by Henry Mayhew, published from 1851 to 1865, called *London Labour and London Poor*. It is said to be the first sociological study of its kind ever attempted.

Mayhew was born, like Dickens, in 1812, and outlived him

by seventeen years, dying in 1887. He was a journalist, playwright, and humorist, and in company with Mark Lemon he founded *Punch* in 1841. But we would not remember him today if he had not also been a sociologist of extraordinary curiosity and industry. If anyone imagines that *The New Yorker* invented the Roving Reporter and the Profile, let them consider Mayhew's claim; he was doing that sort of work, and doing it superlatively well, a century and a half ago. The full four volumes of his study have been reproduced in facsimile by Frank Cass & Co, Ltd., London, in 1967; an admirable series of extracts called *Mayhew's London, London's Underworld*, and *Mayhew's Characters* appeared under the editorship of Peter Quennell in 1951.

Mayhew is the perfect journalist—an able writer, curious, busy, and objective. His writing is free of cant, even on subjects which made some of his contemporaries brim with it. Compare Mayhew on prostitution in London, including his verbatim reports of what street women told him, with what Dickens has to say about Martha in *David Copperfield*. Dickens knew the truth, undoubtedly, but he writes what his readers wished to believe: a girl who has lost her virtue is beyond redemption, she loathes herself, she contemplates suicide, and she is extremely likely to die of a disease which can only be diagnosed as Ingrowing Remorse.

Mayhew, on the contrary, reports that in 1857 the population of London was roughly one million persons, of whom fifty thousand were prostitutes by profession; servants, milliners, makers of artificial flowers, and other girls earning small wages and occasionally prostituting themselves were not included in this reckoning. Of these girls he judged that the majority took to their profession because they were lazy, stupid, or because they liked it. Remorse gnawed them far less than resentment of the police and moral reformers.

Dickens frequently represents the very poor as eager for a

measure of respectability and religious instruction. Mayhew reports that the destitute and the poor street traders cared nothing for religion and regarded marriage as an unnecessary preliminary to domestic life. The costers and the street traders in general lived in reasonably monogamous concubinage with the women of their choice, acknowledged their children and brought them up with kindness, according to their lights. They were almost entirely analphabetic, but they were far from stupid, and in politics they were Chartists—that is to say, socialists—to a man. Toryism and the more practical Reform doctrines did not belong to their level, but a cut above them, among the poor tradesmen of the lower middle class.

In his introduction to *Bleak House* Dickens says: "I have purposely dwelt upon the romantic side of familiar things." A study of Mayhew shows how romantic was his attitude toward criminals. Evil as Bill Sikes is, and contemptible as Noah Claypole is, they are creatures of romance when we measure them beside the rough facts of the London underworld known to Mayhew. Tom All Alone's, the ruinous rookery inhabited by squatters, is darkly hinted at in *Bleak House*, but Mayhew takes us inside a dozen such places, tells us what the inhabitants wore, where and how they slept, what they ate, and how they passed their leisure time. It is nasty but fascinating reading. The trades they plied! His description of the Scaldrum Dodge—an imposture by means of which a beggar might outfit himself with a loathesome and alms-compelling sore—of the Choking Dodge, and the arts of the professional writers of begging letters are better than anything of the sort in Dickens; they recall Defoe at his best.

It is the low life, however, rather than the criminal life, which presents us with the most amazing facts. Queen Victoria, it appears, had both a Rat Catcher and a Bug Catcher, working under royal warrant. They were not often needed for direct attendance upon the Royal Household, though the

Bug Catcher once captured a single bedbug in the chamber of Princess Charlotte, with her fascinated assistance.

Less exalted persons, but respectable insofar as honest work makes a man respectable, were the Pure-Finders. "Pure" was the name given to dog's excrement, which was used in the tanning and preparation of fine leathers for glove-making and bookbinding; in London in 1851, there were between two and three hundred men and women who fared forth every day with buckets to collect this valued substance from the pavements. None used shovels, though a few of the more fastidious wore a glove on the working hand. A full bucket of the best pure—the limey as opposed to the sticky—fetched a shilling at the tannery. A pure-finder did not consider himself at a social disadvantage beside, say, a doll's-eye maker, or a crossing sweeper, and might fittingly think himself the moral superior of a vendor of obscene snuff boxes (imported from France and sold chiefly to "fast" young men).

The pages of Mayhew are a huge peepshow of Victorian London as it really was, and not as the novelists of the day were compelled by convention to represent it. It is not too much to say that the general reader who delights in Dickens, Thackeray, Surtees, Trollope, Cockton, Lever—yes, and perhaps also George Eliot—cannot squeeze the fullest flavor from his favorites unless he has some knowledge of Mayhew. He primes the pump of our creative imagination. To him, therefore, our homage and our thanks. He was not a novelist, but a sociological journalist. Yet after a perusal of his masterly pages, we come to the novelists who were his contemporaries fresher, better informed, and capable of a deeper understanding, a richer enjoyment.

Inconsistency of Julia

In *Sylvester Sound* Cockton makes one of those sudden changes in an important character which are of such frequent occurrence in Victorian novels, and surprising until we recall that they were written for publication in monthly numbers. Even Dickens and Thackeray were hasty workmen by the standards of modern writers, who make Flaubert their model and toil over their manuscripts, trying to get rid of anything which might look like an inconsistency. But when a "number" had left the author's hands, nothing could recall it, and if his story changed its nature in writing (as stories are so apt to do), he had to cobble it up as best he could. It is well known that when the original of Miss Mowcher, in *Copperfield*, complained to Dickens of the injustice of his portrait of her, he repented and made amends; but he could not rewrite, and so the somewhat sinister dwarf of the earliest appearance inexplicably becomes a lovable dwarf later. Thus, also, Julia Smart, the beautiful barmaid in *Sylvester Sound*, who collects rings from infatuated medical students and is described as a "decoy-duck" for her employer, becomes a good girl of superior mental attainments very shortly afterward, falls in love with Sylvester, and when he cannot love her in return (inequality of station), sinks into a consumption and dies thus:

> "Sylvester," he heard her say, "I soon shall be no more. I feel that every hope of my recovery has fled: the only hope I cherish still is, that we may meet in heaven! God forever bless you! I die happy, Sylvester—quite happy now that you are near me! Pray for me, Sylvester—pray for me. Angels of light are waiting now to bear our prayers to heaven!"

Sylvester, who was deeply affected, knelt and prayed with fervour: her mother also knelt and prayed—and Julia ceased to breathe.

A conventional and almost perfunctory Victorian deathbed scene—but what is it doing in a comic novel? And what about the deaths of Grimwood, Whitely, and Raven in *Valentine Vox*? In the novels of the great Victorians such incidents are introduced with art; in Cockton they are plainly a means of getting rid of inconvenient people. But apparently his public, which was a large one, was ready to accept them, as it accepted and made much of death in life itself.

Gusto for Death

DEATH OCCURS today on the same general principle which governed it a century ago; for every living creature there is a death apiece. But our novelists do not approach the theme with the gusto which marks the Victorians. Birth is still popular in novels; an experienced reader becomes quite a theoretical midwife. Is it because we know a little more about the physiological processes of death, and thus cannot be led to believe in rhetorical deathbed farewells, followed by immediate expiry, as was the case with Julia Smart? Or did Victorians really die differently? There are plenty of people living who recall the eagerness with which the "last words" of the dying used to be seized upon and widely repeated. The human spirit is remarkably accommodating; have "last words" ceased to be coherent and memorable simply because they have gone out of fashion? Have deathbed scenes ceased to hold the imagination because so many of them take place in hospitals, which are demonstrably unsuited to poignant intimacies? Does the presence of physicians and nurses, professionals in death, who cannot for their own sakes encourage drama, inhibit the dying and the bereft alike?

The most likely explanation seems to be that Victorians regarded death psychologically and theologically; we consider it to be almost entirely a clinical, final affair. In novels, at least, Victorians died when their lives were at an end—which is to say when their taking off was most significant and affecting both to themselves and their survivors; they died in the certainty of an afterlife upon which, as with Julia, and such characters as Eva St. Clair in *Uncle Tom's Cabin*, they offered anticipatory comment, sometimes of a prophetic nature. What about ourselves? Physicians of a psychosomatic turn of mind think that some people at least choose their time of death, but few characters in novels do so. As for an afterlife, there has been a decline in the general acceptance of it as a certainty, and though a few rationalists may be pleased, to many people this has added a new terror to death. We are reluctant, in the main, to consider the disappearance of ourselves and consequently of all we feel and know. Every man's death is, literally, the end of a world if he dies without hope. We have exchanged Gone Elsewhere for Gone Nowhere, and as novel readers, it gives us no pleasure to dwell on it. If there must be a death in one of our novels, we prefer that it have the least possible emotional charge.

So also with the Dying Child, so popular in the fiction of a century ago. We can have little experience of the evanescent, frail charm which childhood had for the Victorians, who lost so many of their large families; modern medical science has made our children hearty and durable; any good pediatrician would have little Paul Dombey out of that wheelchair in a couple of weeks, taking swimming lessons in the wild waves instead of bothering his head to know what they were saying. In reality no parent would exchange the young roarer of today for the pathetic little Paul of yesterday; in the novel, happily, we can have the best of both worlds, and may even look sourly upon our young when we lift our eyes from the page, because their rude health does not dispose them to be imaginative.

A Victorian Proposal

IF THE WRITERS and readers of a century ago were less queasy about death than we, it must be said that we far outreach them in our appetite for sex. There seems to be no end to the varieties of sexual involvement in which we can interest ourselves, and no limit to the amount of more or less lubricious detail we will accept in describing them. Not so the Victorians, and if we laugh at them for it, they may be laughing somewhere at us because we lack their gusto for death. The great psychologists of the era wrote perceptively of the relations between men and women, and what is between the lines is as masterly as what is on the page. But less gifted novelists approached the theme as though to handle it with tongs. Cockton shows the style very well. Valentine Vox, in his crusade against human folly, makes an excursion backstage at a theater, where several gentlemen, all described as old, are trying to make assignations with the dancing girls. Like the fine boy he is, Val "throws" his voice into the ears of some of these graybeards, saying "Wait for me, love, in the hall!"; he then goes to the hall and watches the scene of their disappointment "without being by any means satisfied that its tendency was to promote the cause of virtue or to cultivate those feelings which bind man to man." Even the most ardent escaper-into-the-past finds it hard to admire Valentine unreservedly, as Cockton plainly expects us to do.

What of Valentine's own pure passion? Although the women in Cockton's books are not well realized, he has taken some pains to give Louise Raven a character; she is haughty and capricious, and aware of her desirability as a beautiful girl and an heiress. Furthermore, she has no mother (and thus, by Victorian standards, no well-intentioned jailer), so that she is easier to talk to alone than were most wealthy girls of her time. It is interesting that as soon as they become engaged, Valentine sends for his own mother, who becomes in an instant Louise's cherished confidante, and takes on the necessary jailer's duties.

Before this came about, the important scene of the proposal had to be dealt with. Cockton gives us a full-dress treatment, requiring about twenty-five hundred words. Valentine and Louise are taking a walk, and, having got rid of Fred Llewellen, who insists on being with them, the great moment approaches. Louise knows that a proposal is coming, but must pretend otherwise. Valentine "felt very droll, and thought himself very stupid." They sit. Louise plays with the fringe of her Lilliputian parasol, and he wrings the necks of his waistcoat buttons with his watch guard. He says he is thinking of something. Of what? Of *the day.* Louise pretends not to understand, so he takes her hand and calls her a rogue; he means the day on which they are both to be made happy. Are they not happy now, counters Louise. When this pretty subterfuge has been disposed of, she is pressed by her lover to express a preference between May and June. She really cannot. She does not know how to give her answer. Valentine begs leave to teach her to say yes. She will not until her father says yes first. And if Mr. Raven says yes, shall they be made happy in June? She will not reply, because Valentine "is a very teasing creature," and she will have nothing more to say on the subject.

Mr. Raven, of course, says yes with great vehemence. He declines to disguise from Valentine how much he admires him; he knows Louise to be a good girl and all that a man could desire in a wife; he blesses them extravagantly. Yes, the adulterer and child-and-fortune stealer blesses them as sonorously as if he were the saintly Whitely, or the rapturous Uncle John.

That is all there is to it. No doubts, no discussion of earlier affairs, no to-ing and fro-ing, no physical experiment beyond a kiss, none of the complex voodoo which is thought necessary in even the most perfunctory modern novel to clap two ninnies together.

A Victorian View of Marriage

If the Victorians seem to us reluctant to write of the relations of men and women before marriage in anything but the most namby-pamby strain, they amply make up for it by their realistic treatment of the married state itself. And again, if we want to find the characteristic tone of the age, we are wiser to go to the popular rather than to the great. Thackeray and Trollope wrote revealingly of marriage, but we may question if they ever aroused such enthusiastic response as Douglas Jerrold, a capable but lesser man, with *The Curtain Lectures of Mrs. Caudle*. This work appeared in serial form in *Punch* before it was published as a book in 1846. Thackeray reviewed it favorably in the *Morning Chronicle*; presumably he was sincere, though his association with *Punch*, to which Jerrold was also a popular contributor, may have had some influence on him. Dog does not eat dog, even among book reviewers. But it is surprising to us that the well-bred Thackeray could recommend a book so coarse and repulsive in tone.

Jerrold was by no means an inconsiderable writer; he was a good and successful journalist, and one of the best known of the practical, carpentering, slapdash playwrights of the day. The theater for which he did much of his best work was the Royal Cobourg, later the Royal Victoria, and now famous as the Old Vic. In his time he passed for a satirist, and his wit was described by his publisher, in advertisements, as "acrid."

A curtain lecture, it is necessary to tell most modern readers, is a character analysis given by a wife to her husband when they are shut up for the night behind the curtains of the Victorian double bed. The book comprises thirty-six elaborate scoldings. We are to imagine the long-suffering Job Caudle, a well-doing small tradesman, burying his head in the pillows while Mrs. Caudle hectors him because he has lent five pounds to a friend; because he smells of tobacco; because he has joined a convivial club called the Skylarks; because he has lent the family umbrella; because he has joined the Masons; because he does not want Mrs. C.'s mother to live with them; because he has had a party when she was from home (the invitation was decorated with a design of a punch bowl, and the motto "When the Cat's Away the Mice Will Play"). Caudle has transgressed because he has bowed to a girl in the street; he has been neglectful in failing to find a rich godfather for Dear Baby; he has forgotten their wedding anniversary; he will not concentrate on their annual holiday; he has shown unmanly cruelty by refusing to smuggle stockings back from France for his wife; he will not buy a cottage in the country, and keep a small carriage; he has flirted with the maid; he will not reveal what is in his will. There is much reporting of what Chalkpit the milkman is doing, and the splendor in which he keeps Mrs. Chalkpit. Mrs. Caudle is consumed with jealousy of Miss Prettyman, daughter of a neighbor, with whom Caudle is suspected of flirting, and she takes pains to let Miss Prettyman know that Job dyes his whiskers. And—Victorian touch—when at last Mrs. Caudle dies because she has disregarded her husband's advice, and ventured into the rain in thin shoes, she dies nagging, warning that Miss Prettyman must not be the second Mrs. C. with "the key to the caddy." These are Mrs. Caudle's "last words"; compare them with those of Little Nell, or Colonel Newcome:

> "Mother, you see, knows all your little ways; and you wouldn't get another wife to study you and pet you up as I've done—a second wife never does; it isn't likely she should. And after all, we've been very happy. It hasn't been my fault, if we've ever had a word or two, for you couldn't help now and then being aggravating; nobody can help their tempers always—especially men. Still we've been very happy, haven't we, Caudle?
>
> "Good night. Yes—this cold does tear me to pieces; but for all that, it isn't the shoes. God bless you, Caudle; no—it's *not* the shoes. I won't say it's the key-hole; but again I say, it's not the shoes. God bless you once more—But never say it's the shoes."

The comic death scene is no rarity in the novels of the Victorians, and in this respect they show a sturdier spirit than we. Birth and death were equally facts, capable of comic or tragic consideration. What was not a fact, to be considered at all, was the ordinary give and take of sex. But the *Caudle Lectures* are characteristic of a large body of their writing about marriage, and if we read between the lines in these accounts of tireless nagging, of "crim. con.," of desertions, of husbands "gandermooning" (seeking the company of light women when their wives were "lying in," as they so often were), we can form a pretty fair notion of the kind of society which sat on the top of the rubbish heap so carefully described by Mayhew. It was no better and no worse than our own, perhaps, but in many important respects it was different, for the pretenses, the areas of shame, the conception of affection and of what was permissible between the sexes at varying periods of their relation were far from our own.

Popular music is one of many keys with which we can unlock some of the secrets of a past era. The kind of song Job Caudle and his friends sang at the party when the cat was away was probably along these lines:

Oh, I met her on a steamer
  As I journeyed to Cremorne;
A crinoline and a pork-pie hat
  Her figure did adorn;
Our glances met, she smiled at me,
  Then, as if unawares,
My arm it slipped around her waist
  While on the cabin stairs.
I ask'd her if she'd go with me
  She said "Yes, if I'd let her";
'Twas just as good as going home,
  Yes, as good, *and a good deal better.*

Who was she, who was thus encountered on the steamer? A milliner, a maker of artificial flowers, an actress from one of the "minor" theaters (perhaps a less fortunate sister of Miss Lucy Glitters of Astley's, who appears in *Mr. Sponge's Sporting Tour* and whom we shall meet shortly), or simply a maidservant whose mistress was temporarily from home?

The Greatest Plague of Life

IF SHE WERE a maidservant, we should be hardhearted indeed if we grudged her any sort of adventure which came her way. Not that domestic service was necessarily hard, for even in a modest household two or three servants might be kept—a nurse, a cook, a housemaid, and possibly also a "rough girl"—but the terms of employment involved much monotony. The Victorians, no less than ourselves, strove to make real the manifestly impossible; they wanted to keep in their houses as many people as they could afford to make their life comfortable, and they wanted these people to be without fault, without idiosyncrasy, and without personal desires. There was no regular "time off"; holidays had to be secured by special permission from mistress, and we know that the holiday was usually granted with many a sigh, and many a murmur about the inconvenience of it. Many servants had no holiday by right, except the middle Sunday of Lent, called Mothering Sunday, when custom permitted them to go home to see their families, if they lived within reach. Otherwise their holiday time came when the family went away on its own vacation, which in a rich household might be for weeks and even months. It was then that the maids might—if the butler or housekeeper failed in the moral supervision they were expected to give—be found on the steamer going to Cremorne.

There were good employers and happy servants; Victorian novels suggest that many of these were found in the country, where a remnant of feudal feeling remained, and where there were fewer people attempting to suggest eight-servant grandeur on a three-servant income. But in London there were a great many "new people" who were not used to as much service as they demanded, and who had a most ungenteel objection to the petty thievery which servants had considered to be their right for hundreds of years. These "new people" felt no shame at seeing a joint of meat appear on their table twice, whereas servants knew that it was beneath the dignity of gentlefolk to face such a thing; the "new people" did not know that gentlefolk had new candles in every stick every day, and objected to the lively trade in long candle ends which was part of cook's perquisites. The war between these mean, ungenteel "new people" and their servants was unending, and upon the whole it tended to be a draw, with honors even.

What it all meant we may learn from a little book written by Horatio and Augustus Mayhew, brothers of Henry, called *The Greatest Plague of Life, or the Adventures of a Lady in Search of a Good Servant* by "One Who Has Been Almost Worried To Death." It is valued now chiefly because its twelve illustrations are in George Cruikshank's best manner, but the letterpress is instructive. Servants were fallible: some of them were Irish, which was apparently not to be borne; they all broke china and blamed it on the cat; many of them drank, and filled up the bottles with cold tea; some of them wasted their time reading; some neglected Dear Baby for soldiers or young tradesmen when they took the little darling out for a walk; some of them were insolent by nature, and most of them became insolent when sufficiently snubbed and goaded; furthermore, they had unsuitable passions, and attracted "followers" who ate and drank everything in the larder. (It is not surprising that many of these followers were soldiers, for in those days these men were not supplied by the army with food between midday and breakfast the following morning; household servants possessed the one unfailing charm—food.) It was a lifelong battle, and if mistress was a greenhorn when she married, and engaged her first Irish drunk under the impression that she was a tender virgin from Cornwall, she was an old campaigner by the time ten years had elapsed. To us today much of the interest of *The Greatest Plague* lies in its portrait of the mistress; her innocent belief that angels could be found to work for eight or ten pounds a year (lodgings and clothing found) is an interesting footnote to any consideration of Victorian idealism.

The Comic Valet

It would be unfair to quit the subject of Victorian service without some mention of another aspect of it which recurs again and again in the fiction of the time, and sufficiently often in memoirs and biography to assure us that it was a reality. It is the Comic Valet. The concept is as old as Christendom, and may fitly be called an archetype. Many of us feel the want of an intelligent, cheerful, resourceful subordinate, who can be depended upon in all crises; a few fortunate souls achieve the reality in one way or another. Such an appendage to the hero of a novel is obviously invaluable. Don Quixote is not himself without Sancho; Don Juan is nowhere without Leporello; Pickwick was but a shadow until he found Sam Weller. The last overt example of this relationship in modern literature is that of Jeeves and Bertie Wooster. The Comic Valet has gone underground for a time, cropping up disguised perhaps as the Invaluable Leg-Man who works for the Great Detective, but we are not deceived. The Comic Valet cannot die, and he is not simply a creature of fiction. He is a yearning deep in the human heart, and occasionally he manifests himself in the flesh as a secretary, or a devoted son; I have even known him to appear disguised as a wife. In the fiction of the Victorians he was simply a body-servant.

Examples are to be found in most of the writers who dealt with the wealthier classes, though Trollope does not make much of the type. There is a shadow side to the relationship; an occasional wicked Steerforth has his sinister Littimer, but in the main the Comic Valet is a funny man. Charles Lever, in his Irish novels, has drawn a gallery of them which has done more than is usually acknowledged to create the type of the witty, resourceful, drunken but essentially "good" Irish rogue—a type which continues in literature through Slipper in *Adventures of an Irish R.M.* to a variety of unworthy modern examples. It is worth noting that this particular sort of Irishman seems to have appeared only to English writers; the Irish write of their rogues in quite a different way. This is not to say that he had no existence; only that an Englishman sees a Celt in a light wholly unlike that in which another Celt sees him.

For an example, however, let us again avoid the beaten paths, and look for our Comic Valet in a really unexpected place, in a novel by George Payne Rainsford James. This extraordinary man is said to have written over one hundred books, and the British Museum Catalogue lists sixty-seven. During one period of eighteen years he produced a book every nine months. Nor were they slight productions; *Philip Augustus*, which contains four hundred and twenty octavo pages, was written in less than seven weeks. James was a highly educated man and a voracious reader, and most of his books were either histories or novels with a historical setting. Like many men of unusual industry (Trollope is a great example of the type), he wrote too much for his reputation. He was popular, but not popular enough to be delivered from the drudgery of hasty work, and he was much mocked by critics, other writers, and persons who pretended to taste. Usually his work was dismissed as flimsy and melodramatic, though it was admitted that he wrote a good sort of prose. Thackeray was one of his chief detractors, and in his series *Novels by Eminent Hands* one of the best of his parodies is Barbazure, which is Bluebeard as James might have written it; it is as deadly and as unfair—and as funny—as only a great parody can be. Lovers of *The Rose and The Ring* will recall also that some of its mock-heroic passages are introduced with the words—"Had I the pen of a G. P. R. James."

The extraordinary thing is that James recognized the justice of Thackeray's criticism, and made appropriate alterations in his style; whatever his stature as a writer, he must have been a man of uncommon evenness of temper, and a most unliterary lack of vanity.

Readers have been content to take it from Thackeray that James was a figure of fun. I should have been one of them if I had not happened to run across a novel which he published anonymously (I do not know why) in Dublin in 1843; it is called *The Commissioner, or De Lunatico Inquirendo*, and the bookseller recommended it only because it contains twenty-seven plates by Phiz (Hablot Knight Browne), the famous comic illustrator. It seems to me to be quite as good as Lever at his best. The story begins on the Moon, whence the Chevalier de Lunatico is dispatched to Earth "with full powers to claim, and send back all deserters from the lunar sphere"—all lunatics, in fact. This sounds unpromising, but it is handled with a dispatch, a delicacy of humor, and an avoidance of ostentatious fantasy, which is engaging. The Chevalier sits down on a moonbeam, slides quickly to earth, and becomes engaged at once in a picaresque romance.

To enjoy *The Commissioner* it is not necessary to put one's critical faculty to sleep; it is only necessary to ask the usual questions—what has James tried to do, has he done it well, and is it worth doing? He has tried to amuse his reader with a lively tale; he has done it with unobtrusive but thoroughly professional skill; so far as I am concerned, this is excuse enough for a novel. The plot is complex, and is assembled on the principle which served the Victorians so well—the style which resembles the composition of a *napoléon*—a layer of melodrama and a layer of farce, and so on until the right thickness is reached. As a stylist, in this book at least, James is free from the fustian which afflicted so many of his contemporaries, and which becomes pathological in such a writer as Cockton; there is about his prose some hint of the familiar, easy, yet elegant style of Goldsmith. His melodrama is well done, if you are prepared to accept melodrama; when the dissolute young Fitzurse is killed at his wedding feast by the lunatic father of a girl whom he has seduced, I at least was surprised, and there is enough strength in the writing to make the scene horrible. It may interest students of obloquy to learn that in this book, although "D—n" is always so spelled, Fitzurse is called a son of a bitch—a phrase which I cannot trace in Dickens or Thackeray, or indeed in any other Victorian known to me. There can have been nothing inadvertent in such a choice of epithet, for James is extremely careful in his use of words, and employs them expertly for comic effect. As an example of this, we may consider the scene in which the disingenuous Mr. Darius, who claims to have lived among cannibals in New Zealand, dilates to Fitzurse upon the pleasure of eating roast boy. They have passed a child on the road, and Darius replies, in answer to a question as to what he did with his own adopted son:

> "Oh, sir, we ate him, we ate him," said Mr. Darius calmly: "the chiefs and I had a great feast, a sort of farewell dinner; and as there was no fresh meat, you know, I thought I'd give them a treat. He was as nice a boy as ever I ate in my life. I've got his head now in pickle—a sort of tender memorial to him. I look at it very often—but I'm afraid it's too salt to be good eating now. A very nice-looking boy indeed," he continued, standing up in his stirrups and looking after the child. "Now do you think people in this country would fancy there was anything wrong in it if one were to take a griskin out of a boy like that?"

Dickens himself could not have improved on "griskin" at that particular point.

But it was to consider James's version of a Comic Valet that we made this digression. The young man is called Joey Pike, and he is no relation to Sam Weller, though when this book was written, six years after *Pickwick,* there were many weary imitations of Sam to be found in novels. Joey is partly acquainted with French and Italian, phrases of which he uses very freely in his conversation. He is so elegant in manner, and so fresh of complexion, that he is able to disguise himself as a French maid. He is not only funny, he is intelligent; he busies himself on behalf of his master in the best Comic Valet tradition, and he helps to solve at least two of the mysteries which support the plot. In the end he falls heir to a fortune—not a large one, but one hundred pounds a year, which would be large enough—and we leave him about to set out in life, grown to man's estate and ready to continue his adventurous career.

He is useful in managing the machinery of the book, but we never feel that he has been introduced for that purpose; he is one of the best characters drawn by James, who is so obviously an experienced hand at writing novels that this cannot be sheer luck. He is a skillful realization of the Comic Valet archetype: many of the characters which recur in Victorian novels are archetypal, and this explains why, though they often seem far-fetched when looked at from the standpoint of "realism," they carry a conviction to the heart of the reader which bypasses the photographic conception of what is real. An archetype must never be confused with a stereotype; if the Comic Valet character, in the hands of a skilled novelist, convinces us, we may be sure it is because such comic valets, however disguised, existed (and still exist) in the actual world.

The Cynic in the Pink Coat

BEFORE BRINGING these remarks to an end, I want to write of one more author, not well known on this continent, who was a minor master and deserves more attention than he gets. He is Robert Smith Surtees. His name is known, and booksellers do a briskish business in complete sets of his novels because they are illustrated with lively hunting prints which appeal strongly to a certain kind of sentimentality. Who can resist so many red coats? For some reason Surtees is one of the darlings of those printers who bring out lavish sets of standard works, and several editions, all fairly expensive, are to be bought. But does anybody read them? Perhaps I mix with the wrong people, but I meet few who have ever done more with Surtees than look at the pictures by Alken, Leech, and Browne.

He eminently deserves to be read by the particular sort of escapist to whom this chapter is addressed. He carries us into a different, wonderful world which is—a change this, among these Victorian books—realistic in that every line plainly has its roots deep in personal experience, no flights of fancy are attempted, and there is little caricature, save in recording instances when Nature has caricatured herself.

Surtees wrote sporting novels, about people whose chief concern was with country life, fishing, pheasant shooting, racing, and, above all, fox hunting. He knew all about sport himself, but he is not the dupe of sport or sportsmen; the cold and calculating eye which Ring Lardner brought to baseball was not unlike the disenchanted gaze which Surtees bent on the hunting field. He is that oddity, a thoroughly intelligent sportsman; like others of his rare kind, he is willing to forego the pleasures of excluding the nonsportsman, in order to tell him what sport is really like. The least horsey reader becomes vicariously horsey with Surtees, not because his enthusiasm is whipped up with any Yoicks, Tally-ho nonsense in the writing, but because it is so good and true that an air of authority rises from the page. Surtees gives us all his knowledge, so that we find ourselves despising the greenhorns in the field who override the hounds; we admire the sensible caution of the old gentlemen who look for a gap in a hedge instead of leaping over it to probable death; we deplore the chicanery of the huntsman who keeps a wily old fox or two for release when he cannot find a fresh one. We have no right to these fopperies of the field, but Surtees sets us free to try them on, as it might be to try on his pink coat.

This is uncommonly good-natured of an author who has the reputation of being a cynic. But cynicism, like all attitudes of mind, receives as much color from the man who assumes it as it gives to him. Surtees's cynicism is not of the mean, denigratory, life-diminishing order, but is rather a matter-of-factness, a clarity of vision and a detestation of cant.

These qualities may be said to have been bred in him. He came of a good county family of Durham, and succeeded his father as squire of Hamsterley Hall; but before that he had been qualified as a solicitor. Thus he was not impressed by gentry, and some early experiences in the shifts and uncertainties of business life made him watchful. Though, as a young lawyer, he wrote for money, he later wrote simply because he liked it. He was admired for his horsemanship.

All of his novels have their particular charms, but since the late Joyce Cary declared that *Mr. Sponge's Sporting Tour* is a neglected minor masterpiece, it has enjoyed a small new popularity, and we may as well consider it. Briefly, it is the story of Mr. "Soapey" Sponge, a man with enough money to live without working, but not enough to be indifferent to more. Sponge is an expert fox hunter, and he decides to turn his sport to account, so he hires two handsome but vicious horses, Hercules and Multum in Parvo, from a dealer named Buckram, on the understanding that he will hunt them, and sell them if he can, keeping part of the sale price for his trouble. For a generation which has forgotten about horses, it is perhaps necessary to explain that the deception here lies in the fact that Sponge, an expert rider, can manage these horses and make them seem spirited rather than incorrigible, but that they are likely to prove killers to the purchaser. With these two handsome, evil brutes, and one of Buckram's grooms to watch both the horses and Sponge, he sets out on a tour of the lesser hunts, looking for buyers.

The technique, of course, is for Sponge to pretend that his mounts are merely two of a fine stable, and to ride them in the showiest way possible; he finds dupes enough, who covet his horses and persuade him, though pretending reluctance, to sell. At least one of the buyers is glad to pay him to take Hercules back.

As a picture of rural England in the forties the book is reminiscent of Gogol's picture of rural Russia in *Dead Souls*. Sponge meets and imposes on a remarkable group of oddities, but none is so odd that he fails to carry conviction. Lord Scamperdale and his understrapper Jack Spraggon are first-rate creations, and the Hard Hat Hunt which they command is a fine portrait of what fox hunting must really have been like in all but the wealthiest and most aristocratic areas. Another shrewd portrait is of Mr. Jawleyford of Jawleyford Court, a country connoisseur with a very vague notion of sport, but with a gallery of portraits and statues, principally of himself. The maneuverings of his daughters Emily and Amelia, who believe Sponge to be wealthy, and "do the agreeable" in an attempt to enchant him, form an excellent realistic contrast to the falsely romantic nonsense of Louise Raven in *Valentine Vox*. The book is full of good minor characters, like Mr. Jogglebury Crowdy, who believes that he is ensuring the future fortune of his children by carving the heads of the Kings and Queens of England on a series of walking sticks; and the rural editor who writes articles for two papers, quarreling with himself, is an interesting anticipation of the chief plot in C. E. Montague's *A Hind Let Loose*. Sir Harry Scattercash and the theatrical riffraff who join him in playing at being county gentry add another example to the many pictures of theatrical folk which turn up so often in Victorian novels. But the character which holds it all together and gives the book weight is Sponge himself, the self-assured, hard-bitten gentleman crook, whose favorite reading in his leisure hours is *Mogg's 10,000 Cab Fares*—which he is memorizing.

The Author in the Middle

Does it sound dreadful to you? Do you shrink from these people with their elaborately comic names? Do you groan in spirit at the thought of four hundred pages, so much of which is about fox hunting? I can but say—give it a try. For Surtees was a novelist of uncommon abilities, and Surtees stands dead in the middle of this book.

He makes no bones about it. He was anything but unsophisticated in his character, but the convention (so dear to one school of modern criticism) which demands that a writer should conceal himself, should pretend that he does not exist, was unknown to him, as it was to most of his contemporaries. He is in the thick of the book because he knows very well that he is the best thing it has to offer, and that his knowledge and his insight are the marrow of it. "We fancy we hear our fair friends exclaim . . ." he says, without a hint of shame, and proceeds to put his fair friends at ease. He even brings in his illustrator, as at the opening of chapter four:

> We trust our opening chapters, aided by our friend Leech's pencil, will have enabled our readers to embody such a Sponge in their mind's eye as will assist them in following us through the course of his peregrinations. We do not profess to have drawn such a portrait as will raise the same sort of Sponge in the minds of all, but we trust we have given such a general outline of style, and indication of character, as an ordinary knowledge of the world will enable them to imagine a good, pushing, free-and-easy sort of man, wishing to be a gentleman without knowing how.

And was Surtees wrong? He believes in his method, and he makes it work. He never pretends to deceive us into accepting his tale as reality in the photographic sense; he frankly calls upon his reader's creative imagination. He will provide the material for that imagination to feed on, and he will guarantee its authenticity. The Muggeridge Hunt failed for exactly eighty pounds; he knows why, and he says so. He gives us the speed of a hunt—"four miles in twenty minutes; pretty good going anywhere, except upon paper, where they always go unnaturally fast"—in such a way that exaggerated accounts of hunting, such as Lever's, are rebuked. And always there is a wonderful vivacity—not a rattling, breathless style, but a true vivacity—and a compression of description which makes us feel that we are being given the cream of the story, and that not a single word less could convey it.

Nobody has ever pretended that Surtees goes very deep into human nature, but like every writer who carries conviction to his reader, he goes deeper than at first appears. And where do we find the depths he stirs? Not so much in his characters, as in ourselves. What Surtees has to say carries conviction, not because it is precisely like any sort of life which we have experienced, but because it finds its answer in that "ordinary knowledge of the world" to which he refers in the passage quoted above. Surtees sounds his string, and we provide both echo and overtones; that is no trivial feat for any writer.

His characters, even the most improbably named, are never flat. He possesses that faculty of impersonation which is one of the best gifts a novelist can claim. When he writes about a man, he becomes that man, while retaining his watchful, chronicler's identity as well. The late Sinclair Lewis had the same faculty, and in our day Joyce Cary, Pamela Hansford Johnson, Angus Wilson, and Peter De Vries—to name only a few—have used it with excellent effect. It is comparable to the art by which an actor is both himself and another man while he is on the stage. And, as a way of presenting a character to the reader, is not this method of impersonation, in a writer who has the gift for it, fully as good as the method of building the character up "from within," leaving us with some acquaintance with his soul, but possibly ignorant of his appearance, habits, and tricks of speech? The strength and also the danger of this method of creating character by impersonation is that it may lead to caricature, and taste and discipline are needed to keep caricature in check. Surtees has taste and discipline to a degree not always found among his contemporaries, who delighted in caricature and could not check their exuberance; Dickens comes at once to mind. Yet even Dickens's extremest caricatures have an abounding life, for they are the performances, on paper, of a very great actor—great as clown and grotesque, as well as comedian and figure of melodrama.

Surtees gives us Sponge at full length, and in the round. He is a crook, but he is never more dishonest than is necessary to get what he wants, and there is an engaging absence of real hardness in his character. When he sees Lucy Glitters ride magnificently in the hunting field (she learned her riding at Astley's Royal Amphitheatre, and was therefore a circus queen of a sort), he cannot resist her, and, forgetting his plan of marrying a fortune, marries her instead. He decides that between them they will somehow manage to "make tongue and buckle meet." So, having won a steeplechase (by accident, for he was to receive a consideration for losing it), he and Lucy set up a bookmaker's establishment in Jermyn Street, called The Sponge Cigar and Betting Rooms, "whose richness neither pen nor pencil can do justice to." Sponge is a rascal, but he is also enough of a fool and enough of a man to be somewhat redeemed in our eyes.

The Image of Soapey's Soul

LUCY GLITTERS is a first-rate heroine, if we qualify that term to mean first-rate in relation to her hero. She is pretty, lively, and intelligent, and without being seriously inhibited by virtue, she has standards from which she will not depart. If, as some deeply serious critics have maintained, the heroine of a romance is the Image of the Soul of the Hero—in C. G. Jung's terminology, his Anima—we have found the secret of Lucy's charm, for she is demonstrably the Image of the Soul of Soapey Sponge, and he wins her hand when he is truest to himself. It is this suitability, this congruity of character, which makes *Mr. Sponge's Sporting Tour* an integrated novel, in spite of its rambling, picaresque form.

It is true of the Victorian novels considered in this chapter, and perhaps of all novels which impress us with a sense of their artistic completeness, that the Heroine is the Image of the Hero's Soul; she represents what he wants in life and what he considers good. To recall this from time to time throws an interesting light on much novel writing which seems murky. In *Valentine Vox*, for instance, it is hard for us to like Valentine wholeheartedly, and when we examine the character of Louise Raven, our distaste is clarified. She is his Good Conduct Prize, and she is the Image of his Soul. And what sort of girl is Louise? Cockton has tried to give her the conventional virtues of a well-bred young lady of her time, but again and again, in small but significant ways, she reveals herself as a twister. Not a twister in a very serious sense, perhaps, but when she is Mrs. Caudle's age, Louise will be a thoroughly disagreeable woman. Cockton was never able to draw a truly lovable woman, and this, taken with the strange and tortured themes he chose for his books, and the persistent miasma of paranoid grievance which hangs about them, tells us something of him, though his biography is almost entirely a mystery. What the sore spot was, let some psychoanalytical critic explain, if he thinks it worth his trouble.

A New Vision of the Present

IN WHAT HAS GONE before, it may seem to some readers that I have raked over a handful of forgotten, or almost forgotten, books of the past century, attributing to them a factitious significance by reading into them what is not there. If that is what you think, I have failed indeed, for what I have sought to do is to suggest a method of reading the novels of a past time in such a way as to recover their flavor. Not their first flavor, for nothing will make us into the people who picked up one of these books a few days after it had left the press. But I think that we do these old books great injustice if we bring them nothing but the spirit of Max Beerbohm, looking for absurdity, and determined to feel no fervor. The flavor we may find in them is perhaps even nearer to the author's hopes than that which was enjoyed by his first readers; they saw him through contemporary spectacles, which are as likely as not to have a tinge of green in them; people then and people now very often take up a tale of contemporary life with a slight, unrecognized prejudice against it because it may show the life about them in a way which is not agreeable to the reader. We tend to have set and narrow notions about our own times.

Although I have suggested a reading of old novels as a means of escape and a rest from the present, I have not said that this is all that such reading will bring with it. If it is true, as the Jungians maintain, that much of the past, remoter even than our personal memory, lives on in the psyche, do we not do well to explore and cultivate this sense of the past, with a view to enriching our understanding of the present?

If we find Victorian literature shallow, it is quite possible that we are shallow ourselves, the prisoners of a single age and a single set of literary attitudes. Old novels, it is true, lack the relentless and usually humorless introspection which marks so much modern writing; but because we would not choose completely to relinquish our own attitude, are we therefore to slight all others? In this chapter I have purposely dwelt (except in the case of *Sponge*) on books which are forgotten but which were once thought to have considerable merit. They provide their own mirror of life, their own satisfactory commentary, and to comprehend them, or others like them, is to add a dimension to our own understanding, and find a different way of looking at our own time. To read a few novels written a century or more ago is not to drop our bucket very far into that deep Well of Time from which we may, if we choose, drink deeply. Nevertheless, it is a beginning, and wisdom is no more likely to be confined to the remote, the primordial past, than to the age in which we live. To sup the waters of even a century past may bring a change of vision which is greatly revealing.

·V·

Making the Best of Second Best

Of what use is a University education to a young man unless he comes under the influence of instructors who can astonish him? He needs to be aroused to awareness, not merely of knowledge, but of modes of thinking whose existence he has never suspected. As I sit to write about the pleasure of reading plays, I recall two instances from my days at a Canadian university when I was greatly astonished.

The first of these experiences was provided by a professor of, I believe, chemistry who said to me: "I have read everything in English drama worth reading." He was a Dane who read easily in several languages, and he left me gaping. I had read a good deal of English drama at that time myself—enough to know that it would be many years before I could make any considerable dint in it, without troubling other literatures. But I understand now what he meant. He had read most of Shakespeare and a play each of a few other Jacobean dramatists; he had read the best of the Restoration playwrights; he had read Goldsmith and Sheridan; he knew the early Shaw. He had, in fact, read most of the English plays which are endurable to a man who, in his heart, dislikes the theater. And that was "all that was worth reading"—for him.

The other professor who astonished me, and continued to astonish me for a whole university year, was a specialist in Shakespeare. He contrived to assure us that Shakespeare's bounty was as boundless as the sea, while at the same time making it clear that Shakespeare had not many secrets from him. He pumped us full of A. C. Bradley, but his real critical love was Georg Gottfried Gervinus. After some struggles I found myself resistant to the genius of Gervinus; I simply could not get on with him at all, so I began to intrude into my essays quotations from Harley Granville-Barker. I received a warning; Granville-Barker was superficially enlightening, but upon the whole the opinions of theater people about Shakespeare were to be regarded with suspicion, and if I persisted in the path of Shakespeare scholarship, I would undoubtedly one day discover that the Bard was most fully to be appreciated in the study.

I was politely rebellious. I cared nothing for the study, and wanted the Bard in the theater. My mentor was patient but not understanding; he introduced me to his own great enthusiasm, which was the Closet Drama.

Oh, the Closet Drama! Dreariest of literature, most second hand and fusty of experience! Oh, theater without theater, without action, without emotion except on the most falsely aspiring and gaseous level of the human spirit, without a touch of anything unexpected, dished up in five-act eternities of ennui! Better anything at all in the live theater—better the grossest melodrama, in which the one-eyed Chinaman appears through the trap door and cuts the throat of the butler; better the smuttiest burlesque in which the comedian, seeing afar a beautiful girl, spits into the front of his baggy pants to cool his lust—than the Closet Drama!

But, as you see, I was astonished at the university. I was

astonished to find that there were educated, admirable people who did not really like the theater; they liked an intellectual distillation from the theater, called the drama. I believe that I was born with a passion for the theater, but in my time I have been a dissembler; in order to get the coveted degrees or (real baseness, this) to gain favor with people whom I temporarily believed knew better about such things than myself, I have pretended to love the drama only. But now that time has sowed a grizzle on my case, and I have a black gown, and a red gown, and a rainbow variety of hoods, I need pretend no longer. The drama and the theater are indissoluble, and drama removed from the theater is to me as are those tobaccos and coffee substitutes which are guaranteed to contain no harsh irritants, no tarry residues, no drugs—wholesome, doubtless, but not the real thing.

This is not intended as aggressive lowbrowism. I shall not go on to assert that I would rather see *Ladies' Night in the Turkish Bath* in the theater than read *On Baile's Strand* at home. I greedily choose to do both. But I cannot be blinded to the fact that *Ladies' Night* would be intolerable reading, and that *On Baile's Strand* in the theater (performed, as it usually is, by university groups and other solemn but not theatrically serious people) is a weariness. There is a way of having most of the best of both worlds.

That way is, as you will have guessed, by reading plays. I have read plays avidly since boyhood, and have had countless hours of pleasure from it. Not the full pleasure of the theater at its best, certainly, or a pleasure easily comparable with reading books which are intended only to be read, but a different sort of pleasure which I think is there for anybody who wants it. It has never occurred to me, when picking up a play, to wonder whether it is worth reading, for that is quite the wrong approach; I read it simply because, if the opportunity presented itself, and I had unlimited time and money, I should go to see it performed. I am curious to know why it was produced in the first place, what pleasures and surprises it affords, what it is about. If it is old, I want to know what amused its first audiences; if it is new, I want to experience it without having to wait for a visit to New York, or London, or the rare chance of a touring company, or a glimmer of its quality peeping through the murk of an amateur production. I never think of it as a book, but as a play which I must perform, however inadequately, for myself. My production is a second best, but it is far, far better than nothing. And nothing, in the case of an old or obscure play, is the inescapable alternative. I am grateful to my old friend who admired the Closet Drama because he drove me to investigate the pleasures of play-reading more carefully, on my own account.

Let us agree, then, that reading plays can be a great pleasure, if we do not concentrate solemnly on the "worthwhile," the "significant," and plump always for "drama" as opposed to "theater."

Drama vs. Theater

VERY ROUGHLY, the drama may be called that part of theatrical art which lends itself most readily to intellectual discussion; what is left is theater. Drama is immensely durable; after a thousand critical disputes, it is still there, undiminished, ready for the next wranglers. Theater is magical and evanescent; examine it closely and it turns into tricks of lighting, or the grace of a particular gesture, or the tone of a voice—and these are not its substance, but the rubbish which is left when magic has departed. Theater is the response, the echo, which drama awakens within us when we see it on the stage. I protest against the use of the word "theater" as a synonym for what is disingenuous or unworthy of intellectual consideration; when people say that *Cyrano de Bergerac* is "good theater," meaning to patronize it, I am sorry for them; they have lost their feeling for magic, or perhaps they never had any. There are rewarding realms of feeling which do not lie within the confines of what is intellectually sturdy, and to be unable to experience them is to be the poorer. Ibsen, Strindberg, Pirandello, Beckett, and Ionesco need no help or recommendation; but there are other playwrights and groups of plays which need a friend to speak up for them.

When Bernard Shaw was fighting his great fight on behalf of the plays of Ibsen (and also the kind of plays which he liked, could write, and felt disposed to write), he asserted that he was fighting for drama; it was not until later that we appreciated the great Norwegian's mastery of theater. It was not until very much later that anybody noticed the splendid flashes of theater in the plays of Shaw. He roared against the kind of plays which were presented by Sir Henry Irving, which were all theater, with virtually nothing in them of drama in the sense that we have been using the word here. Irving played Shakespeare just as he played *The Bells*, *The Corsican Brothers*, and *The Lyons Mail*; that is to say, he used every play in which he appeared for the exhibition of his own extraordinary theatrical personality. The proof of his greatness is the delight he gave, during his long career, to hundreds of thousands of playgoers, not all of whom can have been deluded and tasteless fools. Indeed, if you are curious to know what it was that Irving brought to the theater, it is finely conveyed in the obituary essay Max Beerbohm (by no means a naïve critic) wrote about him, called *The Knight from Nowhere*. Shaw demanded drama, and perhaps thought he wanted nothing else: Irving was all theater and considered talk of drama mere literary fal-lals. If people wanted thought, he would provide them with a splendid illusion of thought; that was his art.

There is much to be said for Irving's attitude toward the theater, though not if we regard it as being primarily an extension of literature. To him the book of the play was a scaffold upon which he would hang a complex and delicate illusion. If the scaffold were rough, what of it? Such is the nature of scaffolds. Sometimes, in the modern theater, we long for something of Irving's quality; actors who can fill out a play, let alone create a splendid personal fantasia upon it, are not found every day. Indeed, the theater of our time discourages them. The magician, where he is to be found, is called the director.

Great plays mingle drama with theater most subtly; if, in lesser plays, one or other element must go, it had better be drama, which is the "literary" sister of the two.

Plays As Literature

ARE PLAYS to be considered "literature," in the sense in which poetry, novels, and *belles lettres* are "literature"? In answering, we must give proper weight to the fact that most good playwrights have been eager to have it so; Shakespeare, because he had sold the scripts of his plays outright, is the only playwright of the first eminence who appears not to have cared whether his plays were published. Somehow the idea seems to have taken hold of the public that the publication of plays for readers was little known until Bernard Shaw made it his practice. Every library possesses shelves of books which give the lie to this preposterous notion. It is possible to assemble a large private library of plays alone, all published before 1850. I make no pretense to owning an impressive collection, but I have quite an assembly of folios, quartos, octavos, and duodecimos, all attesting to the desire of playwrights to give their work the dignity of print, and, one must assume, the desire of a considerable number of people to read what they have written.

Some playwrights were eager to be regarded as poets. They wrote their tragedies in blank verse, and they encouraged the notion that a play is in reality a substantial poem, capable of being acted. This pretense has never had very happy results, and it is set at naught by the eighteenth and early nineteenth-century custom of publishing plays in the form in which they were acted in the theaters—usually Covent Garden and Drury Lane, as these were the "patent" theaters, under royal protection. Readers appear to have wanted the text of what they could see on the stage, and such texts are the real Closet Drama—a substitute for, or a reminder of, a stage performance. The Closet Drama so much admired by my fastidious mentor was a hermaphrodite, neither play nor poem, composed by men with no theatrical flair for readers with no theatrical taste; such interest as it possessed was pathological.

The Next Best Thing

In discussing the reading of plays, it may be well to insist once again on the distinction between drama and theater. The lover of drama needs no help from me; he has been amply provided for by scholarly writers who excel in finely balanced theory and the uttermost nicety of judgment, quite divorced from the rough-and-tumble of actual performance. It is the reader who wants some approximation of theatrical excitement who needs a helping hand, and words of encouragement. He needs to be assured that he is not wasting his time reading plays which make small appeal to the austere lovers of drama, and drama only. Often it is the nearest thing to the true pleasure of theater-going that is available to him. We do not all live conveniently near to the few centers where plays are offered, and even if we do, a lifetime may pass without a single production of a play which could give us great delight. You live in New York? You can get to Broadway without too much inconvenience? You have enough money to be able to go to the theater every week if you choose? Lucky you! But how many plays by Congreve have you had a chance to see during the past ten years? How many of Vanbrugh, Farquhar, Otway? You don't care about them? How do you know? They moved men and women to laughter and tears in their own day; how do you know that they might not do the same for you? Let us not equate the unknown with the not-worth-knowing.

If, as is very possible, you live at a great distance from a theater capital, your need is even greater. You are in no position to scorn a second best, which is certainly better than nothing at all, and can be very good in its own way.

You can train yourself to read plays so that they will give you keen enjoyment. The directions are few. First, you must give the play a fair chance; it is not a novel, and it should not be read in scraps; try to complete it in an evening. Second, always read it in a theatrical framework; it was written for the stage, and you must, to the best of your ability, visualize it as a stage production. This takes some doing, for you may not have a strong theatrical imagination. When a play is well performed in the theater, a crowd of experts have all worked to give you pleasure; you will not at first trial provide in your mind a director, a designer, and a cast of talented actors. Do not be disappointed if your early attempts seem a little heavy. If you persist, the art will come, in a sufficient measure, for it is a law of the imagination that the more you want, the more it will provide. Persist, and the reading of plays can become a splendid private indulgence.

Let me warn you, as a rule, against play-reading groups. The sheer physical technique required to make a reading aloud a pleasure is not to be found among people who try it only occasionally, and who have not made a study of the text. Play readings are, as a general thing, prolonged butcheries. Read plays to yourself, bringing all the imagination, feeling, and wit that you possess to bear upon the feat. Be a Gielgud in your own bosom, and do not encourage your friend, the lawyer, to read the role of Hamlet aloud in his courtroom voice.

Above all, read a great many plays, both for the pleasure it will give you and for the mastery that can be gained only in that way. The imaginative skill which you pick up in the reading of a dozen trivial comedies will bear fruit when you attempt a great one; much of the disappointment which undergraduates feel when they first read great plays arises simply from the fact that they do not know how to go about it; such texts demand the most expert work of the most gifted actors and directors to give them life on the stage; why expect them to leap into brilliance at the behest of an unexercised imagination?

Read much, and do not expect every play to be a perfect experience when you read it, any more than you do when you go to the theater. In this department of reading more than in any other, catholicity and bulk are the secrets of pleasure.

Making a Start

WHERE to begin? If play reading is new to you, do not take up some heavy collection of lesser Elizabethans, or a compilation of the noble Greeks, for you will almost certainly lay it down within an hour. In time your taste may turn to these things, but not yet. If you are an experienced reader of novels, and if the suggestion made in the previous chapter about the pleasure of escaping into the not too distant past made some appeal to you, it may be applied to this kind of reading, also. What you will find in the plays of the nineteenth century is rarely drama, in the sense in which serious scholars use that word. But neither, I submit, is it quite such trash as some hasty judges have said. It is what amused vast numbers of people who were no less intelligent than ourselves, and whose notions of sophistication, though different from ours, were no less exacting. For them the theater provided all of what is now divided among the stage, the screen, television, and even wrestling; it was popular entertainment and not, as it is now, somewhat specialized in its appeal.

Where will you find it? Collections of the plays which held the stage in nineteenth-century England are many, and most large libraries have some of them. Within everybody's reach is an admirable collection of ten, made by George Rowell, called *Nineteenth Century Plays* and published in The World's Classics. The American theater of that period is splendidly served by the twenty volumes of *America's Lost Plays,* under the general editorship of Barrett H. Clark. In a volume called *S.R.O.,* compiled by Bennett Cerf, may be found *Uncle Tom's Cabin*, *The Old Homestead*, and *The Two Orphans*. But it is out of the question to give even a short list here; the collections are too numerous; if you want them, librarians and second-hand booksellers will help you find them. I have a considerable number of such compilations, and paid no extravagant prices for them, though I must warn you that if the infection strikes deeply inward, you will spend a great deal of time in search of curiosities. As a suggestion, some remarkable old stand-bys of the theater are to be found, fossil-like, imbedded in the full catalogues of the big play publishers, like Samuel French.

Because the life of a good play is long, and because you do not want to trouble about the neatness of "period" which pleases the scholar, you are certain to run across some plays which were popular in the nineteenth century and were, in fact, written in the eighteenth. A farce like Garrick's *Miss in Her Teens*, though written in 1747, was a favorite for a century because it gave excellent opportunities to an ingenue. The same is true of Townley's *High Life below Stairs* (1752), which had life and point for as long as people kept footmen, and footmen tended to drink their master's wine. *Venice Preserv'd* (1681) appears in several nineteenth-century compilations because it held the stage in a much-hacked version, and so does Charles Macklin's *The Man of the World* (1781) because the leading role of Sir Pertinax Macsycophant was a favorite with many leading actors. (It is of interest that Macklin, who lived to be a hundred, wrote this play and starred in it himself when he was eighty-four; he detested Scotsmen, and in this part, and also in Sir Archy McSarcasm in his other great success *Love à la Mode*, he gave them rough treatment.) Edward Moore's *The Gamester* (1753) had two excellent leading parts in it, and was a recurrent favorite, as was also *The Stranger*, translated by Benjamin Thompson from the German of Kotzebue, "the German Shakespeare" (1761–1819); the part of the morose Stranger (called Count Waldbourg) was a gift to a leading actor who was strong in the "heavy" line, and Sarah Bernhardt (1845–1923) distinguished herself in Baron d'Ange's translation, in the role of Mrs. Clarkson (which part was called Mrs. Haller in the English version). The concluding scene may well be the first of many in which children reconcile estranged parents. These facts are mentioned to show that such plays, quite unknown now, nevertheless had a long life, the reason for which can be discovered by a sympathetic reading.

Some of them would play well today, not as curiosities, but as valid entertainment. Not perhaps Pocock's *The Miller and His Men*, or M. G. Lewis's *The Castle Spectre*, but such a sturdy farce, for instance, as James Kenney's *Raising the Wind*, written in 1803 and played by Irving as late as 1879. It is still fresh because the neatness and point of its dialogue derive from the eighteenth rather than the nineteenth century, and are thus paradoxically nearer to modern taste than the rhetoric of the later age.

At first the lack of what we now consider psychological truth in these plays may offend you. Their conclusions are of the arbitrary sort mocked by that good critic C. E. Montague (1867–1928) when he wrote of "the happy ending dear to the lover of the 'wholesome' play: that known causes should not have their known effects; above all, that in last acts any leopards which gain the playgoer's regard should be left rigged out in snowy, curly lamb's wool, and nice Ethiopians go off at the end as blondes with straight, tow-coloured hair." But Montague wanted drama—serious, meaty stuff—and the Victorians relished theater. Theater is not realistic in a vulgar, wide-awake fashion: it is realistic as dreams are realistic; it deals in hidden dreads, and it satisfies hidden, primal wishes. And if that is not psychological truth, what is?

Telling Situations

ANY PLAY which has survived in print, we may be sure, had a considerable popularity. There were literally hundreds of pieces which never emerged from manuscript. The panic necessity for new material which is the bugbear of television would not have astonished the resident playwright of a popular melodrama theater in the nineteenth century. These men were retained to provide new plays at need and in a hurry. They translated, they stole from the successes of other theaters, they pillaged popular novelists (for there was no law to prevent it), and occasionally, driven to it by sheer desperation, they wrote something original.

One of the best of their kind was Douglas Jerrold, whom we have already met as the creator of Mrs. Caudle. At twenty-two, in 1825, he was house dramatist at the Royal Cobourg Theatre, later to be known as the Old Vic. It was Jerrold who, testifying before a Royal Commission, defined melodrama as "a play having a great many telling situations with a physical rather than a mental appeal." He was himself a master of situation, and he appears at his best in *Black Ey'd Susan* (1829); it was written for a favorite player of the day, Thomas Potter Cooke, who had been stage manager at the Cobourg and also, like Jerrold, had spent his boyhood in the navy. Because Jerrold had been ill-used by the Cobourg manager, Davidge, this mighty success was lost to that theater and appeared at its rival, the Surrey, where it played for the then phenomenal run of four hundred consecutive performances.

Black Ey'd Susan abounds in telling situations, but none excelled the parting of William, the sailor hero, and Susan, his devoted wife, when William is condemned to death for striking his superior officer—in defense of Susan's honor, it need hardly be said. Here is the speech:

> *William:* Susan—you know the old aspen that grows near to the church porch;—you and I, when children, almost before we could speak plainly, have sat and watched, and wondered at its shaking leaves.—I grew up, and that tree seemed to me a friend that loved me.

> Beneath its bows our little arms were locked together—beneath its boughs, I took the last kiss of your white lip when hard fortune made me turn sailor. I cut from the tree this little branch (*produces it*); many a summer's day aboard, I've lain in the top and looked at these few leaves, until I saw green meadows in a salt sea, and heard the bleating of the sheep. When I am dead, Susan, let me be laid under that tree—let me—

A Scottish critic commended Cooke for "nothing overdone; no bad bye-play . . . a power of suggesting emotional stress without the suspicion of a whine." We may presume that it was thus he played the scene which culminates in the speech above. There is nothing much in the speech itself to move an audience; it was the situation, combined with the acting, which did the trick, and made this scene a byword for pathos.

So much so, indeed, that it had a curious corollary in 1872, when the young Henry Irving was consolidating his London triumph in *The Bells*, under the management of an American impresario, Colonel Hezekiah Linthicum Bateman. (Would any playwright dare to put an American on the stage with such a name?) The play which was being molded to fit the rising tragedian was *Charles the First* by William Gorman Wills. The playwright wanted to finish his piece with Charles's denunciation of the traitor Moray after the battle of Naseby; Bateman and Irving wanted one more "telling situation." But what? One night, at supper with Irving and Wills, the Colonel cried: "I've got it! The parting of William and Susan!" Irving, who had played often in the old melodrama, knew at once what he was talking about. "Exactly!" said he, and explained to Wills what was wanted.

The result was a final scene in Wills's play in which the doomed King, on the morning of his execution, bids farewell to his children, concealing from them the purpose of his departure, and at last takes leave of his Queen in these words:

> Oh, my loved solace on my thorny road,
> Sweet clue in all my labyrinth of sorrow,
> What shall I leave to thee?
> To thee I do consign my memory!
> Oh, banish not my name from off thy lips
> Because it pains awhile in naming it.
> Harsh grief doth pass in time into far music;
> Red-eyed Regret that waiteth on thy steps
> Will daily grow a gentle, dear companion,
> And hold sweet converse with thee of thy dead.
> I fear me I may sometime fade from thee,
> *(Queen presses to him)*
> That when the heart expelleth grey-stoled grief
> I live no longer in thy memory:
> Oh! keep my place in it forever green.
> All hung with the *immortelles* of thy love;
> That sweet abiding in thine inner thought
> I long for more than sculptured monument
> Or proudest record 'mong the tombs of Kings.
> *(Soldiers enter, drawing up on either side of door. Bell tolls. Whilst the Queen seems to stiffen in grief, Charles kneels, kisses her, and goes to door.)*
> KING *(mournfully)* Remember!

Irving was greatly praised for the beauty he brought to this culminating speech of a deeply pathetic scene; no critic appears to have thought of the parting of William and Susan, though if Shaw had been present, he might have done so. It may be pointed out that neither in *Black Ey'd Susan* nor in *Charles I* can this "telling situation" be dismissed as having merely a "physical" appeal, if by that word "superficial" or "factitious" is implied. The parting from the woman he loves of a man who is going to his death must touch all but the stoniest hearts, if it is presented with artistic sincerity.

It was the crude handling of such situations, and the brusque way in which all the most popular were crowded into a single play which gave melodrama its bad name. There are plenty of people living now, who are by no means Methuselahs, who have seen some of these old melodramas and romantic dramas acted by players who retained the best sort of nineteenth-century sincerity and skill, and who will attest that they were powerful and moving. They called to qualities in the human spirit—chivalry and renunciation, to name two—which are out of favor at present but which we would be wrong to think of as banished forever. Indeed, if we give ourselves up to some of these nineteenth-century plays as we read them, we may be astonished and pleased at the unsuspected qualities they can awaken in us. To experience deep feeling only in the fashionable modes of our time is to limit ourselves foolishly and to ensure that as the years pass, we shall ourselves become back numbers—for nothing changes so quickly as mere fashion.

An Evening at Covent Garden

WHAT WAS the theater like for which these plays were written? It was generous to a degree which astonishes us now. Consider, as a typical evening, the entertainment offered at Covent Garden on Thursday, November 8, 1832. The doors opened at six, and the performance began at half-past with an orchestral overture. The thrifty people who had paid a shilling for the gallery or two shillings for the pit (which was where the orchestra seats are in a modern house) would be in their places in good time, and so would many of those who had paid four shillings to sit in a box; boxes in those days formed a series of semicircles right around the theater, and were the best seats because they afforded some degree of privacy and the comfort of a movable chair. The boxes on the evening we have chosen would be filled early, because the first play is *The Hunchback* by Sheridan Knowles, and the author himself plays the leading role of Master Walter; the leading lady is Miss Ellen Tree, later Mrs. Charles Kean and highly regarded in America.

The Hunchback became a great favorite of the nineteenth-century repertoire, but in 1832 it was still in its first year of fame. Knowles was not a particularly good actor; he never succeeded in ridding himself of his Irish accent, and the audiences of that day were as critical of speech as audiences in our time are not. He was a successful playwright because he understood telling situations, and could wrap them up in a species of Jacobethan blank verse which actors liked and audiences accepted much as they now accept the verse of some of our own poetical playwrights—with uncomplaining meekness, and occasional bursts of gratitude when the fog lifts.

Knowles also had a sense of the power of myths which marks him as an unusual man. *The Hunchback* is the story of the beautiful and accomplished Julia, who has been brought up by the deformed agent of the Earl of Rochdale; this strange, testy, but wise and good man brings to her Sir Thomas Clifford, a young nobleman with an elaborate sense of honor; they love, and are betrothed; but love and the prospect of being a lady turns Julia's head, and when she learns that Clifford has lost all his fortune and estate, she behaves foolishly.

The cat-and-mouse complications of the plot do not lend themselves to compression; let it be said, then, that Julia agrees in pique to marry a titled oaf, and Clifford suffers with the uttermost nobility. But at last the plot is resolved, for it proves that Master Walter, the hunchback, is the rightful Earl of Rochdale, and also Julia's father; he had concealed this latter fact in order to spare her the ignominy of having to acknowledge a cripple; he is able to make her rich and marry her to Clifford, and has the coolness to describe the agony of the young people, which he has himself contrived, in the main, as "wholesome, though severe"!

This is not the nonsense that so bald a narration suggests. The theme of the proud girl who rejects the worthy but penniless suitor is a good one, and another nineteenth-century favorite, *The Lady of Lyons* by Bulwer-Lytton, exploits it most successfully. The suffering of such a girl is pleasing to an audience, perhaps because there is a special satisfaction in seeing a beautiful woman undergo humiliation. One need not be a student of Jung to recognize in the deformed Master Walter one of those ambiguous monsters from fairytale—wise, seemingly unkind, unpredictable, extremely powerful—who tries the soul of hero and heroine so that in the end his bounty may fall upon them more sweetly. The late George Arliss earned his greatest fame in a series of roles all based on this archetypal figure. The three leading parts in *The Hunchback* are full of meat for robust players; they are the stuff of myth and fairytale, and in the theater these elements never die.

A criticism of Knowles's plays which appeared in *The Athenaeum* in 1847 is of interest. "The *heart* which Mr. Knowles puts into his work lays hold of the hearts of his public; and this is his secret. . . . In fine, counting Burns at the head of the Uneducated Poets (an epithet as we have often said, to which the freest meaning must be allowed) we think that Mr. Sheridan Knowles will keep his place in the annals of the British Theatre as the King of Uneducated Dramatists." This estimate, so well meant and so strangely expressed, must have pleased Knowles and his publishers, for they put it at the beginning of his *Dramatic Works* (1856).

The Hunchback, we may assume, kept the audience busy until close to nine o'clock, at which halfway period in the evening a great many people would enter the theater, having paid half-price. They would be, in all likelihood, young clerks who had been kept at work until eight or so. Only their masters, who dined at half-past four, or five, could come to the early part of the evening. What remained for them to see? Nothing less than a huge masque, written by Knowles and stage-managed by Farley, who specialized in such spectacles, to do honor to Sir Walter Scott, whose death on September 21 was one of the great events of the year. This pageantlike affair "in Honour of the Genius of the Minstrel of the North" was called *The Vision of the Bard*, and anybody who has had any experience of such theatrical tributes to genius will have small difficulty in imagining the course it took. Opening with a view of Sir Walter's burial place in Dryburgh Abbey, the Bard himself appears (Knowles, naturally) accompanied by actresses representing Fancy, the Genius of Scotland, the Genius of England, and the Genius of Ireland, as well as the Spirit of the Mountains (who may perhaps have done double duty as the Genius of Wales and the Isle of Man, not otherwise represented) and Immortality.

The Bard then has a vision, in which he beholds elaborate tableaux from the principal works of Sir Walter—nine of them, all told—and the masque concludes with "A Jubilee, supposed to be given at Abbotsford in commemoration of Scotia's Minstrel, at which the Various Characters in his Dramatic Works are assembled, in Honour of his Memory!" The masque appears to have been mounted with picturesque splendor, and included about fifty principal characters, as well as supernumeraries. Doubtless it made use of the elaborate scenic effects for which Farley was celebrated; let no one suppose that a well-equipped theater of that time was incapable of elaboration, and very probably of beauty, in this department.

Nor was the evening finished when *The Vision of the Bard* was concluded. There followed "a new military spectacle, in two acts, founded on an incident in the early life of John Churchill, Duke of Marlborough, called *His First Campaign*!" and it is worthy of note that the overture and incidental music were the work of Adolphe Adam, remembered as the composer of the still vital *Giselle*. The piece contained a ball, and two principal dancers, male and female, are listed among the cast. We can guess that it was weighted heavily on the side of spectacle, for the pageant master Farley is named as director. As the cast is pretty evenly divided among English, French, and Dutch, we may assume that there was some hearty national fun; the role of "Mrs. Branagan, an Irish Sutler," is played by Mr. Mitchell, and is contrasted with "Gertrude, a Flemish Sutler," played by Miss H. Cawse. The role of "Charley Rowley, an English Drummer," is played by Miss Poole, who, we know from other playbills, specialized in these male roles, which were called "breeches parts."

So there it was—a five-act romantic play, an elaborate masque, and a spectacle with music and dancing, all given in one evening for a shilling, from half-past six to midnight, if you were frugal, hardy, and gluttonous for entertainment. Nor is this ample provision in any way extraordinary; it was the custom of the time. The following year, at the Royal Victoria, we find that on December 18 Knowles played *Macbeth*, which was followed by an Interlude called *A Day in Paris*, in which a Mrs. Selby played five different parts, including a "breeches" one. The evening concluded with the popular romantic drama *The Miller and His Men*, which culminates in a spectacular explosion. It is observable that

Knowles, the leading man of the theater, played in the tragedy only, but such a "utility" actor as Mr. Selby was expected to play Ross in *Macbeth*, a supporting part to his wife in the interlude, and the important role of Grindoff, the miller, in the melodrama—a heavy evening's work. A Miss Forster played the Gentlewoman in the tragedy, a servant in the interlude, and the thoroughly wretched part of Lauretta in the melodrama. Modern actors do not know how easily they get their money.

The Victorian theater was a place where dreams come true, as they now do in movies of the sort which critics despise. It was often ridiculous, shallow, and slapdash, but we miss a special sort of pleasure if we permit ourselves to despise it. Its audiences were ready to applaud wholesale "poetic justice" and ample heroics because that is what they wanted life to be like; the theater gave them the Ideal, and they could be certain that life would rub their noses in the Real. Behind these superficially ludicrous plots rises a world of fairytale and myth from which people have long drawn strength. The Victorian theater held the mirror up to nature, by reflecting not external realities, but rather those inner desires which such realism snubs and thwarts. The present fashion is to assume that the more painful a thing is, the more true it must be. Let me repeat, there is primal truth in dreams, though dreams need a skillful interpreter.

Truth in Melodrama

A THEATER which offered so much was chronically in need of new work of all kinds, and playwrights were many. Most of them were capable hacks, who could cobble up a play to suit any circumstances and any group of actors. They did not rank highly as men of letters; it was well past the middle of the century before their names were put on the playbills. They had to deal with rough-and-tumble production, very often, and had no time for subtleties. A famous story is told of Ducrow, great horseman and contriver of the circus spectacles at Astley's Theatre, which specialized in them. Addressing a playwright with too lofty notions of his calling, he said: "Cut the cackle and come to the 'osses. I'll show you how to cut it. You say 'Yield thee, Englishman!' Then you (indicating another actor) answer 'Never!' Then you say 'Obstinate Englishman, you die.' Then you both fights. There, that settles the matter; the audience will understand you a deal better, and the poor 'osses won't catch cold while you're jawing." Much Victorian melodrama was arranged on those lines, and it is whispered that they are not entirely unknown in the modern theater.

We must face the fact, also, that what seems stagey to us was acceptably lifelike to our great-grandfathers. Nobody would think at once of Thomas Hardy if asked to name a contriver of crude melodrama, but what is more startling, considered in cold blood, than the plot of his much praised *Tess of the D'Urbervilles*? A simple, beautiful country girl is seduced by a flashy villain, complete with silky black mustache, whose first words to her are: "Well, my Beauty, what can I do for you?" and who later gloats "Ha-ha-ha! . . . What a crumby girl!" She has a child, which she christens Sorrow before it dies. She falls in love with a clergyman's son, and after great inner debate, she writes a letter in which she tells him of her earlier affair—but by a trick of fate he does not get the letter. Therefore she has to tell him on her wedding night, and he—with a callousness which makes us detest him—throws her over. When, after she has borne degradation and hardship, her seducer appears again and tempts her back to him, the husband returns, and she, betrayed a second time, kills the seducer, and is hanged. The power of this book cannot be judged from a précis of its plot.

Time, however, teaches us a thing or two. One of its lessons is that the plots of melodrama are shopworn for the excellent reason that they contain deep truths; they have been rubbed thin by trashy writers who have understood them superficially and in terms of "telling situations," but for the masters they are still the very fabric of life itself. Anybody who has lived for forty years in the world and kept his eyes open knows that girls are very often seduced, not because they are stupid, but because they are trusting, and that the men who seduce them are often, like Alec d'Urberville, less wicked than emotionally unstable. Prigs like Angel Clare are by no means uncommon, though nowadays they have a different line of fashionable scruple. And a train of unhappy events, once set in motion, is virtually impossible to check. Coincidences like Tess's lost letter can be paralleled in life by coincidences quite as extraordinary, and others which no dramatist would dare to use. Not all people, but certainly some people, live curiously fated lives, in which they seem doomed to carry out actions which bear no relationship to ordinary probability, and are dictated by necessities which have nothing to do with common sense. Melodrama stirs us, and stirred our forefathers, because we sense its basic truth. Twaddle as we may about free will, some of us are bound to live in a context of farce, some in comedy, some in proletarian realism, some in melodrama, and a few—unhappy wretches—in tragedy.

Freud thought that the power of *Oedipus Rex* lay in the universal, unacknowledged fantasy which it showed to us in dramatic form. Is not this true, in varying degrees, of all plays? And which of us has not a buried dream of himself as the hero, the heroine—perhaps even the villain—in melodrama?

Drawing-room Theater

To RETURN to the Victorian theater, it is possible to achieve a convenient bird's-eye view of its range by looking at the plays which were performed by amateurs. Do not suppose that amateur theater was a trifling matter until the Little Theatre movement overcame it in this century. I have at hand a book which will allow us to skip quickly through the range of Victorian amateur drama; it is called *Drawing-Room Plays and Parlour Pantomimes*, and though it is rare, it is not valuable. Nevertheless, I would not part with my copy for any money, because it is one of those secret doors through which it is possible to slip, quickly and unobserved, into a delightful aspect of the past. It was published in 1870 and its editor and compiler was Clement Scott, the drama critic. His purpose, he explains in the preface, is to satisfy a need which is felt everywhere for short plays which can be quickly rehearsed and performed at house parties, especially at Christmas. As we read, we recall those chapters so common in Victorian novels, in which a house party presents a play and invites the neighbors to see it.

The plays, designed for what the Victorians facetiously called Theatre Royal, Back Drawing-Room were written for Scott's collection by some of the ablest playwrights of his day. E. L. Blanchard, editor of *Punch* and a tireless concocter of pantomimes, was one of them, and W. S. Gilbert was another; Palgrave Simpson, Tom Hood, J. C. Brough—their names are familiar to students of Victorian drama, and this book gives us an excellent capsule study of what their public liked. Be in no doubt that in another century a collection of modern plays will read quite as strangely.

Blanchard leads off with an "Induction" which, he explains, may be found useful "to take the place of an occasional Prologue at Private Theatricals, and can easily be modified to suit the circumstances." The scene is the Factory of Fun in the World of Waggery, and the characters have names like Joketta, Witticisma, Punarena, and Whimwag. Their fun is all of the punning variety. It has been asserted by solemn scholars that the unappeasable appetite for puns which the Victorians evinced during the second part of the nineteenth century was the dawn of a literary theater, the pun being essentially a literary device. It may be so. In Blanchard's prologue we also find many concealed quotations from Shakespeare, another Victorian enthusiasm, from which we must conclude that they were better acquainted with the Bard's works than could be assumed of a modern audience.

Not only puns and Shakespearean allusions, but extended parodies were very dear to the Victorians. It is doubtful if there is any modern play so widely and well known that a parody of it would appeal to a chance audience, but in this collection there is a parody of that Victorian favorite *Ingomar, or the Noble Savage* by E. F. J. von Munch-Bellinghausen, translated by Maria Lovell—a drama considered as profound in its day as are the works of Eugene O'Neill or Tennessee Williams now. It is remembered, if at all, by a couplet:

> Two souls with but a single thought,
> Two hearts that beat as one.

It is, very briefly, about a German barbarian living in an early but vague period of history who is domesticated by a Grecian maiden called Parthenia. We are prevented from appreciating R. Reece's parody of it at its full value because Time has so remorselessly caused *Ingomar* to become the best possible parody of itself. But we can raise a faint smile when we see that the noble Greeks bear such names as Sillias and Squintus, and that Ingomar's barbarian companions are called Tagragides and Bobtailos. A *very* faint smile.

Parodying Shakespeare always amuses some people, even when not well done. In this collection we read *Katherine and Petruchio, or the Shaming of the True*, with an odd sensation of having heard it all before—and so we have, in *Kiss Me, Kate*. Age cannot wither Shakespeare, but it stales his parodists with astonishing rapidity.

Not all the plays are comic in intention. House-party theatricals would want sentiment, and this collection of plays provides it, hot and strong, in a domestic scene called *The Pet-Lamb* by Clement Scott himself. He had always a leaning toward the tender, which sometimes degenerated into self-indulgent sentimentality; Ibsen and all the "new drama" of his time were repugnant to him; we get a whiff of his quality in *The Pet-Lamb*. A kindly farmer comes to the assistance of a poor dressmaker and her sick child. This child, Bertie, is desperately sick of a fever, but eloquent and wise beyond his years, and with a hearty relish of his own pathos. The modern dramatist may envy his Victorian brother the ease with which he could meet the problem of Antecedent Knowledge; it was only necessary for a character to say "Surely you recall . . ." or "You will not yet have learned . . ." and then to go off into twenty or thirty lines of flat-footed exposition of the plot. Happy days! How long has it been since a dramatist dared to introduce that infallible tear-jerker, a sick child, into his work? The organized charities of our day have claimed all the brave little Berties for their own, and they have transferred their pathetic appeals from the stage to the advertisement pages.

More subtle than *The Pet-Lamb* is *Fireside Diplomacy*, in which a lady conquers—perhaps "smothers" would be a better word—her restless husband by loving attention and submission. When he is tempted to go out to a party with some male friends (with a possible visit to Cremorne Gardens, haunt of loose women, afterward), she prepares him a supper—one of those suppers which sent Sylvester Sound prowling on the parapets, and small wonder. The midnight snack she offers comprises a lobster rissole, a roasted chicken, and a lemon pudding, to be consumed before retiring to the connubial couch. It works, for as the curtain falls, the husband, delighted with these pretty attentions, is embracing his wife.

I should greatly like to see *Fireside Diplomacy* performed on the same evening as *The Girls of the Period*, from the same collection; this latter is a saucy farce in which two pretty girls dress the brother of one of them in female clothing, so that an elderly French Count woos him by mistake. Apparently there was much concern in the sixties that the girls of the period were approaching life with unbecoming levity. Certainly these girls play a naughty trick on their uncle and guardian. It is interesting, by the way, how many girls in Victorian plays have uncles instead of fathers. Presumably the tricking of a father on the stage would be contrary to public morality, and an uncle was an acceptable surrogate for the family tyrant. Dr. Freud came just in time.

Perhaps the most characteristically Victorian piece in Scott's collection is Tom Hood's *Harlequin Little Red Riding-Hood*, a parlor pantomime written to be performed by children, and a quagmire of puns. Even the cast of characters contains such things as this:

> JACK, the woodcutter, who rescues Red Riding-Hood from the Wolf, quite by axey-dent.
>
> DAME MARGERY, mother of Little Red Riding-Hood, a crusty role, and very ill-bread.

The story of the fairytale is acted out with the uttermost exaction of facetiousness, and then, in a Transformation

Scene (which the directions explain is very simple to contrive, but which sounds as though it might tax the full resources of the Metropolitan Opera), the characters are turned into Harlequin, Clown, Pantaloon, Columbine, and all those other traditional figures through whom the Victorian Christmas pantomime kept its connection with the Old Italian Comedy of the seventeenth century.

A short example of the dialogue in this piece will be of interest, for it conveys exactly the quality of a kind of entertainment, the English pantomime, which is now on its last legs, but which was then at its zenith:

Interior of Grandmother's cottage. On the right hand, close to the wing, a bed with a dummy in it in a large night-cap. Wolf is heard knocking.

GRANNY (*spoken from the wings close to the bed*) Who's there?

WOLF (*Imitating R.R.H.*) Your little granchild, Granny dear.

GRANNY: That child has got a shocking cold, that's clear.

Some carelessness—she's got her feet wet through
With running in the rain or heavy dew,
Perhaps without her bonnet, and of course,
The little donkey is a little hoarse.
Her words she used not croakingly to utter.—
What do you want?
WOLF: I've brought your cake and butter,
But can't come in, the door my strength defies.
GRANNY: Pull at the bobbin and the latch will rise.

Enter WOLF

GRANNY: How are you, little darling?
WOLF: Darling! Pooh!
You didn't bolt your door, so I'll bolt you!

GRANNY: O, mercy! murder! what is this I see?
Some frightful spectre must the monster be!
WOLF: Don't make a noise, for you're a hopeless hobble in;
I'm not a ghost, but soon shall be a-gobble-in!
(*Wolf flings himself on the bed; shrieks and growls are heard. The dummy is removed without the audience being able to see it, as* WOLF *is in front of it.*)
WOLF (*coming down*) I've finished her ere she could angry be with me.
I didn't give her time to disagree with me.

And so on. That children should ever have performed this complicated piece seems extraordinary now, but beyond a doubt they did so, and I for one wish that I might—like Scrooge visiting the scene of Christmas Past—have seen it.

It is likely that more than one of these plays was acted at a time, if the country-house party took its amateur theatricals seriously, for the amateurs were as lavish as the professionals. When Dickens entertained in this way, not only did he and his friends perform *The Frozen Deep*, written by the host and his friend Wilkie Collins, but added to it *Uncle John*, a farce. There was a half-hour interval between the two, during which the guests were given a supper and the program concludes: "Carriages May Be Ordered At Half-Past Eleven."

Victorian Shakespeare

ANY ACCOUNT of Shakespearean production in the Victorian age is outside the range of this chapter. It may be mentioned, however, that Charles Kean (1811–68), the second son of the great tragedian Edmund Kean (1787–1833), was the first actor to attempt Shakespearean productions which were designed and presented with regard for historical truth in costume and setting. He approached this task with more scholarship than taste, and with an utter lack of humor which led him to overdo it. He caused some of his promptbooks to be published, with copious notes to justify his archaeological display; they also reveal how drastically the plays were hacked to make time for the scene changes, and to throw the principal roles into undue prominence. Even on the playbills—still, in his day, large single sheets, rather than booklets in the modern style—he lectured and overbore his audience. The playbill for *Macbeth* carried a harangue in which he justified the scenery and dressing of the piece by reference to Diodorus Siculus, Pliny, Strabo, Xiphilin, Snorre, Du Cange, and the Eyrbiggia Saga. He was under the delusion that he was helping the ignorant Shakespeare by giving his plays the highest historical authenticity the scholarship of the day allowed. To his chagrin the comedy theaters of the day parodied the pedantry of his playbills.

We owe something to Charles Kean and to his wife, Ellen Tree, for the seriousness of their approach to Shakespeare, but the debt is not so great as they themselves believed. In our own time imagination has once again taken control of Shakespearean presentation. But the imagination of our day has been chastened by that long era of heavy, archaeological production; by means of the Keans, we passed from the age when every actor supplied his own costumes, production was a hodge-podge, and acting could drop to the level of the King and the Duke in *Huckleberry Finn*, to a time when artists assist—and occasionally dominate—the scene.

But Shakespeare cannot be neglected in any consideration of what exists to be read about the theater. Those who want a long view of what the best actors of the past did in the plays they valued most will find it in the three volumes of *Shakespeare on the Stage* by the American critic William Winter; they are out of fashion now, but they contain a vast amount of that "fine, confused feeding" which theater enthusiasts love, and enough time has elapsed for us to find Winter's pompous style and heavy moralizing entertaining—in moderate doses. A modern approach to the same material is in Arthur Colby Sprague's *Shakespeare and the Actors* and *Shakespearean Players and Performances*. And there this discussion must stop, for any fuller consideration of the books about Shakespeare in his many phases will run on for unprofitable pages, and will end with a reference to such oddities as *Shakespeare's Knowledge of Chest Diseases*, which was a chairman's address to the American Medical Association in 1950, and a reprint of which I cherish.

Shakespeare Novels

IF A SHORT vagary may be permitted, I should like to suggest that readers on the lookout for curiosities might search for and taste some of the plays and novels which have been written about Shakespeare or which include him among the characters. The yearning to make Shakespeare, the man, real seems to have bitten some writers as badly as the yearning to make him historically respectable afflicted Charles Kean. There are a few world figures of overmastering magnetism whom concocters of fiction cannot leave alone; Christ and Napoleon are easily the foremost among them, but Shakespeare holds a high place. I have at hand a volume of seven hundred and ninety-nine pages, comprising a three-part novel about Shakespeare, published in the United States early in the nineteenth century. It appeared in England first, that being the home of the author, Robert Folkestone Williams, about whom I can discover nothing beyond his name. This first paragraph from the preface gives its theme and the style in which the whole vast work is undertaken:

> Methinks an apology is necessary for adventuring on a subject of the extreme difficulty essayed in these volumes; but the cause of my entering on so notable ambitious a task, will perhaps hold me excused in some measure; for this was it; I had noted with exceeding sorrowfulness, and a becoming indignation, divers small biographers, muddle-headed commentators, and insolent cyclopaedia scribblers, with as scarce a commodity of truth as of wit, garnishing their silly conceits of the noblest heart and brain that ever labored for universal humanity, with a prodigal store of all manner of despicable vileness, and wretched impudent folly; and having had much deep study, and moreover, being possessed of a very boundless love of the subject, I thought I would strive, as far as lay within the compass of my humble ability, to put to shame these pitiful traducers, and set up before the world a statue of this High Priest of Nature, as he ought to be entitled, as like as might be unto the wondrous admirableness of his natural gifts.

In other words, "I'll tell you what Shakespeare was like!" The three volumes, *The Youth of Shakespeare* (1839), *Shakespeare and His Friends* (1838), and *the Secret Passion* (1844), provide a prolonged wallow in pseudo Elizabethanism, Folkestone Williams having enjoyed himself thoroughly in creating a background which would produce the god of his idolatry. He provides much comedy to show us how Shakespeare came by his jokes; he presents prototypes of some of the Shakespearean characters; he shows us Shakespeare reading *The Merry Wives of Windsor* to Queen Elizabeth ". . . the queen once or twice did put up her fan and giggled very prettily . . . ," and pleading with Elizabeth on behalf of his friend Sir Walter Raleigh, and Raleigh's beloved, Bessie Throckmorton; he revels in long, static scenes in which Cotton, Raleigh, Shakespeare, Jonson, Donne, and many others sing songs and recite verses, all of Williams's own composition and all running to many stanzas.

Perhaps the most striking scenes in his book are those which open and close it. At the beginning we are told how the denizens of fairyland met on the banks of the Avon on the night of Shakespeare's birth, that Oberon and Titania might discuss the impending wonder in thumping iambics. (This is followed immediately by a long comic monologue from Gammer Lambswool, the midwife—fantasy alternating with comedy, very Shakespearean.) And at the end of the book, when Shakespeare is dead, the fairies return, wrapped in black mourning cloaks, and sing a Requiem, of which this is the final verse:

> Farewell, then, each loved bud and flow'r
>   Farewell the verdant mead,
> The fragrant air, the secret bow'r,
>   Soft fern and towering reed.
> Bearing, in solemn rite we come,
> Our honoured SHAKESPEARE to his HOME.

Yet another attempt to enter into the mind of Shakespeare which the connoisseur of curiosities should not miss is *The Girlhood of Shakespeare's Heroines* by Mary Cowden Clarke. She and her husband, Charles, were able and assiduous students of Shakespeare, and her *Complete Concordance* to the plays (1845) is invaluable. But in the *Girlhood* (1850–2, in three volumes) she enthusiastically followed that will-o-the-wisp which leads so many Shakespearean scholars into the quagmire—the fantasy of being Shakespeare himself, and of creating, and occasionally correcting and improving, in his vein.

A Shakespeare novel which is of interest because of some unusual and poetic insights, rather than because it adheres to any known biographical material, is *Nothing Like the Sun*, by Anthony Burgess, published in 1964 (the 400th anniversary of Shakespeare's birth). It needs no recommendation, but, as a work of what booksellers call "curious" interest, we may turn to *The Dark Lady*, written by Cothburn Madison O'Neal, Professor of English at Arlington State College, in Texas, published in 1964. It is about a girl named Rosaline de Vere, eighteen at the beginning of the book, who makes her living in disguise as a boy player in the same company of actors as William Shakespeare; she calls herself Ross Allen. Rosaline is a gifted writer, but because the temper of the time does not permit of female playwrights, she uses Shakespeare as her agent, and he sells her work, representing it as his own, and taking an agent's fee. She writes all of the plays which we attribute to Shakespeare (taking an uncommonly short time to do it), she has an affair and a secret marriage with the Earl of Southampton, and she gets herself interestingly involved in Elizabethan and Jacobean politics.

When the book appeared, a few reviewers found this plot incredible; they accused Professor O'Neal of having too little art to persuade them to suspend their disbelief in his assertion that Shakespeare was a precocious girl. Perhaps this was because they knew that the life of literary people is usually devoid of exciting external incident. But of course the heroine of a historical novel must not lead a dull life, and so Professor O'Neal has made the writing of the greatest plays in all literature an incidental part of Rosaline's crowded existence; she is busy with the far more interesting pursuit of love. On page eighty-nine of the first edition, her creator maneuvers her into a sweater, causing the Earl of Southampton to exclaim "Hey, that's no disguise!"—an allusion to the rich amplitude of her bust. And it may be that it is as a sweater girl that Rosaline is most convincing.

The scholarship behind the novel should not be slighted. Professor O'Neal has obviously read several of the plays of Shakespeare, and he seems to have made a special study of the *Sonnets*, which he presents as an ingenious love diary, part of which is written by Rosaline, part by Southampton, and two (the bad ones with all the "Will" puns in them) by Shakespeare himself. The poet is a minor character, a good-hearted chap, but severely limited. "Face it; you are adequate in bit parts, and you make a handsome king," says his fellow actor, Richard Burbage. Shakespeare faces it, and is a kindly agent for Rosaline.

The dialogue is of interest, as revealing how far the poetry of the Elizabethans soared above the daily speech even of the most cultivated among them. When Rosaline confronts her father, the Earl of Oxford, and tells him that her revelations might bring shame upon his house, that Elizabethan nobleman and poet replies: "My, my. So they would." When her lover is disturbed, the She-Shakespeare rallies him with "Now, Hal, don't get upset." We are told of the Earl of Essex, by one of his mistresses: "He has a lot of girls worried." This colloquialism unquestionably brings the characters very near to our own time.

Not that psychological insight is lacking. Savor this description of Rosaline's emotions upon completing *Hamlet*:

> When she had finished, she sat perfectly quiet for nearly an hour, reviewing her play in its totality. She still was not sure of her future decisions, but she did know more about herself than she had ever known before. She wondered if other readers would feel the same, find themselves in *Hamlet*, perhaps reject suicide as he had done,

or maybe put off their personal problems until it was too late. Of one thing Rosaline was sure: after she had written *Hamlet* and read it through, she herself would never be quite the same again.

The more we know of Rosaline, the more we marvel that so lively a girl could be persuaded to sit still for nearly an hour, even after finishing *Hamlet*.

But the psychological insights of the novel are many. Our relief is great when Southampton, having fallen in love with Rosaline when he believed that she was really a boy, and having kissed her ("she responded, open-mouthed, with all the pent-up passion that had been rising in her awakening body"), feels his manhood revolted by what he has done, and strikes her, while wiping his lips; this incident reassures us about Southampton, and doubles our pleasure when the seeming boy cups his hand around her firm bare breast, thereby spilling the beans and speeding the plot. We may contrast this with the scene in which Queen Elizabeth, an unsanitary old party and very much down on ambitious women, scratches herself under the breast, and a later scene where King James I says some hard things about women, being himself of imperfect masculinity. It is in such scenes as these that a novelist can take us right into the heart of history and reveal the artist's superiority to mere outward rank. But the pleasures of this novel are so many that it would be impossible to record them all here, and we must pass on.

Puzzle of Published Criticism

On, to a kind of reading which has come greatly into favor during the past fifty years and which, both in its relation to the theater and in itself, presents a puzzle. I mean published theater criticism. Not criticism of drama, which is as old as Aristotle, and is an honored branch of the criticism of poetry, but criticism of specific productions of plays, and often of plays of slight merit. Every year a few such books appear, and are obviously bought and read. Publishers sometimes say that they do not pay, but they go on bringing them out, and it is always significant when publishers produce books on which they expect to lose money; it is an indication that they think that such books are in real, if small, demand, and that they give distinction to their annual lists.

These books of theater criticism now exist in formidable numbers. By far the greatest number of them are comparatively modern, for the profession of theater critic is a modern one—as modern as newspapers, to give it the benefit of every doubt. It is amusing that the critics themselves, having risen to extraordinary eminence in the world of the theater, and possessing immense power (especially in the United States), seek to extend their history backward. It has always been so; whenever a new god rises to power, it is the job of those who worship him to provide evidence that he has always existed. James Agate, eminent as a critic, brought out an anthology, *The English Dramatic Critics* (1932), acknowledging his debt to an American scholar, Professor Charles Harold Gray; he sweeps theater criticism back to 1660 (though his first example is dated 1664), but we observe that of the three hundred and sixty-four pages of the pocket edition, it takes only eighty-two to bring us to Leigh Hunt, writing in 1807, and really copious theater criticism does not begin for another fifty years. For a century, then, men have been hired to comment on theater performances, and for the last eighty years they have sought to give life and authority to their work by publishing it in books.

What kind of men are they? Superficially they appear to be of all kinds, and some of them—Max Beerbohm is a notable example—profess to have little liking for the theater. This must be taken with a grain of salt. They may not like the theater, but they all seem to be fascinated by it, which is a different thing. They all seem to like the power they wield, and they would be more than human if they did not recognize that they are envied, and that there are hundreds of young men who hanker for their excellent seats, their prestige, and their freedom to say what they please with an insouciance denied most other journalists by the laws of libel, not to mention those of good taste. To comment freely upon, and even perhaps to jeer at, another man's face; to appraise boldly and publicly a woman's figure and attractions; to dismiss as worthless the efforts of a score or more of artists, musicians, designers, choreographers—not to speak of writers—and all of this in the name of Duty—this is work given to few, and sometimes it may be uncomfortable work. Would they do it if they truly did not like it?

What leads a man to become a theater critic? A psychoanalyst once suggested to me that a psychoanalytical investigation of criticism might be greatly enlightening. Where are the wellsprings of this branch of letters, which has become a profession during the past half-century, and asserts its importance so vigorously? Criticism of all kinds flourishes in our day as it has never done before, and especially in the realm of literary criticism there are those who boldly insist that their work is "creative." The familiar justifications of criticism need not be rehearsed here; connoisseurship based on practiced taste, guardianship of high standards in art, education of a less experienced public—we know them all, and we admit them all, but do we find them a full and sufficient explanation? Some of the very best of their kind have been most conscious of the pitfalls of their trade. Hear Ernest Newman, great music critic: "The really dangerous people are the practitioners of the amusing trades of criticism, who can somehow or other persuade themselves that they are not ordinary rule-of-thumb workmen, but priests inspired direct from the oracle's mouth." Of course all critics deny any such delusion of inspiration when taxed with it, but it is only in the grossest cases of the messianic delusion that the patient brazenly declares himself to be the Messiah; usually he just behaves as if that were the case, and perhaps not even the critic knows what goes on in his mind when he is bent over his typewriter.

Our concern, however, is what they publish for us to read. If we go through much of their stuff, we quickly find that the critics fall into two groups. There are those who take the celebratory line, who write best about what best pleases them; of this type James Agate (1878–1947) was a fine example. He did not consider himself a first-rate judge of plays, but he successfully asserted his claim to be regarded as a great connoisseur of acting, and his many books of collected criticism burn with a splendid and infectious enthusiasm. These celebratory critics usually concentrate on players, rather than plays. The other large division of critics may be called judicial, and their best writing is usually about what they have not liked. They very often write at length about the play, dismissing the actors with a word or two. This group is much more numerous than the former, and includes some great names: Shaw was a judicial critic, and so was Max Beerbohm; George Jean Nathan also belongs in this group, and the remarkable nine volumes called *Theatre Book of the Year*—which covers Broadway from 1942 to 1951—is in total effect one long howl of despair and disdain. These men are subdued by the good, and put in their best form by what is bad. It is a curious cast of mind, but we should not attach undue importance to it; we all find it easier to be eloquent and amusing about what has displeased us, though we do not all make professional capital of it.

Where criticism really disgusts is not in the work of these remarkable men, but in the journeymen of criticism. Among these the celebratory attitude is scarcely to be found, for to be pleased is, to little minds, to appear uncritical; the judicial line, in their hands, tends to become carping and denunciatory, so that the theater critic has become, to a great part of the public, an amusing common scold. It is these journeymen workers who bring to the theater Shaw's scorn without Shaw's moral indignation, and Beerbohm's ennui without Beerbohm's delicacy of perception. At their basest such men are mischievous parasites on an art; at best they come under the censure of Peter Ustinov, who says: "All arts are inhibited, in our day, by those who know too much and feel too little; it is inhuman to judge everything alongside perfection."

"Who know too much and feel too little"—yes, but we would not wish a critic to feel much and know little. All criticism is introspection, said Wilde; we do not long value the introspection of bleeding hearts uncontrolled by cool heads. Yet it is this necessary intellectuality of the critic which makes him, in the end, such an unsympathetic figure. "Nobody has ever erected a statue to a critic," said Sibelius to a young composer. The critic must be reconciled to his necessary, ambiguous role, and however much he may caper, joke, and posture for us in his writings, we are unlikely to forget that he is a man who may, at any moment, tread heavily upon our dreams—unworthy dreams, foolish dreams, stupid dreams, sometimes—but still dreams. The critic is the duenna in the passionate affair between playwrights, actors, and audiences—a figure dreaded, and occasionally comic, but never welcome, never loved.

As they feel too little themselves, they encourage us to feel too little, also, without giving us any compensatory acuity of taste. Therefore, if our pleasure lies in reading which is related to the theater, we should take care to read at least a few of the celebratory critics, and Agate's anthology, already mentioned and cheap to buy, will soon show you who they are. Unfortunately, so far as I know, no American counterpart exists, though George Oppenheimer's *The Passionate Playgoer* (1958) contains a section of criticism. Celebratory criticism is wonderfully stimulating to read. And, to be just, so is the best of the judicial criticism, as well. Criticism of music may be good, and sober. So may criticism of pictures. But a theater critic, at his best, always tries to rival the actors; he may not be conscious of what he is doing, but he is always trying to give a show, and the richness of his vocabulary and the gemmy incrustations of his imagery reveal it. Their writing ranges from the illumination of Shaw and the elegance of C. E. Montague to the uproarious and anarchic prose of George Jean Nathan, but always it is on the baroque, rather than the chaste, side.

Dramatic Imagination

SUCH READING, however, should ideally be balanced by much reading of plays, and, as I hope I have already made plain, not solely of those plays which are of assured "literary" value. We shall not develop dramatic imagination by feeding solely on what literary critics think best, for many of them have no dramatic imagination at all. Indeed, it is a rare quality; theatrical producers would pay princely salaries to anyone who could, infallibly, say what plays in manuscript would be successful on the stage. But producers have no such insight; directors have it but fitfully, as witness some of the things they toil to put on the stage; actors are quite capable of rehearsing a play earnestly without much knowledge of whether it is good or bad. A cultivated taste in literature is no guide, for the vice of the literary mind is excessive subtlety, just as that of the theatrical mind is trivial profusion. So when we read plays, old and new, that have been presented on the stage, we must bring, so far as we can, a theatrical rather than a literary judgment to bear on them. Even when we tackle a piece so strange to modern taste as Dion Boucicault's *The Colleen Bawn* (1860), or so much in advance of modern taste as Samuel Beckett's *End Game*, we must try to imagine it and feel it in stage terms. And it is here that reading the good critics will help us, for they tell us what has been done, and how it has been done, and what the quality of theatrical excitement is like.

The theater, more than other arts, is afflicted by the foolish notion that what is contemporaneous is necessarily best. The latest, the newest, is demonstrably superior, for is it not the most recent thing we have thought of? Obviously the actors of the past must, at the greatest pitch, have been somewhat funny, for is it not a fact that we alone possess the magical secret of presenting life on the stage in a really artistic fashion? Part of the price the theater pays for being forever young is this youthful notion that the past is quite done with, and that we shall never drift toward the past ourselves. The newest comedian is the funniest; the last tragedian to arise is the most poignant; the most recent mode in production and mounting is the most expressive ever. Those who think otherwise are incapable of contemporaneity, and must be discounted. But would it not be a good thing for the theater if more of us who make up its audiences became less narrowly contemporaneous in our tastes and sympathies? If we know something, sense something imaginatively, of the theater of the past, and if we equip ourselves by reading much of the theater of the present, shall we not have some influence on the theater of our time? Why do we not try?

The theater is ever changing, and a century from now it will be as different from that which we now possess as is that

Covent Garden where we considered *The Hunchback*, in 1832. It may very well be the theater of which some of us dream, in which masterpieces which do not suit large audiences, or which are for special tastes, or which are not masterpieces at all but delightful bits of tinsel out of the property basket of the past, are to be commanded at will.

Is this fanciful? Well, what would Charles Kean have thought of a form of theater—a shadow theater, admittedly—which allowed *Henry V* to be performed in a boundless landscape, with scores of real horses? Great things can happen in a century. We may yet have all sorts of plays, most feelingly presented, merely by pushing a button. Uneconomic? It would have been uneconomic a century ago to make musical performances of curiosities such as concerti for the glass harmonica, or sets of madrigals, available in everybody's living room. But we have them now. Thus we may hope that our grandchildren may see *The Miller and His Men* or *The Castle Spectre*, the poetic tragedies of Yeats, or even Henry James's interesting failure *Guy Domville*, if it should be their pleasure to do so.

Meanwhile we are not without resource, for we can read any play we choose, and give it a respectable kind of life in our imagination. It is not the theater of today, but it may be a preparation for a vastly richer theater in the future. If we cultivate and feed the dramatic imagination, we shall speed the time when cultivated and catholic taste is not thwarted by the lunatic economics of a theater which is increasingly clumsy and ill-suited to our needs.

·VI·
The Hue and Cry after a Good Laugh

A FELLOW GOING into the dark held out both his arms to defend his face; coming against the door which stood outright, he ran his nose against the edge thereof; whereupon he cryed out, *heyday, what a Pox, my nose was short enough just now, and is it in so short a time grown longer than my Arms?* (1686)

A RICH old Miser finding himself very ill sent for a Parson to administer the last Consolation of the Church to him: Whilst the Ceremony was performing old *Gripewell* falls into a Fit; on his Recovery the Doctor offered the Chalice to him; *Indeed,* crys he, *I can't afford to lend you above twenty Shillings upon't, I can't upon my Word.* (1739)

WHY is a chrysalis like a hot roll?—Because it's the grub that makes the butter fly. (1860)

THE ANATOMY of Kissing: bus—a kiss; rebus—kiss her again; omnibus—kiss all the girls in the room; blunderbus—kissing your mother-in-law; syllabus—two girls kissing each other. (1900)

Well, reader, have you laughed yet? All of the above have been considered very laughable in their time. Or do you like contemporary jokes only, like this one, which a sixteen-year-old girl tells me is the rage at her boarding school: A motorist stopped beside a car which was in the ditch, and was surprised to see that its owner had four kittens hitched to the grille with string. "You can't think those kittens will pull your car out!" said he. "Why not," said the man; "I've got a whip, haven't I?"

Is there any theory of humor which covers all of these jokes? If there is, I do not know it. Yet I have wasted a good deal of time reading learned essays by men whom the world has admired as philosophers and psychologists, who have attempted to explain what humor was, and why people liked it. They have exerted themselves to track the cause of laughter down, to stuff and mount it. None of them, to my knowledge, has bothered to consider why people want to laugh, and seek laughter eagerly—almost pitiably.

Laughter Need Not Mean Humor

CERTAINLY it is not my intention to attempt yet another theory of humor. I am happy to accept the fact that most people laugh sometimes, and that there are millions who are almost feverish in their search for what they call "a good laugh"—a benefit which they seem to value much as neurotically constipated people value a movement of the bowels. I accept also the fact that no single class of joke will make everybody laugh. And finally I am not prepared to believe that readiness to laugh is necessarily evidence of a sense of humor, whatever that may be. My feeling about the sense of humor is comparable to that of the depth-psychologist about the Unconscious—I have some empirical knowledge of it, and I have made some attempts to explore it, but I am not able to offer a comprehensive definition of it. What little I know of it suggests that it is not something which a man possesses, but rather something which possesses him; it is constantly in operation, it has a dark as well as a light aspect, and its function is by no means that of keeping its possessor in fits of chuckles; it is daemonic in character, and, like a daemon, it is most respected by those who best know it. Like a daemon, also, it resents all attempts to put it in chains, and the biographies of many humorists give evidence of the vengeance which the daemon wreaks upon those who set it to drudgery.

Later in this chapter we shall discuss a few men who have had a sense of humor. They are not so many as might be supposed. Great numbers of people claim this gift—for they believe it to be a gift and not something as ambiguous as the three wishes in a fairytale—but it may safely be asserted that those who casually lay claim to a sense of humor are unlikely to have any such thing. They are much more likely to be people who enjoy a good laugh. Let us examine some of these good laughs.

We need not go about it with the thoroughness of the research scholar who must return from his quest bearing the lifeless carcass of popular fun, in order to claim a doctorate as his reward. We need not rake those thousands of collections and anthologies of jokes and funny pieces which so often seem to belong to the pathology of humor, and which are only acceptable to the gluttonous appetite of a boy who is just discovering that laughter may be associated with reading. A handful of books will do for us.

Good King Charles's Golden Days

THE FIRST COMES to hand for no better reason than that I have cherished a copy of it for fifty years, having bought it in a junk shop when I was an undergraduate. But it is a good representative of the popular jokebooks of the seventeenth century, and its name is *Nugae Venales, or a Complaisant Companion, Being new Jests, Domestic and foreign Bulls, Rhodomontados, Pleasant Novels, Lyes and Improbabilities*; it was printed in London in 1686. In his preface the compiler, John Head, frankly confesses that it is a selection from earlier works to which he has added some translations from the French. We may take it, then, as representing the ordinary wit of the Restoration, for Charles II died the year before it appeared. It is an example of that kind of book, common until this century, which made its appearance in the capital, and thence found its way to the provinces, where it might do duty for several generations to give the local squire a reputation as a man who knew a few good stories. In *She Stoops to Conquer*, ninety years later, we meet Squire Hardcastle, whose conversational stock-in-trade was a reminiscence of Prince Eugene, and whose wit was one story about "Old Grouse in the gun-room"; there is plenty of Prince Eugene and Old Grouse in *Nugae Venales*.

As so often before in this book, I must warn the reader, and myself still more, against the easy trick of making fun of these old jestbooks because they are not precisely to modern taste; to do that would be to commit ourselves to what is merely contemporaneous, which is a pitiful slavery, unworthy of anyone who pretends to any taste in literature, however humble, or understanding of life, however small. What we must constantly keep in mind is that all of these jokes were at one time thought funny; *Nugae Venales* was a popular work which ran through several editions, and when these are found now, they are in that smeared, tattered condition which tells of a book which has been cherished, carried in the pocket, and almost read to pieces. What are these jokes of 1676–86?

They do not lend themselves to quotation here, for to our ears they are either gross or flat. Here is one which is characteristic of many, though more delicate than most:

> A LADY sent her servant to the Play-house to know what play was acted that day, the fellow asking the question, he was answered go tell your Lady *'Tis pitty She is a Whore,* the fellow misunderstanding and thinking this was spoke of his Lady and not the Play, replyed, *'tis pity such a parcel of Rogues, Rascals, and idle Sons of Whores should be suffered to abuse honest Women after this manner.*

Not that jokes of this general type are unknown now. I recall the widely quoted objection which was raised by a celebrated English actress to the title of a play which was successful in London shortly before the Second World War: "But my dear, who can possibly bring herself to tell anybody 'I'm going to *We At The Crossroads*'?"

Another from Head's collection:

> MR. CHURCH another time was telling his friend that his wife was with child, and withall, so big, that he could not choose but wonder every time he lookt upon her; *you need not wonder* (said his friend) *doe you not know your Wife hath a Church in her belly?*

We need not continue, to quote the one called *Upon a Close Stool* or the one called *On a Fart*. Anybody who has lived in a country district before the general acceptance of radio and television can reconstruct the atmosphere of *Nugae Venales*. Cuckoldry, maidenheads, excrement—these have long been the staples of those hearty men and women who love a good laugh. Here is one which, we may presume, passed as fashionable repartee:

> A GALLANT standing in a maze, a Lady askt him what he was thinking on? he said of nothing; what do you think on said she when you think on nothing, *faith,* says he, *then I think on you and the inconstancy of your Sex.*

This is the matter, though not the manner, of the Restoration dramatists. But at least one of the rustic jokes sounds like a condensation of a chapter from Erskine Caldwell:

> A LANDLORD askt his Tenant how many children she had; three said she; two of them, *Will* and *Tom,* are pretty Boys, but Diggory is a great loggerheadly Lout, and in troth Landlord, *methinks he looketh as like you as if he was spit out of your mouth.*

It is common to complain of the brutality of some of our ancestors' fun, though if we think about the jokes of our own time, we may find them equally harsh. But ours are in the fashion of our time, and theirs are not. Here is an example from Head which I like, but which some readers may find distasteful:

> A FELLOW and a wench taken together one evening suspitiously in a pound together, were by the Constable committed, and the next morning brought before a Justice; but they standing both obstinately in their innocence the Justice called the Wench aside, and promised her

faithfully, if she would confess the fact as guilty, she should go unpunished for that time. By his subtle insinuation she confessed the truth, whereupon the Justice commended her, and sent the fellow to prison: at length as she was taking her leave thinking her self at liberty, the Justice called her back, and askt her what the fellow had given her for her consent she told him (as it pleased his Worship) he had given her half a crown. Truly woman, said the Justice, that doth not please my Worship; *for though for thy fornication I have acquitted thee, yet for thy extortion I must of force commit thee, for taking half a crown in the Pound;* and sent her to the house of correction to bear her friend company.

We do not make a humorous specialty of the Bull nowadays; as Head explains in his preface, a Bull is a remark which gores and murders sense. Here is one:

PRYTHEE said one, why dost thou wear one of thy Stockens the wrong side outwards? O (said he) it hath a hole on the other side.

Nevertheless, we should be wrong to think that the Bull is unknown in our time. Frequently it appears as a mixed metaphor, as in an editorial I read recently which purported to see the fine Italian hand of the Bank of Canada upsetting the apple cart of the stock market. And it is only a few weeks ago that a civic official assured me that a public body was trying to thrust a lame duck (in the form of a police chief) down the public's throat. The Bull is surely due for a revival of popularity.

We do not recognize the Rhodomontado as such, though the style is familiar:

> I SWEAR, Villain if I come to thee I will give thee such a blow with this battoon, it shall drive thee so far within the Earth, that there shall nothing remain of thee above it, but thy right hand to put off thy Hat when thou shalt see me pass that way.
>
> IF I COME to thee, with my Foot I will kick thee so high into the Air, that hadst thou with thee ten Cart-load of bread, thou should'st be in greater fear of starving than falling.

A type of joke now virtually unknown except among the very learned (and I confess I have heard very few examples there) is the Latin pun, or classical allusion. Head provides a curious example, because the joke is really in English, and puns upon the Latin sounds, without reference to the Latin meaning.

> A RICE-FOOL being brought to the Table, the Guests doubted what it was; one wittily said *Per risum multum poteris cognoscere Stultum.*

Even those who know Latin in its modern pronunciation may miss that one, so perhaps it should be explained that "*risum*" would have been pronounced "ricem," and the proverb means: By his excessive laughter thou art able to know the fool. Possibly it is necessary to explain that "fool" also means a messy pudding, still to be encountered in England.

The Original Joe Miller

MORE TYPICAL of the Latin joke is this one, from the first edition of *Joe Miller's JESTS or the WIT'S Vade-Mecum:*

A LADY coming into a Room hastily, with her *Mantua*, brush'd down a *Cremona* fiddle, that lay on a chair, and broke it, upon which a Gentleman that was present burst into this Exclamation from *Virgil:*

Mantua vae miserae nimium Vicina Cremona. (Ah miserable Mantua *too near a Neighbour to* Cremona.)

We can imagine that this gentlemen's reputation was much augmented by his happy inspiration. He was lucky to live when he did; a few years ago I had to answer some searching questions to a Customs official about a book which I had with me, printed in Latin, and which the official suspected to be Russian; it was a jestbook, as a matter of fact, and I was so foolish as to say so, forgetting that a Latin joke is as strange to the modern imagination as a unicorn or an amphisbaena.

The Joe Miller whose name lingers on as a synonym for old and unfunny jokes lived from 1684 to 1738, and was a very good actor, famous in his day as a low comedian and a popular companion, counting Hogarth as one of his most intimate friends. He was illiterate, and "his principal object in marrying was to have a wife who was able to read his parts to him"; he must have been a quick study and she must have been a good wife, for he occasionally acted two brand-new parts on two successive days. But though he was funny on the stage, Joe seems not to have been a great joker off it, but rather one of those pleasing eccentrics who are the butt of other men's jokes, and upon whom jokes of a particular type are fathered. The jokebook which bears his name did not appear until after his death, and owed nothing to him; it was compiled by the playwright John Mottley, who used the pseudonym of Elijah Jenkins, for a publisher named T. Read. It was a hack job, and the jokes were chiefly cribbed from earlier collections. But it has become the most famous of all jestbooks; there were at least ten editions in the eighteenth century, and the number of jokes was increased in each one until the original two hundred and forty-seven had risen to more than five hundred; editions of Joe Miller were many in the United States, and a New York version of 1865 contains twelve hundred and eighty-six jokes. A lithographed facsimile of the original was published in London in 1861, and was advertised as "for connoisseurs"—perhaps to distinguish it from a *Family Joe Miller*. The original would not be regarded today as a family book, for the well-worn themes of fornication, killing dogs, breaking wind, having one's ears cropped for theft, anti-Papist jokes, and jokes about cuckoldry comprise the bulk of the fun.

Yet it ill becomes us to be self-righteous in our criticism of Joe. Have we not our own vein of sadistic jokes, and jokes in which the uttermost realms of sexual perversity are explored? To each age its own notion of "a good laugh."

A few of the jokes in Joe are no worse than those we hear from the television wits, but the technique of joking has changed with the times. Consider, for instance, Number 201 from the original Joe:

> A PERSON enquired what become of *such a One? Oh! dear,* says one of the Company, *poor Fellow he dy'd insolvent and was buried by the Parish: Died insolvent* crys another, *that's a Lie, for he died in England, I'm sure I was at his Burying.*

This trick of going on after the point has been made is common in the book, and suggests that in the eighteenth century they got them later and enjoyed them longer. This is a humor more robust, less nervous, but also slower moving than our own.

Nowadays we do not much relish anecdotes about historical characters and people long dead, such as Joe's Number 215:

> *Apelles,* the famous Painter, having drawn the Picture of *Alexander* the Great on Horseback, brought it and presented it to that Prince, but he not bestowing the Praise on it, which so excellent a piece deserv'd, *Apelles* desired a living Horse might be brought; who mov'd by Nature fell a prancing and neighing, as tho' it had actually been his living Fellow-Creature; whereupon *Apelles* told *Alexander, his Horse understood Painting better than himself.*

The fashion in comic nationalities has changed with time. Joe has no jokes about Scots or Jews, but he has several about the Irish; in the eighteenth century the English had the notion that the Irish were stupid, an opinion which they reversed sharply a hundred years later, taking the line that all Irishmen, whatever the evidence to the contrary, were resplendent wits. But in Joe's day the Welsh were thought very funny; I never hear jokes about Welshmen today, except among the Welsh. But to our ancestors, Welshmen were always good for a laugh, for they were thought to speak oddly (according to Joe a Welshman always said "hur" when he meant himself, and a century later Cockton, in *Valentine Vox*, makes his funny Welshman speak in this way; actually what Welshmen used to say was something a little thicker in sound than the "Ah" which Americans of the Deep South are supposed to say when they mean "I"), they had terrible tempers, and they were mad on genealogy. Our age has seen the utter decay of the funny Welshman, and the rise to a rivalry in eminence of the Witty Irishman and the Pawky Scot; the Welsh, after all, had only Lloyd George, whereas the Scots had Harry Lauder, and irresistibly droll Irishmen are legion.

Some of Joe's jokes live. Consider good old durable Number 72, which used to appear in a game called Literary Conundrums when I was a boy:

> A GENTLEMAN eating some Mutton that was very tough, said, it put him in mind of an old *English* Poet: Being asked who that was; *Chau--cer,* replied he.

And Number 57 has been told of countless celebrated men, including Wilkes:

> Poor *Joe Miller* happening one day to be caught by some of his Friends in a familiar Posture with a Cook Wench, almost as ugly as *Kate Cl--ve,* was very much rallied by them for the Oddness of his Fancy. Why look ye, said he, Gentlemen, altho' I am not a very young Fellow, I have a good Constitution, and am not, I thank Heaven, reduced yet to *Beauty* or *Brandy* to whet my Appetite.

Joe appears more than once as the hero of these rib-binders, as in Number 4, which is typical of a lot of eighteenth-century fun:

> JOE MILLER, sitting one Day in the Window at the *Sun-Tavern* in *Clare-Street,* a Fish Woman and her Maid passing by, the Woman cry'd, *Buy my Soals; buy my Maids:* Ah you wicked old Creature, cry'd honest Joe, *What are you not content to sell your own Soul but you must sell your Maid's too?*

Inlanders may like to know that "Maid" was an old name for skate and shad.

Let us beware of a superior weariness in examining these few jokes from the original 247; it is their form rather than their substance which makes them different from the kind of thing we read and hear every day. The great wit of the eighteenth century has come down to us as brilliant as when it was new. But Joe's jokes are not the golden guineas, they are the coppers of that age—so much more common and so much in general use. Joe puts us in communion, not with Johnson and Goldsmith, but with Squire Hardcastle, and with the people who frequented the Exchange, the taverns, and the alleys of his time.

Heyday of the Pun

THE PRINTED JOKES of the nineteenth century were not so bawdy as these. It was the century of the riddle and the conundrum. In mid-century appeared a book called *Puniana*, advertised as "An Awfully Jolly Book for Parties." Example:

> WHY is a wide-awake hat so called?—Because it never had a nap and never wants one.

Families in which tradition is strong often cherish a few of these, which come down from generation to generation. Here is one which has lived in good health in Australia, and which (from internal evidence, as the scholars like to say) cannot be much less than a century old:

> A FATHER, a mother, their Child and a monkey tumbled down on a walk, and each broke a knee; where did they go for repairs?—The Father went to Africa where the Knee-grows, the Mother to Ireland, where the She-knees are, and of course the Child went to the butcher for a

Kid-knee. (The monkey went to the bank for an Ape-knee.)

We should not reject this sort of thing without giving serious thought to the present fad for jokes about the Little Moron. (Why did the Little Indian Moron sleep with his head toward the campfire?—To keep his wigwam.)

Do these Victorian puns cost you a groan, reader? If so, can you say why? Hear what Max Beerbohm, a critic probably as fastidious as yourself, has to say on this matter. "A good pun, properly used, is one of the best bells in the jester's cap. Why its tinkles should be received, in all places and on all occasions, with groans of mock despair, I have never been able to understand." Let us remember that one of the most deservingly admired wits of recent times, Ogden Nash, has used the pun so ingeniously as to give it virtually a new dimension.

Jestbooks of the nineteenth century were many. One remarkable compilation may keep our attention for a moment, because it originated neither in the United States nor in Britain, but in Australia, and was the work of that indefatigable bookseller, E. W. Cole of Melbourne (1832–1918). *Cole's Fun Doctor*, in the two volumes in my possession, contains seven hundred and ninety-one closely printed pages of jokes of all sorts. Its index of subjects is extensive, containing themes for fun which have, for one reason or another, disappeared today, such as Women's Rights, Mormons, Servants, Bicycling, Princes, Bustles or Improvers, and Men and Women with Tails. Funny Sermons (a separate section from Funny Negro Theology) are offered on such texts as "They shall gnaw a file, and flee unto the mountains of Hepsidam, whar the lion roareth and the wang-doodle mourneth for its first-born"; this text comes from "second Chronik-ills." It contains such typically nineteenth-century descendants of the classical or Latin joke as:

Boyibus kissibus
Sweet girliorum
Girlibus likibus
Wanti somorum

And it is rich in those question-and-answer jokes which are still the staple of newspaper joke columns:

> *Literary Matron:* What does Shakespeare mean by his frequent use of the phrase "Go to"?
> *Matter-of-fact Husband:* Well, perhaps he thought it wouldn't be polite or proper to finish the sentence.

For the present, that is sufficient about the "good laugh." Only a curmudgeon is utterly indifferent to it; only those to whom laughter is the most serious thing in the world attach great value to it (as in the case of the film called *The Perfect Furlough,* which advertised "287 certified laughs"). But has it anything to do with a sense of humor? It is possible to "get" all the jokes in a television program, or even to laugh the two hundred and eighty-seven laughs of the funny film, without ever initiating a joke or experiencing laughter which has not been provoked by something external to oneself. A sense of humor, surely, is something which permits its possessor to perceive jokes which are wholly or partly personal; a man who has this much admired sense ought occasionally to laugh—perhaps inwardly—when others are not laughing. What is he otherwise but the creature of the jokesmith?

Hitard's Theme

CHILDREN sometimes demand to know who invents jokes, and often their elders think this question naïve. But the children are right; somebody must, at some time, think of and set in motion all jokes, even those which are so old that they seem to have groped their way upward from that Universal Unconscious of which Dr. Carl Jung thinks we all partake, and where the memory of the race lies hidden. Embroidery upon a joke and variations upon the Ur-Joke are simple compared with the invention of a new joke.

It may perhaps have been Hitard, court jester to Edmund Ironside, who in the eleventh century conceived a joke which, if Hitard had been able to set it down, might have run thus (I translate from Norman French into the English of a later period):

> SAYS John-a-Nokes to John-a-Stile, "Who was yon beauteous damsel I saw ye with yestre'en?"
> "Nay, by St. Dunstan," cries he, "that was no beauteous damsel, but mine own ill-favoured dame!"

The joke having been started on its long career, it no doubt served many a jester, so far divided as Muckle John at the court of King Charles I, and Blind Harry the Minstrel, groping the narrow tracks of the Scottish Highlands. Undoubtedly it came to America with the Pilgrims, and was suppressed. Perhaps it was among some laughter-loving Indian tribe that it was preserved, in the form of pictographs, in its most familiar form:

WHO was that lady I seen you out with last night?
That was no lady, that was my wife!

Unquestionably it served *Punch* as the dialogue accompanying some exquisitely drawn illustration:

OLD GENTLEMAN (*enquiring his way at the door, and confronted by Miss Emily, aged four, and temporarily a fugitive from the nursery*): May I speak to the lady of the house, my dear?
EMILY (*gravely*): No lady here; only Mummy.
(*Collapse of Old Gentleman.*)

The jokesmiths have worked many variations upon Hitard's Theme (as we may call it). Such as:

TWO MUSICIANS meet.
"Whose was the piccolo I seen you out with last night?"
"That was no piccolo; that was my fife!"

It has appeared as a cartoon, of the fashionable one-line caption variety. An Eskimo woman is shown standing in an attitude of menace over her prone spouse, who has a hangover. She says: "Who was that lady I thawed you out with last night?"

Hitard's Theme never appeared in *The New Yorker* as one of its celebrated series of Letters from Colored Maids, but there is plenty of time.

True Humor Uncontrollable

THE SENSE OF HUMOR, as opposed to the mere ability to see the point of a formal joke and laugh at it, cannot be dissociated from the rest of a man's personality. The fun of a bitter man, or a mean man, or a cruel man, is his sense of humor, true enough, but it is not something which we covet; a man's sense of humor is as clearly indicative of what he is as his grief, or his capacity to love. A great sense of humor can only exist in company with other elements of greatness.

Nor is a sense of humor something which can be turned on and off at the main. Many people believe that some subjects are humorous and others not. Aristotle, in his *Rhetoric*, quotes Gorgias Leontinus, whoever he may have been, very pointedly on this subject. "Humour is the only test of gravity and gravity of humour, for a subject which will not bear raillery is suspicious, and a jest which will not bear serious examination is false wit." In short, there is a time and place for jokes on every subject. But there are so many of these supposedly forbidden themes that much public joke-making is confined to a handful of subjects which vary from age to age—cuckoldry, excrement, and Latin puns in the eighteenth century; cheese, mothers-in-law, and onions in the nineteenth; these are fixed stars in the firmament of mechanical humor. But a sense of humor is not a thing which we can control completely; many people, in painful situations, have been overcome by a sense of the ridiculous, as was Bernard Shaw at his mother's funeral; sincere grief cannot utterly quell it. A man with a sense of humor may nevertheless be deeply serious in his attitude toward life. Stephen Leacock, writing of his imminent death, was serious, yet he wrote without losing his sense of humor, which was in that instance evidence of his courage. Such a man is no mere joker; his sense of humor is a glory which he carries with him to the end.

It is this uncontrollable quality which shocks people who have very little sense of humor of their own, and as a usual thing they reserve their highest admiration for people who are demonstrably and reliably serious—which frequently means merely solemn. Perhaps this is because humor is a thing of intellect rather than emotion, and people in general are more impressed by emotion than by intellect. And can we say that they are wrong? The deepest feelings of mankind are not humorous, and although Freud has shown the Unconscious to be pranksome and witty in a manner which suggests James Joyce, it is remorselessly serious in its effects. Humor is a civilizing element in the jungle of the mind, and civilizing elements never enjoy a complete or prolonged popularity.

Pitfall of Humorous Writing

"GRIEVE and the world grieves with you; laugh, and you laugh alone," writes Sean O'Casey, who ought to know. But like so many striking sayings, it is a fruitful half-truth, rather than a law. Everybody can share in grief, and grief can be feigned; but laughter can only be shared by those who are of like mind. It is precisely in this that the pitfall lurks for the comic writer; he understandably wants as many people as possible to be of like mind with himself, and so, when he writes his funny piece, he is greatly tempted to throw in a few onions and a mother-in-law to swell his audience. He may begin with a true sense of humor, strong and individual, and from this his early work springs; his audience is made, and his task is to keep it and, if he can, to increase it. This will certainly be a struggle, and unless he is a resolute man, he will adulterate his humor with mechanical fun. It may be some time before his defeat is perceptible, for the applause is mounting; but then the fashion changes, and when jokes about onions give way to jokes about flogging kittens, he is a back number.

Such defeat is everywhere to be observed. Which of us has not seen the newspaper man who is given a column of his own, and who sets out happily to fill it with accounts of his domestic adventures. His wife is pressed into service as a comic character—a Fluffy Pinhead, or an Amusing Nagger; his children likewise are coined in his mint, and appear as knowing little creatures who see through him and have slight regard for his opinion. He himself stars as an inept carpenter, a fellow who cannot replace a fuse, a buffoon who attempts to paper his own walls. For a while the columnist is delighted with what he can do, and he may be funny enough in his hand-me-down clown suit. But unless he can change to something else, he will find that what seemed an inexhaustible freedom has become a slavery, for this masochistic self-mockery is extremely difficult to maintain at a high level, and in time only those who like mechanical fun will read him.

Although this cult of the Columnist as Fool is common in North America, it has had a long day in England, too, where it was until recently associated with Gentility. For a quarter-century between the wars *Punch* was full of this sort of thing; its readers could not get enough of the Genteel Humorists. A. A. Milne was probably the best of them, and because it was his true vein, and because he was a fine craftsman, he was very good. But his imitators—how shuddersomely awful they were! They all wrote about their Aunt Agatha, and her cats, and their bloody little whimsical children, and quarrels with their deaf gardener about whether to plant the garden with erysipelas or night-blooming hysterectomy, and how amusingly ignorant the lower classes were, and how laughably eccentric and vulgar anybody was who had more money than themselves; they wrote in an ecstasy of middle-class refinement; they gave the impression that they ate without evacuating, and reproduced their kind without intercourse; their sense of humor found vent in an epicene titter. Yet two generations seemed to find pleasure in the work of these comical capons.

The masochistic vein, in which the writer is the butt of his own fun, is easy for the mechanical humorist, and it is a trap for the lighthearted writer who is not really a humorist at all. But in the hands of a man of genuine abilities, it can be very funny. Consider the work of an Irishman, Patrick Campbell, whose work is not well known in the United States. He was a masochist, but subtle, and he drew blood other than his own. One of his best stories is a tale of his own boyhood; he is trying to learn ventriloquism, and is discovered by a cruel schoolmaster who makes him demonstrate before a class of howling schoolboys for twenty-five minutes. This is very, very funny; it also chills the heart with horror at the cruelty of the master, and gives the reader that terrible, unmistakable shiver which we feel when we recall and relive past humiliations. A writer who can do this is, of course, very far from our newspaper columnist, the Clown of the Suburbs; he is an artist, who bares his heart and bids us laugh; we do laugh, but we bleed a little at the same time.

The Scholarly Humorist

THE ANTITHESIS of this masochistic humor is—no, not sadistic humor, but scholarly humor; the masochistic humorist is right in the middle of what he writes, but the scholar stands well to one side. This is a kind of humor which is never a drug on the market, for scholarly humorists are few. In the United States the finest in this kind was certainly Morris Bishop; in England I think the palm must go to Daniel George, whose real name was D. G. Bunting.

Real scholars, as opposed to mere pedants, are often immensely jolly men, fond of broad jokes, and fond of narrow and involved jokes—but not at all fond of lead-footed, obvious "good laughs." In his book *Lonely Pleasures* Daniel

George gathers together his essays on a wide range of curious subjects. He was a deeply and curiously learned man, and one of the few critics of our time whose good opinion was a great compliment. One receives the impression from his writings that he made it his plan to read any book whatever that no one else can bear to read. He sought dated books of travel, moribund theology, discredited science, and outmoded poets, and from them he culled the little gems which he published in two wonderful anthologies, called *Alphabetical Order* and *A Peck of Troubles*. His essays are not intended primarily to make you laugh; Daniel George does not crack jokes. Rather, the climate of his mind is so salubrious, so invigorating, that dull thoughts and heavy cares are dispelled by contact with it.

And is not this the true end of scholarship? It is to make us wise, of course, but what is the use of being wise if we are not sometimes merry? The merriment of wise men is not the uninformed, gross fun of ignorant men, but it has more kinship with that than with the pinched, frightened fun of those who are neither learned nor ignorant, gentle nor simple, bond nor free. The idea that a wise man must be solemn is bred and preserved among people who have no idea of what wisdom is, and can only respect whatever makes them feel inferior. Daniel George can tell you what wisdom is, and what scholarship does to a man who is well suited to it.

Humor a Dangerous Profession

IT IS the uncontrollable quality of humor which makes it so dangerous as a profession. Robert Graves says, very justly, that the poet who seeks to live by poetry will certainly lose his gift, and the White Goddess will cease to smile upon him because she does not permit her lovers to count on her favors;

that is why Graves earned his living as a writer of novels, and took whatever came to him through his poetry as luck money. I like his way of expressing this belief, and believe in it myself, but if it is too rich for your taste, let it be said that poetic inspiration cannot be forced, or compelled to flow tidily in the most profitable channels. This is true of humor, also. The man who sits down at his desk, saying "I shall have been funny to the extent of 1500 words before lunchtime," will shortly find himself grasping in desperation at mothers-in-law and onions. He will become the victim of a formula. Even so original and, at his best, brilliant a wit as S. J. Perelman could not escape this professional hazard from time to time. It is one of the most striking elements in the career of James Thurber that he was able, so far as I know, to avoid anything mechanical or forced; it is also observable that Thurber's output was not large, which suggests great restraint on his part, for the demand that a humorist produce funny pieces is both pressing and flattering.

Career of a Popular Humorist

It may not be out of place here to consider the career of a humorist of great gifts who yielded to this demand. The late Stephen Leacock (1869–1944) was one of the most popular humorists of his time, and an examination of his work shows that he was, at his best, worthy of the admiration which was lavished on him. His humor was plenteous and bountiful, flowing in the greatest tradition, not of wit, not of irony or sarcasm, but of true and deep humor, the full and joyous recognition of the Comic Spirit at work in life. If a name must be attached to it, we may perhaps call it nonsense, that sudden upward flight from sobriety and fact which delights and illuminates. The word which occurs over and over again in contemporary references to his work and descriptions of his public lectures is "fun." It is a word which is somewhat out of favor at present, for in our nervous age fun is not well understood or valued. But the quality with which Leacock delighted his readers and convulsed his hearers—call it nonsense or fun—resists any accurate analysis.

He knew it very well. Consider this passage:

> Once I might have taken my pen in hand to write about humour with the confident air of the acknowledged professional. But that time is past. Such claim as I had has been taken from me. In fact, I stand unmasked. An English reviewer writing in a literary journal, the very name of which is enough to put contradiction to sleep, has said of my writing, "What is there, after all, in Professor Leacock's humour but a rather ingenious mixture of hyperbole and myosis?" The man was right. How he stumbled upon this trade secret, I do not know. But I am willing to admit, since the truth is out, that it has been my custom in preparing an article of a humorous nature, to go down to the cellar and mix up half a gallon of myosis with a pint of hyperbole. If I want to give the article a decided literary flavour, I find it well to put in about half a pint of paresis. The whole thing is amazingly simple.

Thus lightly he turns aside the comment of a critical jackass. On another occasion he offered this advice on writing. "Writing is no trouble: you just jot down ideas as they occur to you. The jotting is simplicity itself—it is the occurring which is difficult."

Oh, that he had left it at that! But in one of his worst books—the one called *How To Write*—he includes two embarrassing chapters on how to write humor. He could no more tell anybody else how to write humor than Jupiter could tell them how to turn into a bull or a swan, and for the same reason—it was his special gift, his godhead, not susceptible of analysis or explanation, and not communicable to anybody who wanted to be like him.

Leacock's first humorous book was *Literary Lapses*, which was published in 1910, when he was forty; he wrote fifty-seven books altogether, and though a few of these were works on political economy (the subject of which he was professor at McGill University in Montreal from 1908 to 1936), most of them were books of what he called "funny pieces." He was proud of this huge output—proud as only a Canadian who has also been a farmer can be of antlike industry for its own sake. All his life long he got up at five o'clock in the morning, to work. He declared proudly in *Who's Who* that he published at least one book every year from 1906 to 1936. That his work became mechanical and stale and that there was sometimes an hysterically forced note in his fun were less to him than that he wrote a funny book every year. In *Arcadian Adventures among the Idle Rich* and *Moonbeams from the Larger Lunacy* he mocked industrialists who did not know how to relax, but he was quite as much under the compulsion to work, to produce, as they. He did it because it made money, of course, but also because he had an addicted public which would buy any book which had his name on it, and which seemed never to tire of fun which was in his vein, whether of the first sprightly running, or of the mere dregs. Every popular humorist has these uncritical readers; they are attracted to a writer by the special quality of his work, and they want that special thing repeated, even when it has grown forced or stale. To such readers nothing is more baffling than a writer who insists on trying something new, who experiments or improves. Is the writer to be blamed if he obliges them?

Not by me. There are critics who sit in judgment upon a writer's life, sagely putting a finger on the point where he went wrong, was false to himself, let popularity and the flattery of publishers and public lead him from the strait path. Let such critics look to their own careers, if they have indeed careers to look to. It would certainly be better if a writer like Leacock knew always what was best to do and what would look best in the eyes of posterity, but such unnatural foresight cannot be required of any man.

Humorist's Climacteric

NEVERTHELESS, we may observe that in writers more fortunate or more sagacious than Leacock, who have won at least a part of their reputation as humorists, there occurs a development which is of great interest; at some point in middle age the brilliant and often nervous quality which distinguished the humor of their early work gives place to a humor of a different nature; the source of the writer's humor seems to have changed, and what he draws from this new well is of a fuller flavor. If this change does not take place, the humorist may lose his power and his faith in himself, as it appears that the late Robert Benchley did; with the human instinct to see a natural law in a personal misfortune, he said that few humorists kept their touch after fifty. He was partly right; few of them keep the same touch. P. G. Wodehouse is an example of a man who maintained virtually the same style and quality of humor through a long working life; furthermore, he seemed well aware of what he had done and how he had done it. But less conscious craftsmen who are greater artists seem, if they are lucky, to approach and pass a climacteric in middle life which leaves them changed for the better, though it rarely leaves them humorists pure and simple. After this crisis, it is evident that humor is an important aspect of their work, but not the whole of it.

Why this should be so I cannot pretend to explain, except in such generalities as that experience of life deepens perception. An interesting observation on this topic is that of the philosopher, fashionable at present, Sören Kierkegaard, who writes:

> The more one suffers the more, I believe, one has a sense for the comic. It is only by the deepest suffering that one acquires true authority in the use of the comic, and authority which by one word transforms as by magic the reasonable creature one calls man into a caricature.

Complementary to his is Thurber's remark that "humour is a kind of emotional chaos, told about quietly and calmly in retrospect." Emotional chaos is not pleasant; distillation of that chaos afterward may perhaps be pleasant in some of its aspects, and undoubtedly gives pleasure to others.

In considering works of humor, or partly of humor, it is often possible to distinguish the works of men over forty from those of their juniors by this increased emotional quality alone. It is this which distinguishes Goldsmith's *She Stoops to Conquer*, written when he was forty-three, from Congreve's *The Way of the World*, written when he was thirty; both are masterpieces, but one is unmistakably a masterpiece of maturity. Similarly, we are not surprised to find that *The Canterbury Tales* is the work of one who was, for his time, an old man, any more than we are surprised that Thomas Mann's last book and finest work of humor, *Felix Krull*, was completed in his late seventies, although he began it in his comparative youth. This quality of maturity shows itself in humorous books of such widely differing kinds as *Gulliver's Travels*, which Swift wrote when he was fifty-nine, and *The*

Wind in the Willows, written by Kenneth Grahame when he was forty-nine.

The change may be observed in the work of many writers of the first rank. The Mark Twain who wrote *The Innocents Abroad* at thirty-four was not the man who wrote *Huckleberry Finn* at forty-nine. Nor was the Dickens who astonished the English-speaking world with *Pickwick* at twenty-four the same Dickens who turned the corner with *Bleak House*, written when he was forty, and was in the main stream of his later development at forty-eight, when he wrote *Great Expectations*. It is not increased knowledge of life alone—what Kierkegaard characteristically calls suffering but what may more moderately be called distillation of experience—which brings about this change; it is an alteration in the writer's attitude toward himself which shows in his means of expression and the themes he chooses.

Growth in Waugh and Huxley

A WRITER in whom this change is plainly marked is Evelyn Waugh, who was acclaimed as a brilliant humorist when he produced *Decline and Fall* when he was twenty-five. But it should have been evident in his succeeding works that he was not a humorist and nothing else; no humorist of any consequence is ever merely funny. Yet there were readers who were taken by surprise when, in *Brideshead Revisited*, Waugh produced a deeply serious book, in which there were fine humorous passages; he was forty-two when it appeared, and the time for a change was at hand. His subsequent work was increasingly serious, and never more so than in *The Loved One*, written when he was forty-five. Humor in Waugh is a mode of expression rather than a cast of mind.

Even more might this be said of Aldous Huxley, who was

thought very funny when, at twenty-seven, he published *Crome Yellow*; his reputation as a brilliant wit was increased by every subsequent book until *Eyeless in Gaza*, written when he was forty-two. Many of his novels since that time were enlivened by a wit which is undimmed, but which is not the most striking characteristic of his style or his thought; but readers who could not stay the course fell away from him, and there are people so foolish as to underestimate his later quality as a philosopher because he was once a humorist—or seemed so to people who must label and ticket authors.

Tragedy Rises to Balance Comedy

WHY DOES this change take place? Perhaps a clue is afforded by the theory put forward by Sigmund Freud in *Wit and Its Relation to the Unconscious*. This is anything but an easy book to read, for it suffers greatly by translation into English, and it is apt to overwhelm us with that ennui which is inseparable from books which try to explain why things are funny. But it makes two points which are relevant here. The first is that humor is a way of giving expression to things which would be intolerable if they were said directly. "Out of my great sorrows I make my little songs," wrote Heinrich Heine; the humorist might say with equal truth: "Out of my great disenchantments I make my little jokes." The second point made by Freud is that the humorist's object is to strip away, momentarily, the heavy intellectual and moral trappings of adult life, including so many things that we regard as virtues, and to set us free again in that happy condition which we enjoyed in the morning of life, when everything came to us freshly; when we did not have to make allowances for the limitations or misfortunes of others; when we dared to call a thing or a person stupid if they seemed stupid to us;

when we lived gloriously in the moment, without thought for the past or consideration for the future; when we were, indeed, as the lilies of the field. I said above that humor was daemonic; this is how its daemonism works. As the tragic writer rids us of what is petty and ignoble in our nature, so also the humorist rids us of what is cautious, calculating, and priggish—about half of our social conscience, indeed. Both of them permit us, in blessed moments of revelation, to soar above the common level of our lives.

Why, then, if the gift is so great, does the humorist seem to abandon it, or relegate it to an inferior place, in middle age? The answer is that he does not do so; rather, he balances it against another quality which has arisen in him and demands expression, and that quality is a sense of tragedy. This second quality, this late-comer, is not sufficiently powerful to alter the quality of his work absolutely, but it gives it a background of feeling which is sufficient to turn the brilliantly humorous young man into the richly but fitfully humorous middle-aged one.

It is not necessary to dwell at length on the nature of this difference, for it appears clearly enough in literature. One of the most brilliantly and coruscatingly funny books in English is James Joyce's *Ulysses*, which was published when its author was forty, but which had occupied him for many years before that. There are so many things to be said about *Ulysses* that it is sometimes forgotten that it is a great comedy. Nevertheless, it is the great comedy of a young man. Whether the kind of change which I have been describing here is evident in *Finnegans Wake*, completed when he was fifty-six, I do not feel qualified to say. If we seek a great comedy to contrast with *Ulysses*, let us turn to *Don Quixote*, which Cervantes wrote when he was fifty-eight. This is the comedy of a man past that climacteric which brings humor to its fullest ripening. A sense of tragedy, a sense of the evanescence and dreamlike quality of life, and a sense of the imminence of death may all be found in the work of young men, though not often in their works of humor; but in the comedy of older men these things are to be heard, not aggressively, but as a continuing pedal point, supporting the other harmony, whatever it may be.

The Many Faces of Humor

NOT ALL, or even most, discussion of humor can be carried on at the level of *Don Quixote* and *Ulysses*, for there are legions of people who do not care for either of them, and these people also insist that they appreciate humor, and so they do. There are countless grades and classifications of humor, and we had better agree to allow that name to whatever makes people laugh, or smile, whether we like it ourselves or not. There are people who like the fun of the television comics, though the mechanics of its contrivance are often cynically obvious. They are the same sort of people who, a century or more ago, provided happy readers for such remorseless jokesmiths as Theodore Hook and Thomas Hood. And what are we to say of a man like Sydney Smith (1771–1845), who was perhaps the greatest wit of his time, and whose mind seemed to move in an atmosphere of the most delightful and high-hearted humor? Yet Smith was entirely serious in his attitude toward life, and devoted himself to the cause of political and social reform as tirelessly as if he had been the most lugubrious of killjoys. There is reason to think that he might have achieved his ends more surely if he had not been incapable of dullness; his wit was at once his joy and his handicap. What are we to say about those people, frequently of blameless life, whose favorite humor is heavily spiced with indecency? Their fun is not pornography (it is interesting that pornography is rarely cast in a humorous mold), but most of it never sees print. The six volumes of D'Urfey's *Pills to Purge Melancholy* seem chiefly to be aimed at them, and much farce, old and contemporary, is for their enjoyment. They are the people who cannot contain themselves when an old maid on the stage says: "I've asked the Vicar to help me with my inner tube." Most of their humorous currency harks back to *Nugae Venales* or Joe Miller, and has a submerged, but vigorous, life.

Snobbery and Humor

WHAT ARE WE to say about snob humor? *The Diary of a Nobody* by George and Weedon Grossmith (1892) is unquestionably a very funny book; its revelation of the triviality and timidity of Mr. Pooter is managed with great skill; Mr. Pooter is not mocked, he is revealed. We feel superior to him, but we do not scorn him. The touch is gentler, but no less sure, than that of Arthur Kober in his stories about Bella Gross and her family which have appeared in *The New Yorker*. Does anyone think that the Pooters or the Grosses are inadmissible subjects for humor? But if we want to consider a genuine and, in my opinion, inexcusable instance of snob humor, we must give some attention to the career of Amanda Ros.

The facts of her life, briefly, are that she was born Anna Margaret McKittrick, at Ballynahinch, County Down, in 1860; for a short time she was a schoolmistress, until she married Andrew Ross, the stationmaster at Larne, in 1887. She lived at Larne for the remainder of her days, and wrote several books, of which *Irene Iddesleigh*, *Delina Delaney*, and *Poems of Puncture* were published at her own expense. They achieved some success with a small but influential group of people who appreciated their peculiar badness, and before the First Great War there was something of a cult for her work among the smart set in London. After the war the Nonesuch Press brought out a splendid edition of *Irene Iddesleigh*; *Delina Delaney* appeared in Chatto and Windus's famous Phoenix Library; and Aldous Huxley wrote an essay, *Euphues Redivivus,* which called attention to her extraordinary style. She now called herself Amanda Ros as being more aristocratic than her name in its original form. She engaged in a lifelong controversy with her critics, showing herself to be an unusually vigorous and abusive fighter; she died in 1939.

Why all this fuss about a bad writer? Well—she was a bad writer of genius. She was not negatively bad, in the sense that she was dull, or inexpressive, or trite, or lacking in inspiration; she was exuberantly, voluptuously bad—her badness was supereminent and supererogatory; if it is really true that extremes meet, she was so bad that she was good. Her books are funny, and to some people they are exquisitely and refreshingly funny.

A biography of her called *O Rare Amanda* was written in 1954 by Jack Loudan. In it he makes this judgment, from which I strongly dissent: "Amanda is the most perfect instrument for measuring the sense of humour. Alert and quick-witted people accept her at once: those whom she leaves entirely unmoved are invariably dull and unimaginative. She is for people who do not always expect reason, who are ready to enter her world without disputation, and to accept her magnificent incongruities." I object to this sort of criticism which says, in effect, that if you do not enjoy Amanda Ros wholeheartedly, you have a dullard's sense of humor; that is critical bullying.

Bad writing, however extraordinary, is only amusing up to a point. To enjoy it further, simply because it is bad, seems to me like an unpleasant kind of snobbery. Prolonged displays of ineptitude are embarrassing to sensitive people; the off-key singer, the grammarless orator—after a short time we cease to smile and begin to sweat. I can only read two or three pages of Amanda Ros before I am so ashamed for her that I cannot go on. This is not, I think, an unusual condition of mind, and I do not believe that it is incompatible with a literate creature's sense of humor. Does it really show such a very keen sense of fun to enjoy the spectacle of a woman making a fool of herself, in print or otherwise?

The game of baiting Amanda Ros began when Barry Pain, a critic and humorist now virtually forgotten, wrote a review of *Irene Iddesleigh* in 1898 called "*The Book of the Century*"; it is a labored piece of work, heavy-handed and cruel. For a popular reviewer to mock an inept book by a professional writer may be a duty, and even an agreeable duty; but need he go out of his way to poke snobbish fun at a foolish woman whose vanity has led her to pay for the printing of a silly novel? What Amanda thought about it may be read in her reply, which is published as a preface to the 1935 edition of *Delina Delaney*. It is a transport of galumphing sarcasm; it shows her at her most conceited and most inept; if she had been hurt and had retired into silence, Pain's act would have been unkind enough, but she trumpets and tramples like an enraged elephant, and the critic and author put on an unedifying show.

Pain's review called attention to *Irene Iddesleigh* and *Delina Delaney*, which followed it in 1898. Copies of these books were not easy to obtain, but people got hold of them, and even copied long passages by hand. Amanda became a literary craze among a select group, which included a number of literary people, a few politicians, and some society leaders. They met to read her work aloud; it was a mark of distinction to be able to quote her long, tortured sentences. People of name wrote to her, some of them so civilly that she mistook their interest for serious appreciation, and became extremely vain because of it. And it must be said that some things that were said and written about her, such as Huxley's essay already mentioned, were not malicious but sprang from a genuine interest in the pathology of prose. Nevertheless, it was not a kindly form of snobbery which led so many people who should have known better to make sport of this crazed Irishwoman.

I use the word "crazed" in its primary sense. Although in most respects Amanda Ros was sane enough, and could be amiable when she chose, she showed unmistakable signs of madness in relation to her work; in the mealymouthed phrase of modern psychiatry, she was a "disturbed personality." She had delusions of grandeur, and when annoyed, she was abusive and foul-mouthed. Every editor, of magazine or newspaper, has had experience of the type; at best they are nuisances and at worst they are alarming lunatics.

But when all this has been said, an element remains in Amanda's work which compels attention. It is Irish prose, diseased. There are times when we read Joyce, or Brendan Behan, or more particularly Sean O'Casey, when another voice seems to cut in, like an interfering station on the radio; it is the voice of Amanda. I yield to no one in my admiration for the specifically Irish lyric style of writing at its best, but it readily becomes a mannerism, and degenerates into a word-sodden howl. It slithers greasily from simile to simile; it throws up adjectives in ragged, messy heaps; it piles on the agony until the effect is first comic and then intolerable. It strains for effect; it flings words into incongruous and distasteful unions; it drivels and it mumbles and it breaks into sudden, unmannerly screams. It is the sort of thing Joyce has caricatured superbly in the Nausicaa passages in *Ulysses*, and which O'Casey slips into in the worst passages of his autobiography. But it is Amanda's accustomed and best manner; she can do it all the time. Unquestionably, bad writing on this level commands respect and curiosity, and Amanda stands as a perpetual warning to all writers with even a sixteenth part of Irish blood in their veins.

But funny? It was snobbery more than a sense of humor which made a cult of the cracked old Swan of Ballynahinch.

Humor Short-winded

AMANDA'S WORKS were full-length novels, and they were funny, to the people who found them funny at all, by inadvertence. Many a writer might envy Amanda's power to be amusing for so long a stretch; the problem of writing a comic novel is, among other things, a matter of length. So many of their kind collapse when they are two-thirds completed, and sometimes the efforts of the despairing writer to keep up interest to the end are pitifully apparent. Undoubtedly it is much more difficult to sustain the comic tone for the length of a book than it is to produce a romance, or a book of modestly tragic quality. It is this difficulty which accounts for the frequency, and also for the popularity, of those comic books which are novels only in the broadest sense, being in fact collections of short stories in which the same characters appear.

Such a book may be extremely unsophisticated, like *Peck's Bad Boy*, or it can be the book in which a generation finds its ideal of sophistication mirrored, like *Chronicles of Clovis*. George Wilbur Peck must have been a remarkable man, for he is one of the very few people with an openly confessed sense of humor ever to make a mark in politics; at the peak of his career he was Governor of Wisconsin. *Peck's Bad Boy and His Pa* (1883) was familiar and popular until well after the first Great War; it concerns the Bad Boy, who harasses his Pa with a variety of practical jokes, such as putting ants in his liver pad, writing him "mash notes" in a female hand, getting him arrested, causing him to fall into the cistern, and hiding a deck of cards in the handkerchief which Pa will certainly flourish at the prayer meeting. There are frequent allusions to the drollery of rheumatism, of Limburger cheese, of sewer gas, and of being kicked in "the bosom of the pants." It enjoyed the kind of popularity which later attached itself to Chic Sale's little book *The Specialist*; in fifty years it may be hard to believe that millions of people laughed so much at a string of anecdotes about building privies.

Humor of this kind, and of all kinds, constantly refurbishes and renews itself, appearing in the form most congenial to the age. Doubtless that is why the *Chronicles of Clovis*, which was so much appreciated from its appearance in 1911 until, perhaps, 1925, is so little read today; that kind of fastidious and elegant approach to life has little to say to us at present, though the delicacy of the craftsmanship could bring these stories back into favor at some future time. But we may doubt if anything will restore popularity to H. H. Munro's best venture into the novel form, *The Unbearable Bassington*, for it suffers from the failure of vitality which is the characteristic disease of the comic novel undertaken on this high level.

Failure on the Highest Level

FAILURE OF THIS kind is too common to be a matter for reproach; regret, rather, is what we feel. Consider the striking example of *Zuleika Dobson*, which also appeared in 1911; in it Max Beerbohm has tried to write a gently satiric novel about Oxford, which he has enlivened with all the wit and elegance of style which were his. He began it in the nineties, then let it lie fallow for twelve or thirteen years, so there can be no pretense that he let it out of his hands before he had done his best with it. It has a brilliant beginning—so good that at each rereading I pluck up new hope—but it goes badly to pieces in the middle, and even the fine ending cannot redeem it. It is a daring book; no author who was looking for easy popularity would choose mass suicide as his theme; Beerbohm is not one of those who think that certain subjects must be untouched by comedy. Further, although the English like to be rallied on their snobbery, it was courageous to make the whole undergraduate body of Oxford commit suicide because the example was set by a Duke. The book is full of splendid scenes, of which my own favorite is Zuleika's banal performance as a conjuror and the success which her beauty and charm win for this dreadful entertainment. The style is masterly, for it is unceasingly witty without blinding the reader by a display of fireworks—candlelight on fine silver is rather the effect. But all these splendid and enviable qualities cannot make it a good novel which we can read without some weariness. Would not many writers think themselves lucky to fail so splendidly? No: nobody but a fool wants to fail when he sets to work to write a novel, and it is the hope that he may succeed where others—in so many ways his betters—have failed that keeps him going.

It is not the delicacy of the workmanship which robs *Zuleika Dobson* of a sufficient vitality to sustain the whole novel; there is plenty of steel in everything Beerbohm wrote. A more robust approach would not have saved it, any more than it saved *Cold Comfort Farm* (1932), Stella Gibbons's satire on novels of the Gloomy Pastoral School. It is very entertaining for its first hundred pages; the impact of matter-of-fact, brisk, clear-headed young Flora Poste upon the brooding, guilt-ridden, passion-torn Starkadders of Cold Comfort Farm is extremely funny; good phrases and fine strokes of satiric invention abound; but the book cannot continue in this high strain, the plot has to be resolved by some unsatisfactory wrenches, and we finish it with gratitude, but not with the satisfaction which comes from a first-rate invention thoroughly carried out. What we remember are the successful passages, not the whole.

A Neglected Masterpiece

AN UNDESERVEDLY neglected novel which is satiric in manner, and which carries its satiric intention triumphantly for its full length, gaining rather than losing strength as it progresses, is Osbert Sitwell's *Before the Bombardment* (1926). It is not pitched in the high key of *Zuleika Dobson*, and it does not achieve its effects by extravagance, as does *Cold Comfort Farm*: the author has found precisely the tone and the method for carrying out his intention, and the result is a minor masterpiece. Why, then, is it not more widely known? Why is it so seldom referred to when these things are discussed? I think it may be because of the subject, which is little understood by the generality of readers; people will happily read novels which deal with unfamiliar matter in terms of romance, but to appreciate a satire, most of us wish to have encountered the subject at first hand, or in some nonsatirical piece of writing.

Before the Bombardment is a study of that almost forgotten creature, the Paid Companion. Miss Teresa Bramley is a clergyman's daughter who, finding herself alone in the world and with very small means, takes a position as Companion to Miss Cecilia Collier-Floodgaye, who lives in a hotel in the seaside resort of Newborough. She is oppressed, because the nature of her position implies some oppression, but in no gross or farcical sense: she is also an oppressor, because she is of a somewhat superior social position to her employer, and she has delicate means for making this superiority apparent. There are inevitable jealousies between the two ladies, for when the companion seeks friends other than the woman she is paid to befriend, she is guilty of a special sort of disloyalty; similarly, the companion feels both a professional and an emotional tie with her employer, and seeks to defend her from the unsuitable or unworthy people who wish to know her on a wholly personal, nonprofessional level. There arises, inevitably, the question of Miss Collier-Floodgaye's will, and the extent to which Miss Bramley may hope to figure in it. There are connections of the employer, in whose eyes Miss Bramley of course appears as a designing woman, wielding that vague but dreadful power, "undue influence." The comedy is worked out with delicacy, but not with that frail delicacy which means lack of vitality. And although the intention of the novel is satiric, the satire is not so heavily pressed home that the terrible pathos of the situation is falsified or mocked. The truth which lies beneath the artificiality is never denied or distorted.

It is here that we are able to put a finger on the quality which divides the successful comic novel from the brilliant failure; there is an inevitable artificiality about such a work, as indeed there must be about any work of imagination; but in the realm of the intentionally comic the artificiality is more obvious than in novels of romantic or tragic theme. In the comic novel the artificiality can be such a joy to the craftsman and such a release to the wit, that he is tempted to sacrifice truth. Truth in a comic novel need not mean a dreary adherence to such trite and timid philosophies as:

> There is so much good in the worst of us
> And so much bad in the best of us

That it hardly behooves any of us
To talk about the rest of us

That kind of thinking is for the sentimental funnyman, and finds its expression in such deservedly forgotten work as that of J. K. Jerome. But the comic writer, no less than the tragic writer, must bear in mind our common humanity, and relate his work to it as it appears in his own experience. It is the lack of this quality in *Zuleika Dobson* and *Chronicles of Clovis* which robs them, for all their brilliance in execution, of the highest achievement.

It is no accident that the best novels of one of the most inventive and successful among American humorists, Peter De Vries, are related in the first person. A writer may choose this method of narration for many reasons, and nobody believes that the "I" of the story is the "I" of the writer; nevertheless, a man who is writing in the first person even of a creature of his own invention has a potent force at work upon him which prevents his work from escaping into the realm of the inhumanly clever. Mr. De Vries produces excellent comic effects by his revelation of his central character, his narrator, in several aspects—as he sees himself, as he hopes the world sees him, as he discovers, to his dismay, that the world actually *does* see him. His narrator—in *The Tunnel of Love*, in *Comfort Me with Apples*, in *The Mackerel Plaza*, and in *The Tents of Wickedness*—is a man of lively intelligence, scornful of his achievement, doubtful of his effectuality with women, and given to fantasy; the complexity of this invention serves the author well, for he is able to present both his principal character and his story on several levels. They are obviously accepted on several levels, as well, for his admirers range from people who like "a good laugh" and nothing else—people who see De Vries as a successor to Thorne Smith as a purveyor of their favorite kind of fiction—to people who find an image of themselves and a comment on an aspect of modern life in these complex entertainments. They are constructed with ample but unobtrusive craftsmanship, they do not suffer from the sags which are the characteristic faults of comic novels, and they are amply sustained by that essential humanity which alone seems to be able to keep such novels from falling apart, and from being remembered in terms of incidents and phrases, rather than as unities.

By Lo Possessed

THE DEVICE of narration in the first person is used with remarkable effect in the most discussed comic novel of recent times, *Lolita* by Vladimir Nabokov. Is it comic? I think it is. People who hold that some subjects cannot, under any circumstances or however treated, yield comedy think otherwise.

The book is about a theme which does not seem, on the face of it, comic; the narrator is a man whose sexual appetite is confined to girls of between nine and fourteen. He is not a monster or an indiscriminate ravisher; he is desperately in love with his Lolita; Humbert Humbert is a man in the grip of a demon. His obsession, though not rare, is one upon which society frowns—the same society, of course, which permits the frankest exploitation of "little girl" appeal in fashion and advertising.

Books about men gripped by sexual mania are common; incest, homosexuality, satyriasis, and what not are always cropping up in novels, which, clumsy though they may be from the literary point of view, are often greeted with solemn commendation for their frankness. The attitude of such authors reminds me of the story about the little boy who burst into his mother's living room when she was entertaining the parson at tea, eagerly exclaiming: "Hey, Ma! We caught a toad, and we bashed him and squashed him and put him through the lawn mower till"—at this point spying the parson—"until God called him Home." Their novels are liberal of gaudy incident and sickening clinical detail, but these writers are careful to let us know that they abhor what they record. This trick of construction is called "sincerity," and is much praised by critics and readers who want to eat their nasty cake and have it too. I honor Vladimir Nabokov because he will not play this crooked-minded trick on the simple, and wrote *Lolita* as a comic novel.

Why not? The line between tragedy and comedy is thin, as we have already observed, and as many a bad performance of a stage tragedy proves. So thin is it that some writers of special insight—Chekov, Ivy Compton-Burnett, and Joyce Cary (whom we shall discuss in more detail shortly)—have made that borderline their special realm. What comedy of great stature lacks a root in tragedy? *Othello* and *The Merry Wives of Windsor* have a common theme; *Don Quixote*, the comedy, draws hotter tears than *Faust,* the tragedy. The difference between comedy and tragedy is less often one of theme than of the prevailing color of the writer's mind.

Life is a comedy to those who think, a tragedy to those who feel, says Horace Walpole, but it is not quite true. Nabokov feels for his ridiculous, obsessed pursuer of little girls, and he makes us feel, too. Humbert Humbert is a man of intellect and sensibility in the grip of a mania which he knows to be reprehensible, but which he cannot help; he is also the toy of those ridiculous, farcical elements in life of which we are all a prey, but of which we are usually happily unconscious. His plight is comic, and it is as comedy that it is presented. The victimization of Humbert is not cruelly displayed; there is great understanding and pity in this novel.

If the Lolita whom Humbert Humbert pursues, and for

whom he makes a scoundrel, a doormat, and a fool of himself had been an innocent child, debauched by a grown man, we might well have shuddered. Before World War II the late Stephen Haggard wrote a novel about the reciprocated love of a man for a charming girl-child, and although it was done with some skill and much tenderness, it made my flesh creep. But Lolita is not innocent. She is a shrill little gold-digger who has already, at twelve, lost her virginity to a thirteen-year-old tough whose mother runs a girl's camp; it was not a seduction, but a co-operative activity, in the best summer-camp tradition. When Humbert Humbert at last gets Lolita to himself, it is she who seduces him. Incredible? Ask any candid magistrate.

Who is the victim in this relationship? Lolita, who grudgingly exchanges what she does not value for unlimited ice cream, sight-seeing, and travel, or Humbert Humbert, who exchanges money, time, and self-respect for the favors of his darling? Lolita makes him toe the mark by threats of exposure and prison; Humbert keeps her somewhat in check by counterthreats that if he goes to jail, she goes to reform school. From one point of view, she is victim, and he a monster: but with equal truth she is the exploiter, and he the slave. The comedy of their situation lies in the fact that according to convention (and the law is, and must be, conventional) he is grossly culpable and she a legal "infant," unaware of the nature of her actions; but their situation is so unconventional that we must pity Humbert, enthralled to her body and soul, whereas she regards him with neither affection nor distaste. Humbert is a madman, but his madness is of that unmercifully incomplete kind which creates deep wretchedness, as well as hilarious comedy.

Nabokov writes with style, and style—as distinguished from verbal and syntactical foppery, which is sometimes mistaken for it—gives a dimension to a book which can be disquieting when exercised on such a theme as this. Many authors, on the North American continent, write as if they were apprentice blacksmiths making their first horseshoe; the clank of the anvil, the stench of the scorched leather apron, the sparks and the cursing are palpable, and this appeals to those who equate sincerity with sweating ineptitude. Nabokov is more like a master swordsmith making a fine blade; nothing is amiss, nothing is too much, there is no fuss, and the finished product had better be kept away from children. Like the late Bernard Shaw, he writes as if every reader were as intelligent as himself, and this is disquieting to some intellects. Nevertheless, that is the real sincerity, not to be confused with the fake sincerity which springs from clumsy craftsmanship and a shared loutishness between writer and reader. Virtuosity, so much admired in some of the other arts, is at present unfashionable in literature. Can it be that those who feared the book and banned it felt that something horrifying—something far beyond the anthropoidal simplicities of *Peyton Place*—lurked beneath that gleaming surface?

What lurks there is nothing worse than the spirit of comedy, but as has already been suggested, that can be quite bad enough. This is the daemonic comedy which is so terrible to those who regard humor as, essentially, something which hurts nobody's feelings, a gentle sweetener of life's cup. The humor which whistles up the skirts of Mrs. Grundy like an icy breeze, and blows the judge's robe right across his eyes, is not for them.

Some critics, who were eager to show their liberality of spirit by lallygagging over a once banned work, have called *Lolita* a great book. It is sufficient to say that it is a book of unique quality. There will long be people who will find it very funny; the plain fact that it is not for all readers has nothing to do with the matter, and is, rather, evidence of the originality of its comedy.

The Greatness of Cary

TELLING A STORY in the first person is not a formula for success in writing comic novels, but it serves the true comic novelist well, despite the often discussed handicaps inherent in the method. One of the few really great comic novels to be written in this century, *The Horse's Mouth* by the late Joyce Cary (1944), is cast in this form. It was interesting to observe that the film which was made from this book in 1958 was compelled to leave out virtually everything which makes the book great, but there was quite enough comic incident and comic character left to make a film well above the ordinary level. The story of the novel is sufficient but of minor importance; an elderly painter, Gulley Jimson, is so obsessed with the problems of his art that he subordinates every other feeling and obligation to it; he is literally a man possessed, and from this central fact springs everything that happens to him. In the novel it is this demoniacal possession which is always foremost, and we see his misfortunes, his friendships, the scrapes in which he involves other people, always as minor matters. In the film these incidents had to be brought into sharper definition, and the character of Gulley, though still the most important, lost stature.

The novel is a triumph of impersonation, and it is part of an even greater triumph, a trilogy (*Herself Surprised*, 1941, and *To Be a Pilgrim*, 1942) concerning the relationship of three people; each book tells part of the story as it appeared to the narrator, with differences of emphasis and point of view which make them seem to be three stories, though in fact they are one. The trilogy is a triumphant exposition of the truth that we are all, unwittingly, playing supporting roles in each other's personal dramas. The tragic sense of life, the human predicament, the "sense of otherness"—all the sable generalities which are brought out to justify works which are aiming at tragedy and which so often succeed only in arriving at gloom—are all apparent in Cary's trilogy, but in its totality it is seen through a temperament which is serene, distinguished, and courageous, and so it emerges as great comedy.

Much of this comedy is based on a truth which other writers have found tragic—the isolation and essential loneliness of human life. The three principals in the trilogy are all, at the end, alone. Mrs. Sara Monday of *Herself Surprised* is last met with in prison, where she has gone because she pilfered from her employer, whose mistress she also was. Not he but his relatives discovered and disgraced her. She is astonished to discover, after the court proceedings, that she is what the world calls a criminal, for nothing that she did seemed to her wrong, or malicious, or contrary to the pity she felt for Mr. Wilcher, who was so pathetic and who treated her so well. Her memoir is written in short chapters, in a sweet, countrified vocabulary, and with occasional passages which recall her favorite author, Charlotte M. Yonge. She did not think of her peculations as serious . . . "it was a case of little by little" . . . and she blames "my flesh" for her sexual involvement with Wilcher and with Jimson. It is between the lines and in the other books that we discover what a conniver and a temptress she has been. She sees herself still as a country girl with a special, appealing, fresh beauty, who "could not refuse any pleasure." She does not recognize the portrait of her which the judge gives in his summing up of her case.

So also with poor old Wilcher, whom we meet in *To Be a Pilgrim* as an old man, bemused by what has happened to his life, which seems so much at odds with all his intentions. He is invalidish and in the care of his twenty-six-year-old niece, Ann, who is a doctor and an unsympathetic girl whose intellect has developed at the cost of her emotions. To her, Wilcher is a man whose mind is going and who has been caught indecently exposing himself; this fact, which is uppermost in her mind, is a triviality to Wilcher, and in the light of what we learn about him, we see how trivial it really is. The role of elderly "care" is forced upon him by his juniors, whose values in life are so different from his own, and whom he cannot reach in conversation. The failure, as he sees it, is all with them, but we know better. When we leave him, he is being murdered psychologically, in his best interests, and by what passes with Ann for kindness.

When we consider the trilogy we are struck by the fact that Gulley Jimson, though vital to the lives of both Sara Monday and Wilcher, has only the vaguest recollection of them. Sara is to him little more than a woman who unjustly acquired some of his pictures, which he wants to get back and sell in order to paint more. Jimson has a recurrent sense of persecution. Of Wilcher he remembers little and cares less.

We leave them, Sara in prison (but, with her usual luck, selling her memoirs to a newspaper), Wilcher a prisoner of his chilly niece, and Jimson dying, having been hurt when a mural collapses. In the long years behind them these three worlds have met but never mingled.

Related thus, we hardly find this theme comic. But are there comic themes, or only comic writers—men whose quality of mind and means of expression are comic, without thereby being any less compassionate or understanding or profound than the writers of tragedy? When we have finished a great comic creation, like Cary's trilogy, we feel a lightening of the spirit, a reaffirmation of the splendor and sacredness of life, no less than that which follows our reading of a great work of tragedy. It is a long way from a good laugh; it is a glory in the breast.

Hunting the Unicorn

AT THE BEGINNING of this discussion I disclaimed any intention of formulating yet another theory about humor. If there is a theory which will cover everything from the "good laugh" (which is so much a mechanical and conditioned response to the mere idea of a joke that an audience in a television studio can be induced to roar merely by holding up a placard which suggests that a joke has been made) to the subtlety of Joyce Cary's comic trilogy, it will have to be discovered by somebody else. I cannot believe that it is an entity separable from the rest of human character; surely it is an aspect of some minds, varying in degree and quality with the composition of those minds. It may be, as some psychologists say, the result of a special quality of tension between the Conscious and the Unconscious; but suppose this is so—this precious tension cannot be cultivated or brought into being simply because we have a theory about its nature. As Sean O'Casey suggests, there seems to be far more human identity in grief than in mirth, and this in its turn should make it clear to us that mirth is something other than the antithesis of grief.

It is not even as though we could count on any stability in our own sense of humor. There are many of us who can guffaw at a funny story, at a limerick, or at a pun (What was Joan of Arc made of?—She was Maid of Orleans) and still be moved to quite another kind of pleasure by, for instance, such a novel as *Anglo-Saxon Attitudes* by Angus Wilson, or one of the superb rhapsodies of word-play which are called novels by that too little recognized comic genius, Gwyn Thomas—*Now Lead Us Home*, *No Frost on My Frolic*, to name but two. In our teens we roll about in glee at some modern equivalent of *Peck's Bad Boy*; in our twenties we think that the farthest reach of sophisticated humor is to be found in the harshly ironic comedies of Miss Ivy Compton-Burnett; when we are in middle age, it may well be the Cary trilogy which delights us; in our sixties we may turn to Dickens, or *Don Quixote*, or even the brutalities and buffooneries of Smollett; and in old age, what is it we seize upon to beguile the long nights?—it may perhaps even be *Peck's Bad Boy* again. The search for the sense of humor is as fruitless and as enduring as the hunt for the unicorn; the really wise man knows that the unicorn, being no reality but a life-enhancing myth, must never be hunted, and may only be glimpsed by the well-disposed and the lucky; it cannot be captured, and it is encountered only by indirection. He who insists on hunting the unicorn will certainly discover, when at last he is sure that the fabulous creature is in his net, that he has snared a laughing jackass.

·VII·
In Pursuit of Pornography

It is with reluctance that I begin this chapter with some comment on book collecting, for I do not know how I shall avoid the many pitfalls which lie in the path of all who approach that subject. Hobbyists are likely to be bores to those who do not share their madness, and I am not writing this for other collectors, nor am I trying to make converts. But it is a plain fact that anyone who has ten books on a shelf which he has bought and kept because he likes them is a collector on the humblest level, and his books are, in a special sense, a reflection of himself. It is of collections of books as reflections of their owners that I wish to write. But the temptation to wallow and disport myself in the purple prose of the doting collector is strong, and it will need all my vigilance to resist it.

The trouble is that books have always been what the jargon of the sociologist calls "status-lenders." Books are likely to lay bare unsuspected foolishness, even in people who do not read them. "It's an education just to look at all those books," said a man who came to hang curtains in my library; he was sincere, he was awed, he wished to pay tribute to something which he believed to be good, and he also wanted to show that, though not a reader himself, he was a fellow of fine feelings. "Books are my husband's one vice," said a woman to me, pleased as Punch—as she might well have been had her statement been true. "Why don't you read a book?" say parents to their troublesome children, as who might say: "Why don't you take a tranquilizer?" There are great numbers of people to whom the act of reading a book—any sort of book—is wondrous; they speak of the reader in the tone of warm approbation which they use otherwise when referring to pregnant women, or the newly dead. And how often do we meet the man who prefaces his remarks with: "I was reading a book last night . . ." in the too loud, overenunciated fashion of one who might be saying: "I keep a hippogryph in my basement." Reading confers status.

Books for Prestige

HOW MUCH MORE, then, does the acquirement of rare books add to the prestige of the collector! They need not be very rare; a shelf of first editions of the better sort of modern novelist is quite enough, though it is even better to have some books by reputable dead authors, preferably bound in leather. What matter if the edges be trimmed so that the margins are destroyed, and the binding a tasteless horror? Plenty of people will be impressed.

Another collector, a little higher up the ladder, will not be impressed, however, and it is at this point that the real dog fight for status begins. He takes down the first edition of *Vanity Fair*, for which his host paid $130 at Ladrone's in New York, and remarks brusquely that two of the plates are substitutions, and that the trimming and rebinding have robbed it of all bibliographical interest. "A good reading copy, of course—if that's all you want," he says, and leaves his host a prey to rage and envy, demoted to the ranks of those who collect books merely to read.

Thus it goes, up and up the ladder until those dizzy heights are reached where rich collectors vie for Gutenbergs or First Folios, and where a single note from Lewis Carroll saying "In my heart of hearts I have always detested that little prig *Alice*" can command a sum equivalent to the annual salary of a union executive.

The world of book collectors is a curious mingling of dreamy charm, poison-fanged competition, and snobbery. It reveals itself in the books they write. How winning they are as they confess their lifelong passion for the gentle Elia (they mean Charles Lamb) or Miss Austen (they mean Jane, but they are so courtly that they cannot bring themselves to use her first name). How polysyllabically rude they become when writing of Samuel Johnson, and when they tackle Gibbon, how their prose squirms and undulates as they struggle to catch the rhythm of his splendid music! But behind all this posthumous courtship of the literary great we are conscious of another and very different spirit; it is that of the junkman with his wretched cart and his gloomy howl of "any ol' rags, any ol' bones, any ol' bottles?" They write gleefully of their "finds"—meaning books which they have acquired for ridiculously less than their value to collectors. Nobody would grudge them the reward of expert knowledge and long searching if only they were less unctuous about it, if only they could refrain from rubbing their hands in print. But always in these books the haggling, overreaching sharper is at war with the self-honoring booklover, and the struggle is a disquieting one to the noncollector, who wishes that they would come down flatly on one side or the other.

The collector, however, must haggle, must boast, must croon over his treasures, because it is his nature. And a very peculiar nature, too. Time and again booklovers have written of their libraries as harems and of themselves as sultans, holding captive the beauties who exist for their pleasure alone. It is not in the least inappropriate that Casanova ended his days as librarian to Count Waldstein at Dux; he, who knew every art of seduction, thus became guardian of another man's zenana. The eroticism, snobbery, and shameless greed of book collectors can be shocking if we are so naïve as to suppose, like my decorator, that books are, in their influence, solely educative—which is usually taken by simple minds to mean emasculating.

Collecting Condemned

DOUBTLESS it was this mania of collectors which drove Edmund Wilson to write in 1926, when the trade in rare books was at one of its occasional peaks: "There is no special virtue in first editions: one would usually prefer to read a later one in which the printing is up to date, the paper has not faded and the author has corrected the errors. All this trade is as deeply boring to people who are interested in literature as it seems to be fascinating to those others who, incapable of literary culture, try to buy the distinction of letters by paying unusual prices for bibliographical rarities. . . . It may be necessary for a critic or a student—unless he has within reach a large library—to accumulate a considerable number of books; but it is doubtful whether any first-rate man of letters has ever gone in for collecting books except on some special subject in which he might happen to be interested . . . it is easier for a camel to pass through the eye of a needle than for a collector of first editions to enter the Kingdom of Literature."

Disgust has forced Mr. Wilson to take an extreme position,

and I do not think that what he says is true. There *is* a special virtue in first editions; they are the form in which the author first saw his work, the form in which it was acclaimed or neglected by his contemporaries, the form very often with the best claim to be considered authentic. To prefer a modern reprint, unless for some very good reason, is bibliographical puritanism, and like all unnecessary austerity, it suggests that its professor is making a virtue of his lack of taste. There are also people, no doubt, who like the meals served on airplanes, eaten out of compartmented trays with plastic knives and forks; such people might assert that their victuals are as nutritious as those served on china and silver, but we should not be likely to heed them to the extent of providing our houses with such nasty things; we eat for pleasure as well as to stoke our fires. We read for pleasure, too, and the desires of hand and eye, though inferior to those of the mind, ask for some occasional gratification. First editions, old editions, and handsome books are aesthetically gratifying.

A Plea for Private Libraries

IT IS NOT necessary to be a lunatic collector, either, to object to the suggestion of Mr. Wilson—one in which Bernard Shaw also concurred—that the existence of a public library makes a private one unnecessary. If we admire a book, we like to own it, and we like to have it at hand whenever we want it. Furthermore, there is about public books a public feel, and even a public smell, which some people dislike. Strive as they may, librarians cannot keep books from being marked and dirtied by some of their borrowers. It has long been so, and one of the oldest books in praise of collecting bears witness to it. I speak of the *Philobiblon* of the good Bishop Richard de Bury, written in 1345, from which this passage comes:

You may happen to see some headstrong youth lazily lounging over his studies, and when the winter's frost is sharp, his nose running from the nipping cold drips down, nor does he think of wiping it with his pocket-handkerchief until he has bedewed the book before him with the ugly moisture. Would that he had before him no book, but a cobbler's apron! His nails are stuffed with fetid filth as black as jet, with which he marks any passage that pleases him. He distributes a multitude of straws, which he inserts to stick out in different places, so that the halm may remind him of what his memory cannot retain. These straws, because the book has no stomach to digest them, and no one takes them out, first distend the book from its wonted closing, and at length, being carelessly abandoned to oblivion, go to decay. He does not fear to eat fruit or cheese over an open book, or carelessly to carry a cup to and from his mouth; and because he has no wallet at hand he drops into books the fragments that are left. Continually chattering, he is never weary of disputing with his companions, and while he alleges a crowd of senseless arguments, he wets the book lying half open on his lap with sputtering showers. Aye, and then hastily folding his arms he leans forward on the book, and by a brief spell of study he invites a prolonged nap; and then, by way of mending the wrinkles, he folds back the margin of the leaves, to the no small injury of the book. Now the rain is over and gone, and the flowers have appeared in our land. Then the scholar we are speaking of, a neglecter rather than an inspecter of books, will stuff his volume with violets, and primroses, with roses and quatrefoil. Then he will use his wet and perspiring hands to turn over the volumes; then he will thump the white vellum with gloves covered with all kinds of dust, and with his finger clad in long-

> used leather will hunt line by line through the page; then at the sting of the biting flea the sacred book is flung aside, and is hardly shut for another month, until it is so full of dust that has found its way within, that it resists the effort to close it.

The Bishop was no book miser, but the founder of a great library, and the passage above comes from the chapter which tells how he wants his books to be used. He is also severe against those who write opinions of their own in margins. His complaints have a modern ring because the faults he abuses persist. Flowers, straws, and unpleasing stains are to be found in public-library books to this day, and I have more than once found a used pipe cleaner in their pages. Librarians say, very properly, that they would rather have books read to pieces than preserved untouched, and we must all, when we need many books, use public collections. But if we truly love books, or indeed if we merely like and respect them, we shall want as many as we can get for our private possession.

Mr. Wilson's protest, however, is against the nonsensical side of book collecting, which is a very prominent side. To me, at any rate, there is a perversity in collecting books without meaning to read them, and it is maddening to meet people who regard books as a form of decoration or a substitute for insulation; I once knew a young woman who would own a book only if it had a white binding, and quite recently I heard a man say that a wall of books was the best firebreak a house could have because they burn so slowly.

The moderate collector is likely to be a booklover of moderate means; he values what books can say to him too much to overvalue their age, their rarity, or their appearance, and because he has no money for such pomps, the temptations of books too valuable to be read (and perhaps unreadable) do not torture him. But he may still have a fine library, and to people who know something of books, it will be a partial index to his character.

Private-press Books

BOOKS NEED NOT be old or particularly rare to have beauty and value. Modern craftsmen can produce them, and if you want to know how and why, *The Gregynog Press* by Thomas Jones gives an account of one of the finest private presses of our time. Perhaps the most famous of the private presses was that which Horace Walpole directed for his own pleasure at Strawberry Hill from 1757; the books and pamphlets he produced are rare enough and fine enough to have been worth forgery after his death. He purposely created rarities; of *Hieroglyphic Tales*, for instance, which he produced in 1785, there were only six copies. But it was in the nineteenth century that private presses began to flourish; there were great presses before that time, such as those of Aldus Manutius and Louis Elzevir, but these men were themselves commercial printers, and not, as were the private presses of our own day and the last century, attempting to produce books which commercial printers could not, for economic reasons, attempt.

The names of the private presses are familiar to lovers of books. Kelmscott, Ashdene, Doves, Golden Cockerel, Corvinus, Eragny, Fanfrolico, Gregynog, Nonesuch, Cuala, Grabhorn—they are well represented in the catalogues of sellers of fine books. They are not extremely rare, but they are rare enough; the handsome Nonesuch editions of the Restoration dramatists—Rochester, Otway, Congreve, Farquhar, Wycherley, Vanbrugh, and Dryden—run from 900 to 1,350 copies each, and the Nonesuch Milton is confined to 1,450 copies in two volumes and 90 copies with the two volumes bound as one, printed on a special paper. The Golden

Cockerel edition of Colley Cibber's *Autobiography* runs to 450 copies; *Covent Garden Drollery*, from the Fortune Press, 575 copies; the Gregynog *Elia and the Last Essays of Elia*, 260 copies. To own any of these books is to have a thing of beauty, and the prices, though not trifling, are very much below the millionaire level.

Not all books in this category are equally worthy of the collector's attention. About the directors and workers of the private presses there was necessarily a strong individuality, which sometimes became eccentricity, and fashionable books were brought out which are merely ugly now. Some presses were long on taste but short on craftsmanship, and their books do not stand up well. An example is *The Paintings of D. H. Lawrence* brought out by the Mandrake Press in 1929 in an edition of 510 copies. The quality of reproduction of the paintings is poor, and the pretentious binding is hardly likely to last a century. The book appeals, however, to the pious zeal of Lawrentians, and if they have luck and twenty pounds, they can get one of the 510 copies; presumably it would suffer the usual sea change before it appeared in a New York shop, and would cost more than the equivalent—say sixty dollars—there.

Another fault of many private presses, in my eyes, at least, was that they were more interested in books as objects to be prized than as volumes to be read, and they chose to bring out in handsome form books which very few people care about. If one wanted to read the *Idyls of Theocritus, Bion and Moschus*, would one choose to do so in the prose translation of Andrew Lang? The Riccardi Press thought so. Does someone pine for fourteen poems by James Elroy Flecker, at eighteen guineas? Darantière of Dijon thought they did. Do you famish for *The Parlement of Pratlers* by John Eliot? The Fanfrolico Press thought that at least six hundred and twenty-five bibliophiles were aching for it. I cannot escape a disagreeable impression that these books were chosen because someone thought he could do a pretty job with them, rather than because the books were wanted for themselves.

Private Presses Crudely Imitated

The private presses had other unfortunate consequences. In the books produced under the influence of Elbert Hubbard we see what Kelmscott mannerism can sink to when not controlled by Kelmscott taste. Thick paper, queer type, lavish ornament, and ragged edges will not make a fine book, though they will make a book odd enough to impress people who know nothing of books and perhaps do not greatly like them. The assurance given in a fancy colophon that the object has been "done into a printed book by the handicraftsmen of the Roycroft Shops at East Aurora" does not make up for the fact that the thing is inconvenient to read and that the binding creates the same disagreeable feeling in the hand as wearing cheap suède gloves. Any booklover would much rather have a decent job done by a commercial printer. The only justification of the private presses is that they can design books of unusual beauty and make them at least as well as the trade publishers; if they fail in this they should give up. Hubbard cheapened the craft he thought to elevate.

The snobbery attaching to the products of private presses has given rise at various times during the past fifty years to clubs or associations which produce and distribute supposedly fine books. They have existed in the United States, and at least one exists in England now. Their books are of uneven merit (as indeed were those of the private presses), but they have always some confession of economy about them, of pinching and corner-cutting. The gold on the bindings is not good enough, and it comes off in powder after a time; the books do not open well; the illustrations—usually called "decorations," for it is beneath the dignity of artists to illustrate any more—may be four scratchy etchings which bear no relation to the text, or woodcuts of a determined and self-conscious naïveté. About them is an air of not being quite first rate, either as commercial books made by a decent publisher, or yet as examples of fine printing; sometimes they are refined to the point of being epicene, and if they are meant to be robust—as when a novel by Fielding or Defoe is offered—they exhibit the false and excessive manliness of the tough homosexual. They are not honest books.

The Inscrutable Portrait

WHEN I WRITE of a collection of books as a portrait of its owner I must hasten to make several qualifications. The idea was first suggested to my mind many years ago, when a university lecturer solemnly assured the class of which I was a member that it was so. He was urging us to become buyers of books, and he was eager that we should spend our money only on good books. He spoke exultantly of the joys of collecting a library as an extension of one's personality. I took him at his word then, but during the intervening years I have seen so many collections of books which did not seem to square with what I knew about their owners that I cannot think of his dictum now without overtones of travesty. There was a time when I fancied myself capable of studying a man's books as I might study his portrait, but I have dismissed such prideful nonsense long since. There is no art to find the mind's construction in the books, as Shakespeare would doubtless have written if he had thought of it.

What are we told by the presence of those pretentious, unreadable, complete sets of Balzac and Daudet, which were sold in the early years of this century to people who had never heard of Balzac or Daudet, but who were persuaded by book-agents that they needed such cultivated trappings? Showy but tasteless in binding, and illustrated with dingy engravings "guarded" by bits of tissue, they still turn up at country auctions in Canada—pathetic witnesses of man's desire to be learned without taking the trouble to learn.

What are we told by the rich man's collection, glowing with bibliographical rarities? Perhaps only that he has a long purse and a good advisor, but we must beware of hasty conclusions. Edmund Wilson's strictures on the collector are too severe; a man is not precluded from taste and literary enthusiasm merely because he is rich; that belief is to be classed with the foolish notion that the real lovers of opera are all to be found in the cheapest seats; it is naïve and uncharitable to dislike the rich merely because they are rich. The wealthy collector may be a mere hobbyist, or he may be of the strain of Richard de Bury, or, in our own time, of Arthur Houghton. And if, as sometimes happens, he is both, with the courtier to the dead, the rag-and-bone man, and the benefactor of mankind all mingled in one creature, we must be shrewd indeed to read his portrait in his books.

Hidden Books

NOR SHOULD WE attempt to do so unless we have seen *all* his books—not only those which are on the shelves, but those which are locked in his desk, or hidden behind the shelves, or tucked beneath the winter underwear in his bureau. Even collectors on a modest scale have something of this sort—a surreptitious *Lady Chatterley* purchased years ago on a visit to Paris, a *Ulysses* bought before it became legal and still smelling a little of brimstone, or a *Tropic of Capricorn* concealed from the children or even perhaps from that guardian of the purity of the hearth, The Wife. What a man considers indecent is an important clue to his character, and although there are exceptions, it has been my experience that book collectors have strange opinions on this subject, and few of them lack a book or two which they think they should conceal.

Books are status lenders, but they are something much older and stranger; they retain a quality of magic for people who are deeply concerned with them, as well as for those who know little about them. Books are often burned; as I write this the fires are cooling in Fort William, Ontario, where all local copies of *Lady Chatterley's Lover* were thrown into the flames at the urgency of a female mayor. But when did we last hear of a picture being burned? What angry mayor has recently smashed a statue? It is the hated book which alone suffers the fate of the witch. The fearful are ready to declare that the young will be perverted by suggestive books, but they rarely turn their attention to the contents of art galleries. Books are thought to have a power not granted to other works of art, not only by the simple but by the learned. Among collectors the possession of a few volumes of doubtful character seems to be a fearful yet irresistible necessity.

It is when we discover what these volumes are that we gape and pop our eyes. A man once favored me with a sight of his unholy treasure, which proved to be a first edition of Cabell's *Jurgen*; perhaps tactlessly I told him that it could be bought half a mile away, in a very good bookshop, with illustrations *à la* Beardsley; the information made no impression on his belief that it was a dreadful yet beautiful book, which must be kept at all costs from the eyes of his womenfolk. Another collector, a wealthy Canadian, appealed to his bookseller in despair; his physician had warned him that he might die suddenly, and locked in his desk was a copy of Cleland's

Fanny Hill, or the Memoirs of a Woman of Pleasure; he had paid $100 for it (though it was a modern reprint and of no bibliographical interest), and the notion that his lubricity might be exposed to his daughters after his death was pushing him toward the heart attack he feared. From *Jurgen* to *Fanny Hill* is a far cry, and between are all sorts of books which apparently sensible people consider heinous.

A concept of obscenity appears to be as necessary to one's view of life as a concept of purity. If we seek to encompass all that we can of the spectrum of human intellect and feeling, we cannot confine ourselves to the reds and oranges; we must know the violets and indigos as well. Which is the wiser course—to attempt to suppress a large part of what occupies the human mind, or to examine and cultivate everything in the mind that can be reached? "Vice loses half its evil by losing all its grossness," said Edmund Burke. Book collectors who are, as I have said above, usually men of strong and mingled emotions offer evidence to support Burke's opinion.

My Search for Pornography

SIMPLE pornography has little appeal for them. When I undertook the writing of this book and planned the present chapter, I attempted to find out something about the trade in pornography, but without much success. I asked a good many booksellers about it, and sometimes my reception was amusing; a few of them thought that I had disguised myself as a pedant in order to gratify the literary passions of a voluptuary, and our conversation proceeded, on their side with "strange *œillades* and most speaking looks" and on mine with mounting embarrassment; they had heard of pornographic books, ha ha, but they never dealt in them—no, never. They had heard of collectors who sought out pornographic books, but they got them in New York, or in London, or in Brussels, or obtained them from Japan—the market was anywhere, it appeared, except where I happened to be. Other booksellers were less jocose and more helpful. One, in an English university city, had handled three large collections of pornography in a lifetime of bookselling.

What he told me about these collections was interesting and pathetic. The mania for completeness had possessed the collectors; if they heard of an item in Port Said, they must have it; if a little book of pictures was popular among sailors in Cape Town, they must include an example in the collection. The result was that when the collections were disposed of, there were a few hundred volumes which might be considered salable, and thousands of pamphlets, booklets, and broadsides which could only be burned; nobody, however eager for pornography, could bother with so much repetitious, ill-printed, crudely illustrated trash. One of these collectors was a clergyman of the Church of England who spent all his fortune on his accumulation; his heirs were lucky to get two or three hundred pounds out of a large library which had cost many thousands.

Another bookseller told me that the pornographic market was a closed and special one, with its own scale of prices. This information complemented what I had been told before about the avidity of collectors in this realm; they have a compulsion toward completeness, and as they seem rarely to be the kind of people who can, or will, go to the places where the cheapest pornography is retailed, they must depend on agents. All pornography, it appears, costs more than any other sort of publication in relation to the expense of producing it; nevertheless, some of it sells quite cheaply in, for example, the ports of the Near East. But by the time these chapbooks or pamphlets have been purchased by agents and sent to buyers in Britain or North America, the original price has been multiplied by five, by ten, perhaps by a hundred. And the collector, to satisfy his mania for completeness, pays.

Several booksellers spoke with admiration of the books—perhaps pornography is not the right word for them—of erotic content which are produced in Japan; I was told that they are often of great beauty and delicacy of illustration. The Western market for them seems to be Brussels, with Amsterdam a close rival.

Commercial booksellers, either of new books or collector's books, have no connection with the pornographic market. Some of those to whom I spoke tried to help me by producing volumes which they considered, for one reason or another, fell within the forbidden category. One was the book of D. H. Lawrence's paintings already described; because the original exhibition of these pictures was closed by the police in 1929, the book could not be freely offered for sale. There is not a picture in it which appears to me to be pornographic, if it is admitted that the nude human body is a permissible subject for a painter. Another bookseller showed me some French copies of Rabelais and Baudelaire, illustrated by modern French artists; on his shelves were many books with equally lively illustrations, but they were not French, and thus were free of suspicion. He also showed me a copy of *The Golden Asse*, with illustrations much milder in tone than those in the Bodley Head limited edition of 1923, which sells without hindrance.

A number of helpful booksellers urged me to make myself known at the British Museum, which has the second largest collection of erotica and pornography in the world, the only superior one being in the library of the Vatican. But they mistook my purpose; I did not want to examine pornography, I wanted to find out how the trade in it works, and in this I failed. Had I been a more dedicated scholar, I suppose I would have taken greater pains. I would have disguised myself as a sailor, a dissolute parson, or a gandermooner, and lurked in the places where such people congregate, waiting to be approached. Adolescents, I was told, bought pornography of a particular kind, and I might have tried to impose myself upon a shady bookseller as a wanton adolescent—the half-baked in pursuit of the wholly raw. But I had no confidence in my ability to assume any of these characters convincingly, or yet to pass myself off as a jaded worldling to whom the costly erotica of Japan might be offered. Neither was I successful in discovering a Fred Hankey to assist me.

Don Quichotte or Dirty Hankey?

FREDERICK HANKEY took pains to surround himself with mystery, and facts about him are not easily come by. He was an Englishman of good family who lived in Paris in the middle decades of the nineteenth century, devoting his energies to the collection of pornographic books, pictures, and images. His austerity and dedication to his work was commended by several of his distinguished clients, and in particular by Richard Monckton Milnes (1809–85), Baron Houghton, politician and poet, best remembered as the earliest biographer of Keats. Milnes's library at Fryston (which he sometimes called "Aphrodisiopolis") contained six principal sections, including English poetry, studies of the French Revolution, theology, magic and witchcraft, crime and punishment, and erotica; Hankey supplied the erotica, and it was at Milnes's house that Swinburne made his acquaintance with the works of the Marquis de Sade. The collection was open to Milnes's guests, and many of them made ample use of it. Richard Burton, translator of *Arabian Nights,* was an amateur of erotica and a guest at Fryston at one time; he referred to the Paris buyer as "poor old Hankey." But to other people Frederick Hankey was a sinister figure; it was the Goncourts who named him "*le Don Quichotte des obscènes.*"

Hankey and Burton exemplify two opposed attitudes toward erotica. To Burton it was a subject for study, a part of the comedy of life, but it was not an obsession and it had no mystical overtones. To Hankey it was a reason for being, a support for his own ruling passion (which was Sadism), and probably the source of the deepest emotions of which he was capable. Burton's own great translation and edition of *Arabian Nights* gained the reputation of a pornographic book principally because of one section of the Terminal Essay in which he discusses the Arab attitude toward sex; he was a fearless man and unaccommodating toward the prudery of society in his time. He paid heavily for his frankness, for it was at least as hard a century ago as it is now for people of conventional mind to recognize that a man can be interested in the vagaries of sexual behavior without wishing to practice them himself.

Milnes's library included most of the classics of erotica; some books were included under that heading which do not seem to modern taste to belong there. Voltaire's *La Pucelle* is not a very dreadful book, and Choderlos de Laclos's *Les Liaisons dangereuses* enjoys a special regard nowadays for its psychological insight. Aretino's *Sonnetti Lussuriosi* are certainly erotic, but the famous engravings which gave rise to them are so little pornographic that one of them is reproduced in Dr. Richard Lewinsohn's *A History of Sexual Customs*. Milnes had the works of Sade, of course, who was a novelty in England in the nineteenth century, and whose influence on Swinburne and Rossetti is described in a letter which the former wrote to Milnes after a reading of *Justine*. "I really thought I must have died or split open and choked with laughing. . . . I literally doubled up and fell down with laughter. . . . I read it out and the auditors rolled and roared . . . screams of laughter." It is a pity we cannot hear that laughter. Was it hysterical? Was it caused simply by the Marquis's rather odd sense of drollery? Or was some of it snob laughter, the amusement of sensitive but not notably mature Englishmen enjoying a book which added to the pleasure of being outrageous the tickle of being outrageous in French?

It is extraordinary to what a degree French culture has dominated some aspects of English literary taste. It cannot very successfully be argued that there is an intellectual sympathy between the two nations. But for more than a century Englishmen of cultivation have felt it necessary to have at least a nodding acquaintance with French literature, although there has been no corresponding impulse to know anything at all about what was doing in Germany or Italy. When Thomas Mann died, several English critics admitted without a blush that they knew little of his work and found it unsympathetic; there was some suggestion that he was a rude American enthusiasm, rather than one of the masters of our time. But not to be acquainted with what is happening in literary France is to feel disgraced, and in the pecking order of literary criticism a Frenchman can humiliate an Englishman just as readily as an Englishman can humiliate an American, and an American a Canadian. One of Canada's most serious literary needs at present is some lesser nation to domineer over and shame by displays of superior taste.

This is not said to belittle French culture, even if it lay in the power of any words of mine to do so. It is said, rather, to suggest that for Swinburne and Rossetti at least some of the pleasure of Sade lay in the snobbery of being smutty in the tongue which they so much admired and to which they attributed exquisite nuance and piquancy.

To those who admire French literature but are not beglamored by it the romances of Sade can become a bore. We read of the Duke of Blangis in the ecstasy of love that "horrible shrieks and dreadful oaths escaped his heaving breast; flames seemed to dart from his eyes; he frothed at the mouth; he whinnied . . ." and we feel that the Duke must have been a tiresome lover for any woman of taste. The selection published by the Grove Press in 1953, with Simone de Beauvoir's essay, gives us a taste of Sade, and there are many for whom a taste is enough. He is sometimes very entertaining, even though we do not roll on the floor and fear that we may split, like Swinburne. But it is overstrained, without achieving the kind of magnitude we find in tragedy or comedy of the first order, and in the end it proves wearisome.

Pornographic Tedium

INDEED, boredom is the effect of any prolonged application to erotic writing, and the most ingenious literary art is hardly able to keep ennui at bay. Boredom is inherent in the very nature of the subject. Sex is not a bore, but books about sex can be. The climax of such books is, necessarily, the same, and repetition lessens impact. Consider such an admired classic of erotica as *Le Sofa*, by Crébillon *fils*. It is a beautifully written book and, as Bonamy Dobrée points out, it has the characteristic of the best French erotic books in that it deals with the body but never forgets the soul. In it a courtier named Amanzei diverts his Sultan, a grandson of Scheherazade, with the story of his adventures; his spirit was for a time confined by Brahma in a sofa, from which he could only escape if a couple rendered to each other the first fruits of mutual affection, using his sofa self as a bed. This is an admirable beginning, but we know at once how it must end, and all the entertainment lies in the deferment of the completion. Every skill is brought to the narrative, but it is possible to feel that the book is too fine-drawn. In William Blake's phrase, one can be connoisseured to death by this sort of thing.

It might be said that any long work in the erotic or pornographic line invites failure. The sturdy favorites are such brief things as *The Bride's Letter*, which persistent tradition attributes to Byron, and Mark Twain's *Conversation at the Social Fireside as It Was in Ye Time of Ye Tudors.* This last work was solemnly produced by a New York bookseller when I asked him about pornography, bound up in baby-blue morocco with *The Old Backhouse* by James Whitcomb Riley and *When Willie Wet the Bed* by Eugene Field; such is one interpretation of the bookseller's term "erotica" on Fifth Avenue.

Again and again I asked myself, as I trudged about looking for some clue to the origin and distribution of pornography, why anybody troubled with a secret trade when so much was plainly for sale which was demonstrably erotica. The trade in pictures—moving, still, colored, and in monochrome—is understandable, for these things are not ordinarily obtainable; but a secret trade in pornographic books—was such a thing really necessary?

What Is Obscenity?

I STRUGGLED, as must everyone who concerns himself with this matter, with the question of nomenclature. When does what booksellers call "erotica" become pornography? Why does the use of common words for sexual acts and objects in *Lady Chatterley's Lover* disgust people who apparently feel no repugnance from novels far less serious in tone, which describe the same things in frivolous euphemisms? But I was no more able to decide these matters than most people who think about them, and was compelled to turn to the professional moralists for definitions.

Those among them who are honest admit the great difficulty of defining what is obscene and separating it from what may have literary value. Only Havelock Ellis makes the obvious point that obscenity is a type of pleasure which mankind has always wanted, and which mankind has always somehow contrived to get, and which mankind may need for the good of its soul. Some degree of earthiness is greatly to be preferred to a wincing daintiness, and the enantiodromia which operates in human affairs will see that we get obscenity, whether we like it or not; we are wise, then, to choose rather than to be forced to accept what fate brings. An international Conference at Geneva, to discuss the suppression of the circulation and traffic in pornography, attempted a definition of obscenity but could not arrive at one, recognizing that emotion and also fashion play so great a part in any idea of the obscene that no single definition can be valid, even in all parts of the western world, at any given time. Levels of education and income also exert an influence. As the old painter Northcote so wisely said to Hazlitt, concerning some supposed offensive matter in a stage play: "The common people sought for refinement as a *treat;* people in high life were fond of grossness and ribaldry as a relief to their overstrained affectation of gentility." Often when discussions of public morality are in progress, we receive the impression that refinement is still sought as a treat by some of the disputants, and that the form the treat takes is a particular kind of prestige, or status. Erotic literature is a species of erotic play, and as the investigations of Dr. Kinsey and his associates have shown us, erotic play is disapproved by people below the college level of education, as a general thing. Reformers and self-appointed civic censors very often belong to the group which does not care for erotic play in private, and is shocked by erotic literature, which is not so private. In any public discussion of this matter somebody's liberty is certain to be abridged, and zealous morality usually wins—for a time.

Even where liberality of thought on this subject would be expected, there are oddities of opinion. D. H. Lawrence, for instance, expressed a high regard for the *Decameron* and would allow it free circulation, but he had strong reservations about *Jane Eyre*, and thought that presentation of Wagner's *Tristan und Isolde* should be restricted because of its powerful eroticism. If Lawrence finds offense in *Jane Eyre*, we can have no quarrel with those people who have, at various times, wanted to ban *Madame Bovary*, *Trilby*, *Nana*, *Leaves of Grass*, and Cellini's *Autobiography*.

The best, because the frankest, definition of obscenity I found was in *Catholic Viewpoint on Censorship* by Harold C. Gardiner, S.J. It consists, says Father Gardiner, "in the intrinsic tendency or bent of the work to arouse sexual passion, or, to put it more concretely, the motions of the genital apparatus which are preparatory to the complete act of sexual union." He adds the qualification that this does not apply to abnormal people, who might be sexually aroused by references to shoes, the hair of the head, the ear, and all the rest of the curious catalogue of the fetishists.

Father Gardiner deserves our thanks for saying unequivocally what he means, but his definition still leaves the matter of obscenity in doubt. Those who find that a book affects them in the way he describes should, he says, put it aside. This recalls a friend of mine, by no means of lewd mind, the son of a Presbyterian minister, who told me that the first book to stir him in the manner described in Father Gardiner's definition was *Quo Vadis*, which he read when he was twelve. This book still enjoys a reputation as a novel of Christian moral force, though it is written in a manner far from the namby-pamby and ignorant style of some later examples of the genre. What was it that aroused sexual feeling in my friend? It was not, as you might suppose, the scene in which the slave girl Eunice presses her white body to the statue of her master, Petronius, and kisses the cold marble; that seems to me to be an erotic scene, but a young reader might miss its significance. No, what troubled him was this passage: "Nigidea, stripping herself to the waist, dropped her drunken childlike head on the breast of Lucan, who, drunk in like degree, fell to blowing the golden powder from her hair, and raising his eyes with immense delight." The description of Nero's homosexual attraction toward the Greek youth, Pythagoras, which is part of the same scene, was not even noticed by this reader at twelve. Here we have a moral puzzle: should he have put the book aside, banishing the vision of the half-naked Nigidea, to return to it when he was sixteen and might have understood the passion of Nero, or until he was twenty-five and could have sensed the perversity of Eunice? And what importance are we to give to the fact that Henryk Sienkiewicz drew the dark side of Roman degeneracy with all his considerable skill in order to throw Christian virtue into greater relief? All definitions of obscenity run quickly upon such rocks as these because the supposedly obscene book is only obscene if it provokes a lewd response in the reader. What legislation or definition is possible in a matter so subjective? As Father Gardiner suggests, a reader may feel a book to be obscene for himself, but he is on shaky ground as soon as he asserts that it is, therefore, obscene reading for anyone else.

Thrill of the Forbidden

What if the reader feels the enjoyment of obscenity to be his right and a legitimate pleasure? Such readers are not, however, all of those who buy the kind of book which is to be found in so many of the lesser bookshops in Great Britain and the continent. (If I seem to neglect the United States in this discussion, it is because bookshops of the small, unfashionable, hidden kind which are so common in Europe are not common there; bookselling in the United States seems to be a less complex and perhaps less interesting form of business than it is in older lands.) Many buyers of books which could be classed as obscene appear to count the thrill of the forbidden or the morally questionable as part of their pleasure. The dubious bookshops of London offer the strangest assortment, to suit as many tastes as possible. Some works of Aristotle jostle a novel by Jean-Paul Sartre; the novels of Paul de Kock, which I would have thought unreadable, still have their public; I was amused to see Edmund Wilson's *Memoirs of Hecate County* in a window between Balzac's *Contes drolatiques* and that dull compilation, *The Heptameron*; nearby were two favorites of such shops—*History of Capital Punishment* and *History of the Torture Chamber*, both by George Ryley Scott. In such shops a few years ago a novel was being offered which had as its theme a supposed homosexual relation among the Twelve Apostles and their Master; this is in a very old pornographic tradition, where a strong whiff of blasphemy is used to give extra zest to indecency.

To me, the books which describe acts of cruelty are especially repugnant, for they seem to be aimed at a taste which has nothing to do with ribaldry or legitimate sexual appetite. One old favorite in this realm is *A History of the Rod in All Countries* by the Reverend William M. Cooper, B.A. It describes every kind of flogging, from that which might kill a sailor or a Russian serf to the whipping of high-bred English girls in boarding schools; it is extraordinary that a man should be able to write five hundred and thirty pages on such a theme, but Mr. Cooper never seems to flag, and his style is one in which an unconvincing disapproval is mingled with grisly jocosity. He speaks of the "romantic and comic side" of flogging, and he is fond of the word "curious" in the sense which dictionaries now mark as archaic. His book is designed to please those who get a thrill out of reading about flogging. They must surely be an odd lot, and as one who went to a school where caning was the regular punishment for serious misdemeanor, I can only marvel at them.

Prurient and Pornographic

As for blasphemy, it is harder to achieve than might be supposed, but apparently many people are content with something less—a mingling of religious prejudice and prurient detail. An old favorite in this class is *Awful Disclosures of Maria Monk, or the Hidden Secrets of a Nun's Life in a Convent Exposed*, which was first published in New York in 1836. When I asked a bookseller in Leeds how it sold today, he replied: "One of our steadiest; we reckon a gross a month. It sells mostly to mill girls; they hand me a shilling and take the book. They're ashamed to name it, but they all read it." The *Awful Disclosures* is to be found in all the lesser bookshops in the large towns of England, though I have been told it is harder to come by in the United States, and I have never seen it on sale there. It is of interest to the student of literature as an example of the pathology of romanticism; it is intended to produce the same sensations as M. G. Lewis's Gothic novel *The Monk*, but it is designed for a puritanical and ignorant readership, and thus is presented as a true tale. It is axiomatic that if a thing is supposed to be true, it can be immeasurably more lurid and crude than if it is labeled as fiction.

Maria Monk was a girl who appeared in New York in 1835 and ingratiated herself with two clergymen who published a paper called *The Protestant Vindicator*, the Reverend George Bourne and the Reverend W. C. Brownlee; she said that she had escaped from the Hôtel Dieu nunnery in Montreal, and that the child she was shortly to bear had been fathered in that institution by a priest. She told hair-raising tales of wicked goings-on in the nunnery, of infanticide on a large scale, of subterranean passages, of the murder of insubordinate nuns. She dictated her revelations to one Theodore Dwight, and as neither of them was blessed with any skill as a writer, the book is without form, style, or climax. When Bishop Lartigue of Montreal granted permission to a committee to inspect the nunnery, the imposture was exposed, but the fight continued for some time; it had reached the point where mere truth was powerless to quell bigotry, and facts had less appeal than malignant fantasy. Maria Monk appears to have been a paranoid young person, and after her notoriety, she disappeared until her death on Welfare Island in 1849; she had been living as a prostitute for some time. But her book enjoys a popularity which better authors might envy, and I think it is because it combines sexual misdeeds with a religious atmosphere in a way which very simple readers can comprehend.

Maria Monk deserves, in my opinion, to be classed as pornography, for although it is not so extravagant in sexual detail as many books which are not so called, there is about it a low and disgusting atmosphere, and an obvious determination to appeal to base passions which the author knows to be base, which is calculatedly pornographic. Not all pornography is so. Consider, for instance, what is one of the most popular of all pornographic novels, *Fanny Hill*.

Fanny Hill and Male Vanity

ITS AUTHOR was John Cleland, who published it in 1750, when he was forty-one. Cleland was the son of a talented soldier and poet, and he received an excellent education, which fitted him for the consular service; but he could not get on as a consul, nor yet as an official of the East India Company, and when he was down on his luck, he wrote his famous novel and sold it to Griffiths the bookseller for twenty guineas; Griffiths is reported to have made a profit of ten thousand pounds on it. The book attracted the unfavorable attention of the Privy Council, who summoned Cleland and, after a rebuke, gave him a yearly pension of one hundred pounds in order that he might be able to make better use of his talents. Whether he did so or not is a matter of individual opinion; he became a journalist, a playwright, and at last a philologist, a scholarly profession for which he was pitifully ill-equipped.

Fanny Hill is not a classic for nothing. It is a pornographic book because it sets out determinedly to excite the passions of its readers; in the phrase of Fowler the Phrenologist, it is calculated to Inflame the Propensities. The story is simple, and is told in letters. Fanny is a lovely country girl of fifteen who goes to London when her parents die. She falls into bad company and is debauched, but she finds a lover named Charles, from whom she is separated by the malignity of fate. During this separation Fanny engages in every sort of sexual misbehavior that Cleland could think of, and he was, as I have said, a man of education and talent. But at last Charles returns, the lovers are united, and Fanny settles down in happy domesticity. What merry evenings she and her Charles must have had, talking over old times by the fireside!

Two things about *Fanny Hill* deserve attention. The first is that it is written in a simple, graceful prose, which has not a coarse word in it, and which is so charmingly turned that we can forgive the heroine anything; a girl who wrote so could not be really bad. Truly, this is an instance where vice loses half its evil by losing all its grossness. The other point to be noted is that it is the work of a man, although it purports to be told by a girl, and from time to time we catch a glimpse of an inordinate male vanity in the amorous descriptions. Fanny describes her Charles, not as a girl might speak of the man she loves, but as a very vain man might wish to be spoken of. The ecstasies which Fanny experiences in the arms of some of the magnificently endowed men she meets are not convincingly those of a girl; they are those of a man worshipping the glory of man. They describe the effect a man might wish to have on a woman. Psychologically there is much for reflection in *Fanny Hill*, and women, when they read it—for they do read it—must smile at a man's extravagant notion of the pleasure he can give.

The book is as different from *Maria Monk* as daylight is from dark. The one presents real evil and corruption, not in its story, but in the mind that lies behind the story; when Maria died, she was a ruin not only in body but in spirit. *Fanny Hill*, frankly sexual in its matter, is so candid and healthy in its revelation of the mind behind the story that we cannot seriously condemn it. To adapt a Victorian phrase to a Georgian book, we laugh and think that it is only pretty Fanny's way!

Purpose of Pornography

Why do readers want pornographic and obscene books, ask the moralists, expecting, as is their wont, that every decent

and responsible person will agree that only perverse minds could harbor such a taste. The answer is plain: such books deal with one of the subjects, like war and religion, about which mankind can never hear enough. Taste governs our choice of such books, as it does in all literature; the man who likes *Mademoiselle de Maupin* is not usually the man who delights in *Eskimo Nell.* The public for *Lady Chatterley* is not the same as for Mark Twain's *Fireside Conversation*, though both use the same forbidden words; the one is the novel of a philosopher and the other is unmistakably the diversion of a river pilot. Nor does the outhouse humor of Eugene Field or James Whitcomb Riley appeal to readers whose interest is sexual rather than excremental; no Freudian needs to be told why. These works, of whatever category, supply an element which is lacking in the lives of most men and women. The demanding and inexorable tension of modern life, especially in North America, and the countless duties which are imposed by getting a living and maintaining the type of domesticity now fashionable, do not bring the satisfaction of some of the heart's deepest desires. These desires are not necessarily reprehensible, but they are at odds with much of our democratic slavery. Our modern way of life has not created the need for erotica, but it has perhaps increased it, and has made possible such a phenomenon as the publication, by a reputable house, of *A Treasury of Ribaldry*, edited by a respected man of letters, Louis Untermeyer, and sold freely in all bookshops. Ribaldry and erotica are safety valves for people who feel the weight of modern life heavily upon them; those whose ideal of civilized man approximates to the ox or the gelding, toiling to drag the plow, do not approve, and this is not the place to try to persuade them that their attitude is a dangerous one for the future of civilization.

Erotic books feed a part of that fantasy life without which

man cannot exist. Contrary to the belief of the fearful, this fantasy life rarely has any manifestation in the outer world; it is a private realm of gratification, where its possessor is supreme and where he enjoys those sweets which real life has denied him—including forbidden sweets. Those who starve the fantasy life in the name of morality do so at their peril; reading has for the past century been the principal ministrant to it, offering, in Carlyle's phrase, "phantasmagoria and dream-grotto" which enlarges life in directions where external and daily living cannot approach. The fantasy life is not an end in itself, but a long road by which we travel toward the deepest truth about ourselves; to close that road is to deny much of the best life has to give.

It is recognition of this need in modern life which has brought so much liberty to the modern novel—liberty which may well be temporary and which, certainly, some writers have abused. The filthier a modern novel is, the better it sells, cry the moralists. This is not quite true; it is only a part of a much wider truth. And why does it never occur to the moralists to ask themselves why there should be such a need today for the kind of book which they call filthy, and which critics untroubled by their preoccupation describe very differently?

Those who complain about erotic books should confine themselves to *Amadis de Gaule*, that old romance whose author, when a man and a woman are left together, writes: "And nothing shall be here related; for these and suchlike things which are conformable neither to good conscience nor nature, man ought in reason lightly to pass over, holding them in slight esteem as they deserve." For the majority of readers the touchstone is one of taste; if an author offends you, do not read him. But it will not occur to any true book-lover, I think, to take another man's book from him.

My search for the sources of pornographic publishing was

not altogether a failure, for I discovered where a good deal of it came from, in a general sort of way. What really astonished me was that so many of the books which form the backbone of the lists of the pornographic houses were classics which could be bought anywhere, legitimately and at a fair dealer's price. There are, of course, a few great rarities, most of them illustrated books, but the unaccustomed buyer, unless he has a very long purse, will not be able to get them. The market in such things is a special and artificial one, and certainly I received the impression that secrecy and condemnation formed part of its charm for the initiates.

Books Are for Reading

As I SAID at the beginning, if you have ten books which you have acquired because you truly want them, you are a collector and your library is in some degree a portrait of you. But few people with the book mania reckon their books in tens; they count them in hundreds and thousands. If you read a great deal you will almost certainly want some books which are out of the ordinary, because of their rarity or beauty. It is at this point that I beg you to be careful. You will be tempted to think of books as objects, not to be read, but to be possessed for show, and when that happens, you are easy prey to those booksellers who deal in harlot volumes, tricked out in pretty skins (which will not last because the leather is not well prepared) and bedizened with gold ornament which resembles nothing so much as the gold paint that used to be daubed on steam-heating coils. All the arts of the horse dealer will be exercised to make old books which are of slight value look like treasures. And if you fall for this trash, you will at last have an accumulation which looks like the background for one of those advertisement pictures in which a model is impersonating an advertising man's notion of a gentleman and a scholar drinking Somebody's whisky. It will not be a library at all, but an adjunct of that pompous buffoonery which is called, by its dupes, "gracious living." You will be surrounded by a bad stage setting, and its effect will be to turn you into a bad actor. You will have committed the great sin of our time, which is to put ends before means, and striving and competition will become more important to you than reading. Be ambitious, rather, to be able to say as a reader what Hilaire Belloc said as a writer:

> When I am dead, I hope it may be said:
> "His sins were scarlet, but his books were read."

· VIII ·
Spelunking on Parnassus

If this were a book about writing, it would be almost obligatory to end it with a chapter called *The Writer Today*, or perhaps *The Writer's Position*. But it is principally a book about reading, and the reader of today is not often so self-conscious as to ask himself whether he is different from the reader of yesterday. As for his position, he is not aware that he has one. His modesty is to be praised, and perhaps I should not tamper with it. For twenty-five hundred years the writer was similarly innocent. When Ovid was exiled to Tomi by Augustus, he did not think that the writer's position had deteriorated; he simply thought he had been kicked out. When the plague closed the theaters, Shakespeare did not prate about the writer's position; he thought business was bad. But in the past century critics and literary journalists have made the writer a present of this mysterious Position, and writers who (in William Faulkner's phrase) enjoy being writers have taken a simple delight in it. It asks nothing of the mind or the creative powers; it is a form of class-consciousness. Those who love not the art in themselves but themselves in art are pleased with such gauds.

The reader has as yet no Position, and God forbid that I should put it into his head that he needs one. The only result would be organization and hubbub of a sort which could do nothing but discourage the clerisy, who, as I hope I have made clear, cannot exercise their influence by gang methods. But in this final chapter I want to discuss several things which concern both writer and reader. The process will not be a dignified ascent of Parnassus, but an exploration of some of its caves. Such ill-lit and sometimes dangerous scrambling through the bowels of mountains used to be called spelaeology, but of late it has become a sport more cheerfully called spelunking. I propose to do some spelunking on Parnassus. Where shall we begin?

Rebellion against Mediocrity

LET US TURN again to the clerisy. If this description applies, as I have said, to people who read with some degree of seriousness but who are not personally engaged in the production or criticism of writing, can the clerisy be considered to have any existence? Is it anything more than a flattering name for the vast disorganization of middlebrows? And even though it can be shown that it existed once, can it ever again be an influence in North American life?

It exists, but is not conscious of its power. If it had to express the taste of its majority, and if that taste were determined by ballot, probably it would emerge most of the time as upper-middlebrow. But no such necessity weighs upon the clerisy; freedom and individuality of taste are among its distinguishing marks. Its power is not that of the pressure group, the national organization with covens of zealots in every city of twenty-five thousand or over, engaged in formal discussions and the passing of resolutions. The clerisy does not nag its elected representatives or send urgent telegrams to its government. It is an element which exists, only as individual men and women, in every part of the population, and its action is that of a leaven. It is a leaven which has often in the past, and may once again, leaven the whole lump. Acting simply as individuals, the clerisy could be influential if it chose to assert itself in the rebellion already well begun by a number of serious American thinkers against the lumpishness, the dowdy triviality, the shoddy *expertise,* and the lack of foundation which bedevils so much of North American education.

This rebellion, the campaign of which has been set forth in Jacques Barzun's *The House of Intellect*, to name but one important book, has dwelt on the dark side of North American intellectual life. Doubtless such emphasis on what is wrong is necessary if we are to be aroused to put it right. But there is a danger in concentrating on what is wrong. It tempts us toward a luxury of despair; the people of the United States, perhaps more than any other nation in history, love to abase themselves and proclaim their unworthiness, and seem to find refreshment in doing so; let us not wallow in a deliciously frightening sense of intellectual inadequacy and then pass on to some new and more fashionable mortification. That is a dark frivolity, but still frivolity. We must avoid the temptation to regard our conviction of sin as an end in itself, and not as a preliminary and a means to redemption. Are things really so black as they are painted?

Do the Other-directed Enjoy It?

A WIDELY READ and much discussed book was published in 1950 by a professor of social science at the College of the University of Chicago, and two associates, called *The Lonely Crowd*; it was a study of the changing American character.

Its range and implications are wide, but what has stuck in public consciousness is its concept of the "other-directed person." Professor Riesman and his colleagues took pains to define their concept, which was by no means so alarming as the sense in which it is now popularly used. The "other-directed person" has come to mean the man or woman who is influenced in the important and unimportant things of life by the attitudes of his "peer-group"—the people of his own age and status—more than by any personal sense of morality or responsibility. In *The Lonely Crowd* it is made clear that the "other-directed person" is emerging, and at the time of writing was to be found only in a few big cities. The authors have taken pains to write of him as neutrally as possible, saying only what he is, rather than what he may become or what he may do to society. But such is the desire to be in the swim, even when the water is dirty and the current is going in the wrong direction, that the notion of the "other-directed person" has achieved a continental popularity, and it is almost a matter of civic pride for every modest settlement to claim a few, just as it must have its delinquents. There are fashions in anxiety and even in degradation.

The other-directed person undoubtedly exists; he has always existed, in some degree, but nobody has thought him sufficiently numerous or significant to arouse disquiet. In less nervously democratic ages the other-directed person was recognized as second rate and unworthy of much notice. Is he utterly sunk in his other-directedness? Does he really like being other-directed? If so, why are books about notably inner-directed persons—Clarence Day's father, and Auntie Mame, to name but two—so popular? Maybe the other-directed person would like to be inner-directed but does not know how. What accounted for the success of a series of movies about an inner-directed and awesomely intellectual man called Mr. Belvedere, who shamed and rasped all the good, simple folk with whom he came in contact? In those movies not merely was Mr. Belvedere endured by the people around him; they were convinced that he was really a "good guy." If intelligent, self-determined individualists can be popular heroes in books and on the screen, who doubts that a great many Americans really admire them? They may not admire them to the point of wishing to be wholly like them, but they acknowledge their existence and their value.

Gloom always confers prestige on the gloomy. Lashing the follies of the time, and prophesying woe are impressive pursuits that appeal to our North American masochism. It is immeasurably more difficult to hold the balance truly, and it is the hardest thing of all to avoid underestimating the intelligence of other people. I do not suggest that Jacques Barzun or David Riesman do so; their attitudes have been clearly stated. But the people who seize upon their ideas, without troubling to understand them fully or to make them their own, are apt to underestimate the intelligence of others, and to exaggerate threats which are too often projections of their own anxiety and sense of insufficiency.

Is the Gloom Justified?

THE DISMAY which is so often expressed about the low estate of reading on this continent may well be such an exaggeration, such an underestimation. Statistics are frequently offered on this subject. One "survey" says that only seventeen per cent of people in the United States and eighteen per cent in Canada are reading books at any given time; the same "survey" says that in England fifty-five per cent are so occupied. It is easy to feel humiliation when we are told that Denmark has seven times as many bookshops *per capita* of population as the United States—but the humiliation does not seem to call into being more bookshops, or better ones. In 1958, it appears, a nonesuch called the Average American read only seven books. Paul Blanshard says that buying books is "almost a monopoly of the cultural upper ten per cent of the population."

Well, what about it? This is a matter on which statistics are of little use. Would the statistically minded be happier if the seventeen per cent who are reading were to be raised to England's fifty-five per cent by a greater consumption of the billion comic books which are printed on this continent yearly? Or by a few more millions added to the twenty million copies of the works of Mickey Spillane which are said to be now in circulation? Statistics on reading are of no value unless we know what is being read.

Over half a billion books in hard covers are produced on this continent every year, and at least a quarter of a billion paperbacks. By no means all of this huge production is trash, and among the paperbacks which must be considered the reading of the young and the people with small incomes, the standard is often very high. A paperback edition of *Shakespeare's Tragedies* has sold over a million copies, and a *Pocket Book of Verse* edited by M. E. Speare has sold more than two million. The paperback section of a good bookshop presents a splendid array of classics, and comparatively new books which have proven their worth, at prices substantially lower than their hard-back originals; a young reader could be fully literate without ever buying a book in hard cover. The great experiment of universal education is advancing, and although some of its effects, as Mr. Barzun so trenchantly describes them, are shocking and dispiriting, a greater part of the population is certainly reading today than was the case, proportionately, a century ago, and there is evidence that they are reading more good books.

(What is a good book, says the sophist, smiling like a wolf

trap. Any book is a good book which feeds the mind something which may enlarge it, or move it to action. A book is good in relation to its reader.)

It is not the purpose of the present work to grapple yet again with the problem of modern education, or to agonize about the other-directed person. Anybody who has been taught to read at all may feel moved to teach himself to read well. Other-directed persons may, if the clerisy will wake up, find themselves directed by "others" who read books. The revolution in communications which was described by Marshall McLuhan cuts two ways; if reading is now on a level with film or television, and if those who set greatest value on reading must realize it, is it not also true that those who chiefly value film and television may come to be interested in reading? The mere convenience of reading as a form of entertainment and instruction gives it an advantage over the other two.

Let us deny ourselves the eerie delights of despair about the shortcomings of others, and get on with our own reading. It is a personal art, and one which we shall spread most rapidly and effectively by doing it ourselves. The first task of the clerisy is not to belabor others to read more, but to improve their own performance. The influence which the clerisy can exert will come by doing, not by exhorting others to do.

An Elite Exists

THIS SORT of argument, I realize, will arouse in some people another of the fears in which the anxiety of our time evinces itself—the fear of an elite. There is, of course, an intellectual elite at work in the world of letters now, and it is principally composed of academic critics. So far as I can see, there is nothing much wrong with it except that it is too small, and too professionally narrow in its concerns. If it can be expanded by the addition of a million or two of the clerisy, literature and criticism will both benefit. There are a hundred elite groups of one sort and another at work in North America today, and without them much necessary work would never be done. It is only when democracy is in the grip of reversed peristalsis that it fears that an elite will rob the Common Man of his presumably God-ordained rights in matters relating to art and letters. The Common Man does not care the toss of a button for such cobwebs. The growth and spread of intellect cannot do a country anything but good, and the Common Man, who is not a fool, knows it.

This book did set out, however, to consider some aspects of writing in the light of the North American world as it is now, after a century of the move toward general literacy. It may be, as Peter De Vries says, that "if there is any one major cause for the spread of mass illiteracy it's the fact that everybody can read and write." It could also be that the other-directed person is merely a glossier version of that section of the populace which used to be called weak-minded. Need we dread it if we are ourselves reasonably strong-minded? But whatever the truth of the matter, writing and the writer have obviously been influenced by the growth of literacy, and it is of interest to look at some of the ways in which this influence has been exerted.

Fortunate Time for Writers

THE WRITER'S CHANCES of having his work published are better today than they have ever been. Nobody knows this better than the book reviewer. It is said by Paul Blanshard in *The Right to Read* that seventy-five per cent of the books published today get no reviewing attention; even the small number of publications which do nothing else cannot hope to consider more than a few of the books which reach them. What are literary editors to do? Only their wildly variable best. It was suggested by the late Alfred Knopf that books should be graded like eggs, and that publishing houses should not offer as First Class what they well know to be Fifth. But of course publishers cannot agree about standards for grading, and even if they could, writers would shriek like mandrakes uprooted if their work were sent into the world marked anything less than Strictly Fresh.

Anything which is not ridiculously incompetent has a chance of being published. Part of the reason is economic; publishers must bring out a certain number of books in order to operate efficiently, and when good books cannot be had, books which are less than good get their chance.

There has been a remarkable increase in journalistic books, which deal with immediately important aspects of politics, or record some new feat of exploration. They have their popularity, if any, within a few months and die. Similarly, there has been a rise in the production of books of the type discussed in the chapter called *Enjoying and Enduring*, which offer new hope for the fat, or the arthritic, or the heartsore. Some of the writers of such books must do well out of them, for they sell in large numbers, and a really valuable one, like Dr. Edmund Jacobson's *You Must Relax*, may hold the market for twenty-five years and run through several editions.

Amateur Autobiographers

THEN THERE ARE the amateurs, usually people who have lived the greater part of a life of some distinction and want to tell about it. They have been politicians, and they are greatly concerned about keeping the record (where is this potent "record" about which politicians feel so much concern?) straight, which means favorable to themselves. Or they have been great physicians, or sportsmen, or generals who have fought the enemy with their swords and now want to fight their colleagues with the mightier pen. Or they have been actors, or singers, or society hostesses whose recollections are a welter of great names and wilted witticisms. There is an increasing number of Revenge Books, in which ex-husbands, ex-wives, and children tell of their agonies with somebody well-known and generally respected. Some are the work of ghosts, and as even with the best ghosts, we see through them. But most of them are the almost unaided work of people who have no true skill in writing.

This is not to say that they are all bad or ill-written books. Some are hopeless, of course—the depressing products of trivial minds. But many are the work of people who have a talent which they have not troubled to cultivate or refine, and though their books are readable, they are disappointing. Most of them have a good story to tell, and a few have some grace of expression, but they do not know how to shape a book. Like amateur paintings, their work often has a surface charm but lacks enduring interest; it is not talent that is lacking so much as professional skill, practice, and application.

Their commonest fault is that they are short-winded; they begin well, but they cannot stay the course. The early chapters of their books are often excellent. Scores of them begin their books with descriptions of childhood which make us catch our breath again and again with their felicity and sympathy and humor, but as soon as maturity and fame have been reached, the books trail off into catalogues of names, experiences dully and cautiously described, and reticences which irritate the reader, however desirable they may seem to the writer.

Does the fault lie in the pattern of life itself? Are we so much more perceptive and individual as children? Do we, when once we have hit our stride in life and found our niche (or our rut), become such dull dogs? I, for one, do not believe it. It is not the material, but the writer's lack of skill which is responsible for these disappointments. When we write of childhood, memory does the work of selection for us; we recall vividly what we experienced vividly. But when we write of our adult life, the desire to appear before the world in a favorable light warps our judgment and censors our expression. Not only do we want to show ourselves to what we believe to be best advantage; we also want to avoid hurting feelings, reheating old quarrels—in short, reliving our lives in imagination and recording them with art. In these amateur autobiographies the adult chapters suffer from a lack of courage and a lack of honesty; to be blunt, they have no artistic integrity.

Honest autobiography is, of course, hard work. Recall the uproar that greeted H. G. Wells's *Experiment in Autobiography* in 1934; here was a book in which the writer did not exhibit himself as his own hero, was not invariably kind about his contemporaries, and made sharp judgments on his parents. Perhaps no other book by Wells aroused so much disapproval and tongue clicking. But the book is still full of interest, for it was written by a man who knew how to keep up the pace of his story from first to last. Is anyone so foolish as to imagine that it was written without pain? Wells's life was a struggle from the beginning; he told us of the struggle when he might have wrapped himself in a cloak of success and given a dull record of his triumphs.

The difference between the amateur autobiographer and the professional man of letters is that the former is concerned with self-approval, the latter with self-revelation. The artist's is likely to be disquieting, but it has a chance of being a masterpiece. The work of the amateur will be, at best, a pleasantly diverting and occasionally informative book.

Scores of such pleasantly diverting books are published every season. It was two hundred and fifty years ago that John Arbuthnot said that biography had added a new terror to death: we may say that during the past century autobiography has added a new and undemanding pastime to old age.

The Kingdom of This World

THERE HAS BEEN a great increase in writing which is intended only to entertain. That "only" needs amplification, for all writers seek to entertain in some measure. Those of whom I speak here are the writers who aim at large audiences, upon whom they lay no burdens. Somerset Maugham is an obvious and good example; for perhaps forty years he was one of the most popular and wealthiest of living writers. He notably achieved the desire of the writer of entertainment; he has a kingdom of this world.

He called himself a teller of tales, and he suggested here and there that he thinks he tells tales pretty well. But he has never claimed to be a philosopher, or a poet, or a prophet, or anything of that sort. It is his admirers who have made the great claims, and they have done their idol harm thereby.

Like millions of other people, I have had pleasure from Mr. Maugham's work, and I cannot be ungrateful to anyone who has given me pleasure, even if that pleasure is not very strong or lasting. I have no wish to join those critics who contemptuously brush Maugham aside, because I have enjoyed almost everything he has written—the first time I read it. But I do not want to read his things again.

I have tried, with the nine novels which are included in the three-volume collection. Until then I had passively accepted the popular judgment that Maugham is a master in the manipulation of plot. Of the nine only one, *Theatre*, was new to me; the others I was re-reading. I enjoyed *Theatre*, thin though it is, and thought the plot deftly handled. But the others, which were twice-told tales to me, seemed full of obvious devices, unjustified changes of attitude on the part of the characters, and the Long Arm of Coincidence had the sinuous virtuosity of an elephant's trunk. The writer says, over and over again, that you can never tell what people will do next, and that humankind is full of surprises. True, but the artist must not imitate life too closely in this respect; Fate may push people around like checkers, so that common men become kings when they reach the other side of the board, but the artist must be more circumspect. Maugham is a masterly conjuror, but we can only be deceived once.

As a writer solely of entertainment he is admirable, and he put his talent to shrewd and completely honorable commercial use. He never skimps on craftsmanship. He made one move toward greatness in 1915, with *Of Human Bondage*; there he speaks from his heart, and his study of the ignominy and bitterness of misplaced love is a fine one. Elsewhere he is the teller of tales, speaking from his clever, cool head.

What of his celebrated cynicism—that quality which seems to provoke such agreeably contradictory thrills of attraction and repulsion in innocent minds? Maugham is no more cynical than most people who have seen much of life and met a wide range of people, but he has taken care to express his well-controlled enthusiasm for mankind in a very amusing fashion. He has nothing of the savage indignation of the real cynic; rather, he is worldly wise. The cynical writer may finish his outbursts in tears, for he is angry and grieved that humanity will not meet his high demands. We find no tears in Maugham.

Indeed, we never find any very strong emotion in Maugham or any wisdom which would cause surprise at a bridge table or a dinner party. He is the lower-middlebrow's ideal of a man of intellect. A great writer must give us either great feeling from the heart or great wisdom from the head. If he can manage it, we like the great writer to give us a style of individual quality to which we can respond. Maugham is curiously without individuality of style; has anyone ever been able to parody him?

It is tempting to say that if Maugham had wished to do so, he could have developed the promise of *Liza of Lambeth* and the exciting partial fulfillment we find in *Of Human Bondage* into true greatness. But it is not for readers to talk so foolishly. Maugham deliberately chose to be a teller of tales, and in that character he must be judged. I do not feel that he merits the adulation of his immoderate admirers, nor can I agree that he deserves the ferocious cudgeling that Edmund Wilson gives him in *The Apotheosis of Somerset Maugham*, where he is summed up as "a half-trashy novelist, who writes badly, but is patronized by half-serious readers, who do not care about writing." I feel, rather, that he deserved precisely what life gave him. His is a kingdom of this world, not of the life-moderately-everlasting which awaits the great writer; we know that he enjoyed his commercial success very much, and which of us who has enjoyed his work would grudge him what he fairly won? Peace to his ashes.

Writers and Money

MAUGHAM LIVED long and well as a professional writer; he did no other work. This makes him a rarity and an object of envy to thousands of writers who cannot make tongue and buckle meet on what they get for their best endeavor. There is always discussion in literary magazines about whether a writer should try to live solely by his writing. Robert Graves insists that a poet who seeks to make money from his poetry will lose any gift he has. Graves wrote novels in order to provide for himself and his large family; in his judgment the White Goddess had nothing to do with prose narrative. But there are writers who take novels just as seriously and even religiously as Graves took poetry, and presumably for them the priestly rule is different. Thomas Mann held in awe a deity fully as potent as the White Goddess—it may indeed have been She, in one of her aspects—and he regarded prose and narrative as more demanding than verse and the expression of lyrical feeling.

This is a book for readers, not writers, and no discussion of the economics of writing has any place here except as it may illuminate the life of the writer in a way which will benefit the reader. But writers enjoy talking about money; correspondence and articles discussing their wants are common in the literary journals. Some of them frankly want a pension without strings; some want money for travel or for a year or two in which to invite their souls. Some, like the English poet Roy Fuller, think that it does a writer no harm to have a regular job which keeps him in touch with nonliterary people and the world about him, and he points out that the writer who does nothing but write too often becomes dependent on his childhood memories, and writes chiefly of the adventures (sometimes dull) of his soul (sometimes of modest growth). Thornton Wilder thought military service useful to the young writer because it put him in intimate contact with nonartists—not "real people," as is sometimes asserted (as though artists were less real than others), but people who are temperamentally unlike himself, and of a more numerous group.

There can be no agreement about how a writer should live and get his money, and these matters are really unimportant;

it is only what is written that matters. If, in order to write, A must forgo all regularity of life, all domesticity and even decency, he is neither more admirable nor reprehensible than B, who finds routine work and the pressure of a full program congenial to his creative work; Verlaine must be himself and so must Trollope. But there will always be people who think that if they live like Verlaine they may perhaps write like Verlaine, or that a civil-service mind and an accurate watch may make them a Trollope; the faith in imitative and sympathetic magic persists not only in the breasts of savages but among the weaker-minded artists of every sort.

The later Victorians and Edwardians had a notion—founded upon a few real people, of whom Rudyard Kipling was one—that a writer was a man who lived comfortably on his earnings, usually in a pleasant house in the country, where he enjoyed a degree of luxury, and the standing of a gentleman. Time and taxation killed the possibility of such a creature; Bernard Shaw was perhaps the last man to live such a life, and he had to be a millionaire in sterling, with a rich wife, to afford it. Yet the charming, old-fashioned picture persists among many people, not a few of whom are ambitious authors. The idea of possessing the means and the milieu for a life devoted entirely to imaginative creation is extremely attractive, especially to the story-telling sort of talent. To sit at one's desk, puffing at one's favorite briar, while dashing off a rattling yarn of adventure—the picture is as absurd as those film biographies of painters and composers.

Nothing But Masterpieces?

ONE PHASE of the reality, for those who can stand it, may be examined in George Gissing's painful novel *New Grub Street*. Most writers today can recognize some of their colleagues among its characters. It is full of bitterness, and the low key in which it is written, rebuking any thought that the writer might have exaggerated his picture to gain effect, gives fearful poignancy to such sentences as that which, for instance, begins chapter eight:

> Of the acquaintances Yule had retained from his earlier years several were in the well-defined category of men with unpresentable wives.

I should hesitate to recommend *New Grub Street* to a writer, but no time traveler who cares to sniff the lingering stench of boiled cabbage in the suburban kennels of nineteenth-century authors should miss it. The failure of, for instance, Alfred Yule in this book is more poignant than the failure of Willie Loman in *Death of a Salesman* because Yule once had high aspirations. A drunken priest is a more pathetic creature than a drunken barber, and Yule had a vocation.

Gissing's novel is a reminder that we have looked briefly at the popularizers, the amateurs, and the entertainment authors, but have not yet given any consideration to the group which deserves our most serious attention; his hero, Edwin Reardon, is an author who strives with all the fervor which is in him to convey to his readers his profoundest thoughts and feelings about the most important matters within his comprehension. He fails, he dies of poverty and heartbreak; all that he touches turns to ruin. But his sincerity is complete, and his determination to hold back nothing in his service to literature is a splendid and awesome example of the egotism of the artist. Virtually all the writing that is done which is of any importance as literature is done by Reardons of one sort or another. They are not often such gloomy, ill-fated creatures as he; some of them pretend to a frivolity which deceives simple readers and simpleton critics. But they are all striving to write a masterpiece. As Cyril Connolly says: "The more books we read the sooner we perceive that the true function of a writer is to produce a masterpiece and that no other task is of any consequence."

Splendid simplifications like this are a tonic to the mind. We think of the vast accumulations of books in the Library of Congress and the British Museum, and wag our heads in solemn approval. How cleansing, from time to time, to rise above the clouds to the mountain peak and breathe its cold, thin air! But—nothing but masterpieces? The great libraries magically shrunk to two or three shelves upon which we recognize perhaps a quarter of Shakespeare's total bulk, standing beside a much reduced *Bible,* the *Divine Comedy*, and a daunting array of such things as *The Lusiads* of Camoëns, perhaps *War and Peace*, and the sonnets of Petrarch? No, no; we are not worthy of a literature composed only of masterpieces. None of us lives at the masterpiece level all of the time, and many people never scramble up to it at all. And thus we are made to recognize that all talk of masterpieces is relative, and that the true function of a writer is to produce his own masterpiece. And the reader—let the critics prate as they may about his "true function"—will read what chimes with his taste and his needs.

This is not to assert that standards of criticism are worthless, and that one book is as good as another if it happens to strike the responsive chord in a reader who has happened on it at the right moment. It is only to say that within the very large confines of that literature which judicious readers and critics have admired in some degree over the ages, there are many sorts of masterpieces, and that their worth must be estimated relatively as well as absolutely.

All that we can safely say here about masterpieces is that it is most improbable that one will be written by a hack, or an amateur, or by a writer whose primary aim is mass entertainment. Whatever their theme and manner, be they masterpieces of wit, of realism, of fantasy, or perhaps of those dark writings in which we recognize, long afterward, that some astonishing insight or prophecy has been concealed, only writers more or less of the Reardon stamp will bring them forth. Let us consider what it is that these writers do.

The Ogre of the Nursery

To use a phrase which would have suited Samuel Smiles, they give the best that is in them to writing. And what is the best that is in them? The psychoanalytical bent of critical thought in our time has taught us that the sources of many kinds of effort can look strange to eyes which see flowers but not the manure in which they are nourished. Those who want to examine one psychoanalytical theory about why writers write will find it in *The Writer and Psychoanalysis* by Dr. Edmund Bergler, who has had a number of writers as patients. Authors are attempting to solve an inner conflict through the sublimatory medium of writing, says he, and it has been his invariable experience that the conflict is that of a psychic masochist at war with his Mother Image. This alarming image is not his real mother, or his mother as she appears in his Oedipus complex, but is rather "that giant ogre of the nursery, the pre-Oedipal mother." We need not examine this concept in detail, but it is of interest that in Dr. Bergler's opinion this inner tension results in the aggressive and rebellious nature which is common to writers. Not, it need hardly be said, that aggression and rebellion necessarily manifest themselves in an obvious fashion; they may be confined to a deep level of the writer's work. But they are there. This cast of mind also, in Dr. Bergler's view, makes writers what he calls "injustice-collectors," people who have a strongly developed sense of grievance, which again need not appear in obvious ways. It must be emphasized that this is by no means the whole of Dr. Bergler's theory, which is extensive and technical. His book has been attacked as if it were intended to explain writers away as victims of an unresolved mental quirk. It does not and could not do anything of the sort. It confines itself to presenting a pattern of mental structure which has appeared in thirty-six writers under analysis, and which Dr. Bergler believes may be common to them all.

It does not explain writers away because it does not take account of the vast differences in achievement which divide them. Though they may all be, in their psychic depths, struggling with the hobgoblin of the pre-Oedipal mother, what comes to the surface exhibits the most extraordinary differences of quality, ranging from mediocrity to genius. Nor can this difference in quality be traced to any cause. It is true now, and may remain true for generations to come, as Freud said in his consideration of Dostoevski: "Unfortunately, psychoanalysis must lay down its arms before the problem of the artist." Dr. Bergler thinks he has discovered why writers write; only that fuzzy word "talent" and the now discredited "genius" carry any hint of why some write immeasurably better than others. The secret remains a secret.

Nevertheless, what Dr. Bergler has to say emphasizes what critics have known for centuries: there is something about writers which makes them not like other men, and which can make them difficult and even downright objectionable. Many of them control this element in their nature, confining it to their work; in others it creeps like a stain through the whole fabric of their lives. This quality has been examined by Edmund Wilson in *The Wound and the Bow*, and his opinions, though different from those of Dr. Bergler, are no more complimentary to the literary brotherhood. As a pattern of the quality which he finds in several authors—Dickens and Kipling are his principal exemplars—he takes the myth of Philoctetes, the archer with the miraculous bow who could not miss his mark; but Philoctetes had been bitten by a snake, and in his foot was a suppurating wound, the stench of which made him so intolerable that his companions left him to die on the island of Lemnos; however, they had to have him in order to win the Trojan War, and were forced to seek him. If they wanted the magic of the bow, they had to put up with the stench of the wound. The literary artist, says Mr. Wilson, is a Philoctetes. Publishers, agents, critics, and other putatively normal people who have to deal with authors have shown a ready acceptance of Mr. Wilson's theory which shows that it crystallizes something long thought, but not previously so well expressed. And truly, where would *they* be without Philoctetes?

What Writers Think about It

WHAT DO AUTHORS think about this theorizing on the deep sources of their work? Generally speaking, they have taken it with mildness, and the greater their ability, the less their inclination to throw themselves into such unprofitable battles. They are interested in writing, not in discovering why they write. As William Faulkner says, the writer has supreme vanity. He does not want to be influenced or taken apart; he does not want the officious help of people who cannot, as he knows intuitively, be anything but nuisances to him. The writer may be a little afraid of the critic, and in particular the young, zealous critic with his shiny, humming intellect and his sometimes astonishingly coarse and elementary feelings, but he knows that this clever creature is powerless to help him. E. M. Forster says of such critics: "They want us to be so much better informed than we are. If critics could only have a course on writers' *not* thinking things out . . ." The writer is vain in the sense that he is determined to go it alone; he is humble in his recognition that he cannot play the clever critics' game of pulling things apart, for he knows that if *he* pulls something of his own apart, he will never get it together again; whereas, of course, if a critic pulls a piece of writing apart, it heals as quickly as its own vitality dictates.

Do writers not care, then, what critics think? Some of them care very much, and are wounded by unfavorable appraisals of their work. The tendency to collect grievances, of which Dr. Bergler writes, leads many authors to resent certain critics with an intensity which would flatter the critics if they knew of it. But even more than the distaste of the most sensitive writer for the most sneering critic is the determination of the author to do his work in his own way, which has no kinship with the critical atmosphere of intellect.

The admirable series of interviews with writers which is done by *The Paris Review,* and published under the title *Writers at Work,* gives testimony over and over again of this independence of the writer's creative faculty, which Faulkner calls supreme vanity. Does Dr. Bergler or Edmund Wilson think the writer neurotic? William Styron says: "The good writing of any age has always been the product of *somebody's* neurosis, and we'd have a mighty dull literature if all the writers that came along were a bunch of happy chuckleheads." Asked to comment on work in progress, Angus Wilson replied: "Fiction writing is a kind of magic, and I don't care to talk about a novel I'm doing because if I communicate the magic spell, even in an abbreviated form, it loses force for me"—which is the kind of talk that does not sit well with critics who do not regard a writer as a magician, but rather as a man who needs to be told what he has said. This magical, or priestly, function of the writer is wryly expressed by Georges Simenon: "Writing is considered a profession, and

I don't think it is a profession. I think that everyone who does not need to be a writer, who thinks he can do something else, ought to do something else. Writing is not a profession but a vocation of unhappiness. I don't think an artist can ever be happy . . . because, first, I think that if a man has the urge to be an artist, it is because he needs to find himself. Every writer tries to find himself through his characters, through all his writing." A vocation of unhappiness—the phrase would please Dr. Bergler. And again, Faulkner: "The good artist believes that nobody is good enough to give him advice . . . No matter how much he admires the old writer, he wants to beat him."

The points upon which the writers interviewed are in agreement are few, but important. Each is convinced that the particular form in which he worked is at once the most difficult and the most satisfactory. All are agreed that writing is a kind of magic, though Angus Wilson was the only one actually to use the word. They are agreed that a writer must shake off the trivialities of external living in order to sound his creative depths, and although they all mistrust elaborate schemes, scenarios, plans, and theses, all have ways of reaching those depths which are, in appearance and perhaps in reality, magical. Each calls up his daemon in his special way.

Not all are so willing to admit that writing is a physically demanding function as Simenon, who writes six books a year and has an examination by his physician before and after each of them; writing excites and exhausts him to a degree which may be dangerous. Nor were many so exacting about writing conditions as Truman Capote, who cannot work anywhere but in bed. But most have preferences for kinds and colors of paper, hours of work, and special conditions favorable to a writing mood. A surprising number of them, in this mechanical age, write by hand, and most of them write legibly and even elegantly. William Faulkner's manuscript is as handsome as those of Edmund Blunden or Fr. Rolfe. None among them like to write for long hours.

Gushers and Tricklers

As WORKERS they may be divided into gushers and tricklers. Thurber was a gusher; for one story which was 20,000 words when finished, he wrote a total of 240,000, and fifteen different versions. It is interesting that the torrential Thurber is the one who talked most about that dread of all writers—drying up. (This ailment, called "writer's block," is discussed at length by Dr. Bergler in his book already mentioned; curing this frightening malady is one of his specialties.) Frank O'Connor was also a gusher; he rewrote some of his stories even after they had been published. The tricklers may be represented by William Styron, who says: "I can't turn out slews of stuff each day. I wish I could. I seem to have some neurotic need to perfect each paragraph—each sentence, even,—as I go along." Dorothy Parker, also a trickler, said: "I can't write five words but I change seven!" The industry of the gushers commands respect; Joyce Cary, Frank O'Connor, and Capote—we see them writing and revising, rejecting pages by the handful, and finally piecing their work together from the mass. But the tricklers have an agony of their own; they cannot continue until the last line written is as right as they can make it. Both methods seem to take about an equal amount of time.

All agree on the willfulness of the material which asks to be written, and the likelihood of a story that began with one end in mind being finished with something quite different. This willfulness is a sign of the vitality of the writer's inspiration, and is not to be thwarted. To make a neat plan and write to it has never been the practice of the Reardons. Henry

James's elaborate scenarios may look like neat plans to the casual eye, but they are in fact drafts—something very different. The scheme, the chart that is beloved of some teachers of "creative writing," is rejected by all of these. William Styron's comments on creative-writing courses are of interest—"a ruinous business, a waste of paper and time." (Perhaps in fairness we should quote a remark in contradiction of this opinion, made by James Jones not to *The Paris Review* but to David Ray, referring to his own tutor in writing, who is Mrs. Lowney Handy of Marshall, Illinois: "She could take any knucklehead and teach him to write.")

These writers are at one in their attitude toward critics; they are not actively hostile, but they resent being mauled by schematizers, symbol-sniffers, and those who patronize each "fresh new talent" and try to establish its "influences" before pushing it into a "school." Faulkner speaks for all. "The artist doesn't have time to listen to critics. The ones who want to be writers read the reviews, the ones who want to write don't have time to read the reviews. The critic too is trying to say 'Kilroy was here.' His function is not directed toward the artist himself. The artist is a cut above the critic, for the artist is writing something which will move the critic. The critic is writing something which will move everybody but the artist." Regarding that last word, he says: "An artist is a creature driven by demons." Thornton Wilder also has a wise word. "The important thing is that you make sure that neither the favourable nor the unfavourable critics move into your head and take part in the composition of your next work."

About conditions of living, the writers vary greatly. Two or three point out that there is no reason why a millionaire should not write well, as, indeed, a few millionaires have done. All condemn the romantic notion that poverty is good for an author. They are cold toward patrons. "The good writer never applies to a foundation," says Faulkner, meaning, of course, the author or the playwright. These writers do not consider scholars, critics, and such riffraff as writers in any serious sense; they are to the Reardons what fleas are to a dog, or sores to the leper saint.

Their social habits are various. Thornton Wilder warns against a limited acquaintance, but Angus Wilson confesses to a distaste for simple, naïve people. Some warn against the pseudo-literary fad of seeking low company, dear to a few authors in every generation who boast of their familiarity with ruffians and women of ill fame. Several of them warn against hiving with other writers, and we are reminded of Dr. Johnson's comment that the reciprocal civility of authors is one of the most risible scenes in the farce of life.

This series of interviews has been given extended attention here because it bears out, in evidence gathered from American, English, and French authors, the general character of the author as described by Dr. Bergler, and as revealed by Gissing in the character of Edwin Reardon. Superficially different, authors who are not journalists, hacks, amateurs, or commercial entertainers belong in this deeply serious, but not therefore solemn, category.

The writer is concerned with life, the critic with writing. As Ibsen says, living is a fight with the dark forces, the bogeys within, and to write is to sit in judgment upon one's inmost self. If the true writer, the Reardon, the man whom Simenon describes as inescapably committed to the search for himself, is a writer because he has the psychic structure which Dr. Bergler describes, or something like it, we must beware of criticism which ventures too far in its attempts to explain him, to give him a helping hand, to put him on the right track. There is a trend to that sort of criticism at present, among the younger men who do not know what the old hands of criticism know. Sometimes this trend is given the odd name of creative criticism. It flourishes around universities, like the damp, pest-harboring ivy which it so much resembles, and it provides for its practitioners a wreath which proclaims a double honor—that of being both critical and creative at the same time.

Lust to Be Creative

THE YEARNING to be creative seems to possess more people in our day than ever before. Peter De Vries in *The Tunnel of Love* has brilliantly caricatured an editor who sets out on an adulterous path for which he has no talent and small appetite, in order to show that he can be as immoral as any of the creative men with whom his work associates him. Life has not given him the bow, but he is trying to fake the wound.

Surely it is a fine thing to be a critic? We need not agree with Dr. Bergler, who says that a critic is, in most instances, an inhibited writer who is filled unconsciously with undigested anger against writers; we need not follow him in his assertion that these critics have a predilection for mediocrity, because the sterile can forgive the mediocre more easily than the talented. We need not—unless we wish to accept the doctor's theory about the psychic genesis of the true writer's urge to write. But even then we may be permitted to postulate a talent for criticism, which is by no means the same thing as a talent for creation. It is the critics who want to have both honey and jam on their bread who trouble us.

The yearning of the uncreative to create is, of course, as old as literature, and is by no means confined to it. Mules of all kinds hanker pitifully for parenthood. Dictionaries of music contain amusing accounts of ingenious machines which were designed to enable people who were not composers to write music. We have all seen those canvases carefully marked out with lines and numbers to assist people who are not painters to paint. Magazines and papers frequently contain advertisements offering to teach people who are not writers to write. Sometimes ingenious methods of inducing creation in those in whom it has not shown itself are carried to extraordinary lengths.

The Handy Method

UNDOUBTEDLY the most famous experiment of this kind in our day was that of Mrs. Lowney Handy. She had a colony where those who wished to be writers might live and submit themselves to her tutelage. This consisted in part of copying, for many hours each day, books which she believed to be good models; the purpose of this copying was that the apprentices (as they were called) might absorb and make their own a body of literature by a method that drove it deeply, but not critically, into their minds. Let those who are quick to scorn this method reflect that it is a mechanical intensification of the one used by Robert Louis Stevenson to teach himself to write. In due time writing began to bubble in the apprentices, and what they wrote was scrutinized by Mrs. Handy.

Mrs. Handy must be accounted fortunate in her first pupil, James Jones, whose popular and financially successful first novel, *From Here to Eternity*, was written in this way. Mr. Jones's later book, *Some Came Running*, contained 1,266 pages and 700,000 words, and weighed two pounds, eleven ounces; longer than *War and Peace*, and nearly twice the length of *Gone with the Wind*, it came within 70,000 words of the length of the *Bible* and is the longest novel ever published. What libraries Mr. Jones must have copied before bringing it forth! Edwin Daly, Gerald Tesch, and Tom T. Chamales were also writers who achieved publication and some popular success by the Handy Method. Inevitably there are malcontents who assert that they can detect in the work of Mrs. Handy's pupils the influence of the writers whom they have so toilsomely ingurgitated. My only purpose here is to call attention to a remarkable experiment, conducted with a rigor that reflects the greatest credit on the fortitude of everyone concerned, and which again presses home the only rule that can be applied to the study of literature—that there are no absolute rules. Whether the writing produced by Mrs. Handy's discipline was the result of stimulation or simulation is for the acute critics to decide, and so far most of them have shown a painful indecision. Whether Mrs. Handy was able to provide at an advanced stage in the psychic development of her pupils a satisfactory approximation of the fearsome pre-Oedipal mother is a matter upon which probably only Dr. Bergler could pronounce.

La Littérature Engagée

TIME AND AGAIN I am forced to the conclusion that if we want intelligent comment about writing and the temperament of writers, we are more likely to get it from writers themselves than from critics. Writers have shown themselves patient in answering questions about their work and their private lives and attitudes. Consider, for instance, the question of the writer's contribution to the political and social problems of his day—what the people who believe in it call *la littérature engagée;* should the writer be involved in political and social movements, and should these in turn find a place in his writing? Since the thirties this question has repeatedly appeared and faded like the Cheshire Cat. Nine English writers, young and prominent, were questioned on this matter by *The London Magazine* in 1957. Not one of them plumped for participation and propaganda, which is what *la littérature engagée* can so easily become. Maurice Cranston said: "*Littérature engagée* is the literature of enlightenment, as well as of commitment, of judgement as well as perception." "The writer's only artistic duty is to find a subject suited to his talent," said D. J. Enright, protesting against the notion that the writer is morally obligated to engage himself in the social and political issues of his time. Roy Fuller said: "The writer's work . . . is to transform the political and social world into the moral world." William Golding said: "I am fully engaged in the human dilemma but see it as far more fundamental than a complex of taxes and astronomy." Philip Larkin said: "Good social and political literature can exist only if it originates in the imagination, and it will do that only if the imagination finds the subject exciting, and not because the intellect thinks it important." Stephen Spender said: "It is surely just as important to try to be outside one's epoch, as to be of it." And Colin Wilson, with an echo of Cyril Connolly, said: "A writer's first commitment is to great poetry and art: in other words, to produce a masterpiece." No quotations are given here from the answers of John Osborne and John Wain, not because they disagreed with the others, or because their replies were not cogent, but because no short extract readily presents itself. These nine writers may safely be said to represent at least one powerful body of opinion on the fuzzy subject of *la littérature engagée,* and as they were not chosen as known opponents of it (indeed, the questions asked suggested somewhat too nakedly that support for *littérature engagée* was expected), their unanimity is striking. So, also, is their attitude toward their art, so much more serious than that of the anonymous questioner.

The true *littérature engagée* of our time is, of course, the vast literature of enjoying and enduring which we examined at length in Chapter Two, and the literature of sex instruction in Chapter Three, as well as the journalistic literature referred to earlier in this chapter. Exhortation on political and social problems abounds. What could be directed more shrewdly toward the heart's desire of millions of North Americans than *How I Turned $1,000 into a Million in Real Estate—in My Spare Time* by William Nickerson? In 1958 it was selling for a time at the rate of 10,000 copies a week. It is sheer romanticism to suppose that only books dealing with unpopular contemporary problems deserve the stylish description of *la littérature engagée;* these are highbrow enthusiasms—the realities in this realm are the books which tell you how to make a million, how to get a better job, how to forget that man is mortal, how to bully the Powers of Darkness (God or Anybody Who Will Listen) to boost your business.

It must not be supposed that the real writers, the Reardons, the men perpetually on trial before their inner tribunal, the men in unceasing battle with a ferocious pre-Oedipal mother, neglect matters of contemporary importance. When these are inevitable themes for them—what Samuel Butler speaks of as the books which will not let an author alone and demand to be written—they write about them, and write well. Nor should it be assumed from the somewhat staid tone of the writers who have been quoted that they are neglectful of experiment. True, they do not experiment as much as some critics would like. Critics like experiment because they weary of attempts to create masterpieces on conventional lines; they feel, understandably, that a new form or an unconventional approach might yield interesting, if not revolutionary, results.

Experiment and the Antinovel

COMPARATIVELY FEW writers, however, are truly experimental in a large sense. They are still leaning heavily on the revolution in material brought about by Freud and his followers, and the revolution in manner which stems chiefly from James Joyce. Small variations on these basic themes content them. There is always plenty of room for experiment, and one realm which has not been explored seriously in our time is the verse narrative.

This is the more astonishing when we reflect upon how many of the good modern novelists are also poets. Some of them—the names of Frederic Prokosch and Lawrence Durrell come to mind—have drawn on their poetic powers to enlarge their narrative scope. But what has been done in this realm which can be called daring? What, for instance, attempts to follow where Browning led in *The Ring and the Book*—one of the most remarkable psychological novels in English, and one of the most neglected great poems? The public taste which once rose so eagerly to the verse romances of Sir Walter Scott, and which gave Byron's *The Corsair* a sale of 10,000 copies on the day of its publication, is not dead; it is asleep, and rouses easily, as the success of Benét's *John Brown's Body* in 1927 plainly showed. Are the breadth of theme or the depth of penetration demanded by verse narrative uncongenial to the poets of our time? Do they lack the gusto and variety and sustained energy which such composition demands? If experiment in form is wanted, here is a realm in which it can be tried, and the possibilities of adventure are boundless.

Another sort of literature which has been little explored and which promises rich experiment is the film scenario. Tennessee Williams's *Baby Doll* has appeared in this form, and so has Dylan Thomas's *The Doctor and the Devils*; both are excellent reading. Is it always necessary that an actual filming should be in prospect for a writer to take this form and use it? Has it not qualities of its own which make it interesting, without reference to actual realization on the screen? In making this suggestion, I certainly do not wish for a Closet Cinema to partner in dowdiness the Victorian Closet Drama, but rather a new attack on narrative which would jettison some of the machinery of the novel. Miss Ivy Compton-Burnett has perfected for her own use a type of novel which is virtually dialogue, with connective tissue little more extended than stage directions. The scenario offers the chance of an equally incisive medium, employed on a broader scale.

A widely discussed experimenter of our time is Samuel Beckett, whose recognition was slow in coming. The material he chooses is not of the kind which attracts the great mass of readers and keeps at bay many of the timid among the clerisy. The interior monologue of an old man on his deathbed (*Malone Dies*) or the anxieties of a decrepit fat woman who is married to a blind curmudgeon whose ambition is to kill a child (*All That Fall*) do not, on the face of it, engage our fancy. But when we have read them, they linger in the mind, not merely because they are extraordinary and rather nasty, but because they have taken us behind the scenes of life and have shown us some aspects of it in a thoroughly unaccustomed light.

Consider his novel *Molloy.* It has been extravagantly praised. M. Jean Blanzat, writing in *Le Figaro Littéraire*, says it is one of the most profound investigations ever written of the disaster of man's destruction. From the first page we are engulfed in confusion and mystery, from which we pluck scraps of communication which after a time assemble into a ghost of narrative. Molloy is an old man, filthy, ragged, and diseased, who is wandering about the outskirts of a city, searching for his mother. He lacks most of the emotions which hold mankind together, and such relationships as he has with people, including his mother, are either violent or indecent. He is suffering from a failure of his legs which at last reduces him to dragging his body through the dirt with his hands. He encounters a man who kills him.

After this point the story becomes the inner monologue of Jacques Moran, a detective who is given orders—why and by whom we are not told—to track down Molloy. Moran is a cruel man who tortures his son with purgatives, and puts on a fantastic dress which includes a huge straw hat with an elastic under the chin, for his chase. He too has trouble with his legs—the "torso-man" whose limbs are failing is a favorite character of Beckett's—and one of his knees makes walking almost impossible. Moran's degradation and sense of loss and failure grow as he pursues his victim. At last he meets a man and kills him without knowing who he is. The man was Molloy.

No place to go for a laugh, you might say, echoing the schoolboy's comment on the works of Matthew Arnold. But baffling and occasionally maddening as *Molloy* is, a laugh is precisely what you do get, from time to time. In this welter of lunatic despair—despair gone far beyond such emotions as sadness or regret—there are humorous flashes worthy of Joyce himself. The atmosphere is nihilist, but not boring or depressing. On the contrary, it leaves me, for one, with a sense of exhilaration and clearer vision which convinces me that *Molloy* and Beckett's other books and plays are true works of art of an unusual kind. But they are not for Nice Nelly; the exhilaration and the fresh vision are bought at the cost of a steep descent into squalor, and abandonment or reversal of all the ordinary values.

This is not caprice; it is the turning inside out of the Classical novel. An English critic, Miss Christine Brooke-Rose, calls Beckett's works antinovels and antiplays; she likens them to *Don Quixote*, *Tristram Shandy*, *Les Faux-Monnayeurs*, and *The Skin of Our Teeth*. The comparison, and especially with *Tristram Shandy*, I find enlightening and helpful. In that extraordinary and delightful work the life of the hero has not passed beyond infancy when, at the end of the eighth volume, the conclusion is reached; as a life of Tristram Shandy it is nothing, but considered from any other point of view it is rich fare. In the works of Beckett every positive becomes a negative, and everything subsides to pointlessness and oblivion; he that is down need fear no fall, he that is low, no pride. That it should be stimulating is superficially strange, but I mean later to return to this point.

Dangers in the Avant-garde

It is by no means easy to distinguish between a valid and a durable literary attitude, such as that exhibited by Beckett, and the quickly fading enthusiasms of the *avant-garde*. Within the past thirty years we have seen the rise and fall of the Angry Young Men in Britain, and the sunset on the Beat Generation of the United States. In both these instances the enthusiasm and the name came from outside the group concerned, and the writers comprising these two coteries were unified less by common aims and sympathies than forced together by foolish adulation and foolish attack. In the March 1958 issue of the *London Magazine* its editor, John Lehmann, confessed to embarrassment at having to tell French inquirers that Kingsley Amis was of Britain's *avant-garde;* Mr. Lehmann did not think Mr. Amis sufficiently ahead of the crowd. Mr. Amis's opinion on the matter was not recorded, which was a pity. He, as much as any writer today, has been the victim of a label and an association which he did not seek, but did not resist with sufficient force. In consequence, his books which have followed *Lucky Jim* (1954) have been scrutinized for new evidence of Angry Young Manhood, and the decline observable in *That Uncertain Feeling* (1955) and even more marked in *I Like It Here* (1958) is due at least in part to this pressure to keep up an attitude. Mr. Amis never was very angry; on the contrary, he was good-natured. But he has been trapped in an attitude. In *I Like It Here* his fancy was exhausted, and he was brought down to the level of bladder and toilet fun, and does not scorn to employ even so jejune a device as a confusion of "word" with "turd." Any tiresome duty or work he classifies as "bum"—a word of titillating obscenity in some areas of English society; there are whole bum sequences in this unhappy book, and he extends his exquisite device by such variants as "buttocks" and "nates." He puts the crown on this drollery by a daring use of "shit." The anti-intellectualism which was amusing in *Lucky Jim* has dropped to the point where he describes that exquisite poem *The Dream of the Rood* as "a piece of orang-utan's toilet requisite." To be wittily scatalogical is one thing; this sort of writing, which might be called *l'ésprit de la chaise-percée,* is quite another. But was Amis wholly to blame? He was labeled as soon as he raised his head, and he cannot wash the label off. Now, old and honoured (the Booker Prize, 1986), the media still treat him as a naughty boy.

Technical experiment as well as attitude can mark the *avant-garde* writer, and can trap him just as surely. Great interest is fittingly aroused by Alain Robbe-Grillet's desire for a prose cleansed of "the myth of depth of meaning in objects"; as displayed in his own novels, *Le Voyeur* and *La Jalousie*, this results in a kind of antihumanism. He is in revolt against an anthropomorphic attitude toward objects which demonstrably have no human feeling; he would, for instance, deplore any reference to a *pitiless* storm, or a *smiling* sun. He will not admit that it is valid writing to say that a village *crouches* in its place; it is situated there, and nothing more. All of which is reasonable enough, and good writers have always taken pains to avoid cheap effects which arise when this style of description is abused. But matter is vastly more important than manner in writing, and it will be interesting to see if M. Robbe-Grillet can maintain this sort of abstinence for long. Matter dictates manner; to work the other way about is to do violence to the writer's inspiration, for it subordinates his creative to his critical faculty. Every writer is critical of his work after he has written it, but he is on unsteady ground when he puts himself to work to demonstrate a critical theory. He may do it once or twice, but it will be strange if he bases his career on it.

These matters of labels, of theories, of the strength or weakness of the *avant-garde* are properly the concern of critics, rather than the clerisy in general. Reading for pleasure, they are concerned with effects, not causes. Are they, therefore, unconcerned about the development of literature? By no means, but they will not follow that development far unless it produces some pleasure for them. Pleasure is not mere tickling of the senses, a good laugh or a good cry; standards of which even the self-conscious and specifically literary reader may not be fully aware have to be satisfied if any book or group of books is going to enjoy a success on a generous scale. The reader must be satisfied; a fine style, a lively plot, interesting characters are of little avail if the book does not persuade the reader that the writer has been honest with him, and such honesty demands a sincere revelation of the writer's mind and heart.

Puzzle of the Best-seller

MINDS AND HEARTS exist on many levels. A glance at the best-seller lists since the beginning of the present century shows us that a bewildering variety of authors, with minds and hearts of every sort, have appealed to great numbers of readers. There is only one common denominator in these books, and it is that the writer has held back nothing that he was able to give; he has striven to make the most direct impact possible on his readers.

It is empty cynicism to say that the greatest success will result when the writer with a cabbage head and the heart of a sheep calls to readers similarly equipped. If that were all, literature would not be an art, and literary success would be predictable and contemptible. The great successes of the nineteenth century rebuke such a superficial judgment; Dickens, Thackeray, Melville, Hawthorne, and Tolstoy were all best-sellers by the modern standard, and they cannot be brushed aside. In our own century we must set against the success of Florence Barclay's *The Rosary* the success of *The House of Mirth* by Edith Wharton. If *Pollyanna* charmed multitudes with its easy optimism, *Main Street* astonished equal numbers by showing what too often lies behind such optimism. If we scorn the sentimentality of *If Winter Comes*, let us recall that Conrad's *The Arrow of Gold* found as much favor. In 1922 Sinclair Lewis's fool-killer *Babbitt* sold hugely, and so did Louis Hémon's spare, delicate idyll *Maria Chapdelaine*. If Will Durant's *The Story of Philosophy* is scorned as a piece of easy popularizing (which I think would be an injustice), the scorners may ask themselves what it was that made Shaw's *Intelligent Woman's Guide to Socialism and Capitalism* a best-seller? *Sorrell and Son* may have enchanted the cabbage heads in 1926, but was it the same cabbage heads who bought *Elmer Gantry* in 1927? There is no way of juggling the best-seller lists to prove anything about public taste. The success of the books named here can only be accounted for in the broadest possible terms; they yielded up the author's meaning with full sincerity, and they found great numbers of readers to respond to what the authors had to give.

Sincerity must not be understood sentimentally; *Queen Victoria* by Lytton Strachey, which was a best-seller in 1922, is sincere in the sense that it conveys its writer's intention single-mindedly, not simple-mindedly. Shaw's *Saint Joan*, one of the few plays ever to achieve the sale of a best-seller in its book form, is likewise sincere, but it is not the sincerity of the stage confectioners whose pieces win tribute as "warmly human" because they do violence to every law of reason and probability. *Good-Bye, Mr. Chips* is one man's sincerity, and *The Bridge of San Luis Rey* is another's; both were best-sellers. Isak Dinesen's *Seven Gothic Tales*, an extremely sophisticated production, and *The Education of Henry Adams*, another, both won popular favor; *The Four Horsemen of the Apocalypse* and *Magnificent Obsession* were their contemporaries, and found their readers, too. There is sincerity in all of them; it is not sincerity of the same kind, but it is the sincerity of writers who meant what they wrote.

The year 1936 brought forth a remarkable group of best-sellers, of which the leader in numbers was *Gone with the Wind* by Margaret Mitchell. Its companions were *The Last Puritan* by George Santayana, *Sparkenbroke* by Charles Morgan, *The Thinking Reed* by Rebecca West, and *Eyeless in Gaza* by Aldous Huxley. One of the most popular tales of adventure in the history of publishing, and four philosophical novels of unusual distinction! Distinguished and, by the standards which the highbrow usually chooses to apply to the middlebrow, not easy to read. Yet they were read, just as, more recently, *By Love Possessed*, *Dr. Zhivago*, and *Lolita* have been read. Certainly it was not that they were "readable" in the sense in which that word is usually employed—implying that they slither rapidly and pleasurably beneath the half-attentive eye. Readable, rather, because they established themselves as worthy to be read, and worth taking some trouble to read.

The quality which seems to me to be common to all of these best-selling books—that of intellectual, emotional, and artistic sincerity—is not, of course, a guarantee of lasting worth. As we look at the list of best-sellers from 1895 to 1900 in Alice Payne Hackett's authoritative compilation, it is like an elephant's graveyard. Who knows now that there was once a best-selling novelist named Winston Churchill? Who reads Sir Gilbert Parker? Did anyone ever really read Theodore Watts-Dunton's *Aylwin*? Indeed they did—best-sellers all. *Trilby* still has readers, though everything about it save the inexplicable charm of its heroine has faded. *Sentimental Tommy*, one of Barrie's greatest successes, is read by a few. Of them all only Stephen Crane's *The Red Badge of Courage* has taken its place among the books which we feel that we ought to read, some time, and some place.

Neglected Works of Quality

Is THERE ANYONE who reads much who can look over a list of the best-sellers of the past without wondering why these books succeeded, when others of equal and sometimes superior merit came and went with little public acknowledgment? Why did a public which seems always ready for another novel of historical adventure permit Salvador de Madariaga's *The Heart of Jade* to slip by it so easily? Why, when carefully wrought novels of philosophic tone are being discussed, is L. H. Myers's *The Root and the Flower* so seldom mentioned? What happened to those readers who declare themselves to be on the watch for originality when Mervyn Peake's two extraordinary imaginative creations, *Titus Groan* and *Gormenghast*, made their appearance? Did *Titus Alone* fare better? Why did Alejo Carpentier's *The Kingdom of This World* and *The Lost Steps* not reach a wider public, which many of the most perceptive critics sought on their behalf? Why does the American public, always hospitable to a humorist of merit, know virtually nothing of Gwyn Thomas, who was, in his special realm, one of the wittiest writers living? How do we account for the respectful ignoring of John Cowper Powys, and for the fact that while she lived, Virginia Woolf was delighted when the sale of one of her books reached 5,000? Inevitably, when thousands of new books appear in England and the United States, not to speak of the rest of the English-speaking world, every year, many must escape notice, but how can great merit be slighted? There are doubtless a variety of answers, but one of them is certainly that the clerisy is not alert, not self-conscious, and unready to make known its enthusiasm for anything which does not appear on the best-seller lists. These lists appear to dominate the attention, and perhaps also the taste, of people who ought to have independent judgments and make them known. Another reason was put testily by an English critic, James Agate. "There appear to be certain literary ponds at which the horse-minded reading public just will not drink, even if you shove them into the water up to the neck."

We may laugh at the past, when Browning circles, reading clubs, and literary gatherings in provincial centers took themselves seriously, but they did have opinions of some sort. We seem now to be content with the domination of a handful of literary supplements to the national newspapers, and a few magazines which carry book reviews of the better kind. These publications are in their turn dominated, to a considerable degree, by the fashions of academic criticism. And thus we arrive at a condition where a highbrow public reads what even higher brows tell it must be read, and a much larger middlebrow public reads the best-sellers and virtually nothing else. If these constitute, as Mr. Blanshard supposes, about ten per cent of the population, and if we assume that forty per cent of the public never read anything at all, there must be fifty per cent or so which reads pocket books, reprints of best-sellers, books of sham philosophy and fake religion, and made

Mickey Spillane the best-read author of his day, and *In His Steps* by Charles Monroe Sheldon the all-time best-seller of American publishing.

Surely we can do a little better than that? To read only what the people we admire and fear (what David Riesman would call our peer group) read, be these peers highbrows or middlebrows, is to be other-directed indeed. And, as I have already said, other-directed appears to be nothing more than a sociological term for weak-minded. Surely if we possess the curiosity, the free mind, the belief in good taste, and the belief in the human race which characterize the humanist, we can choose the books we read on personal grounds, without experiencing unsettling sensations of eccentricity?

A Best-seller Considered

BEFORE LEAVING best-sellers, let us take a look at one of them to see what a prime example of the species is like. *The Robe* by the late Lloyd C. Douglas will serve us well, for it has many of the characteristics which have set the highbrow against this class of fiction. Its theme is religious. It is overwritten. It has sold considerably more than two million copies.

The objection to a religious theme is valid to criticism of the book because such a choice immediately gives the writer an advantage which is, aesthetically considered, irrelevant. Much bad art hides behind Christianity, for to criticize it on purely artistic grounds is to seem callous toward its inspiration; the Sistine Chapel and the fifty-cent chromo, the *St. Matthew Passion* and Moody and Sankey's hymns, *Pilgrim's Progress* and *The Robe*—to millions of people these seem more alike than unlike. To write about Christ is to disarm criticism and leave the way open for excesses which would not otherwise be tolerated.

As for being overwritten, it is a blemish only to the critic of technique. "I love those great still books," wrote Alfred, Lord Tennyson, to his son Hallam; "I wish there were a great novel in hundreds of volumes that I might go on and on." Hundreds of thousands of readers share this view. When they have found something they like, they do not want it to end. Those who succumb to the atmosphere of *The Robe* like to wallow in it. Why not?

Overwritten it may be, but it exhibits remarkable technical skill. Lloyd C. Douglas was a Lutheran Dumas; there is no trick of sensational fiction which he had not at his fingers' ends. He makes no attempt to recreate the atmosphere of Imperial Rome in the time of Tiberius; he desires merely to display certain aspects of it so that he may take his twentieth-century American Protestant reader right into the middle of Rome and invite him to criticize and be outraged. The reader is, by identification with all the good characters, able to despise the might of Rome, to cheek Pontius Pilate, to sneer at the doting Augustus and pimple-picking, spoiled-brat Tiberius, his successor; the reader is invited to apply his twentieth-century Christian standards of womanly conduct to Salome, who tells dirty stories (we are not permitted to hear them), and to revel in his knowledge that this rotten empire will undoubtedly decline and fall. It is no trifling matter to do what Mr. Douglas does, and give his reader the sensation of one bravely asserting the ethic of the First Lutheran Church of Middletown in the face of so much splendor and strength.

The lines between Good and Bad are firm; there is none of that confusing gray which must have made the early days of Christianity such a puzzling time for those who had to live through it and make their decisions in the light of what they actually knew. The Good Romans are good in every respect, save that they lack The Faith, and that is vouchsafed them at last. They are good in that they are exactly like twentieth-century Y.M.C.A. leaders; brought up with slavery, they know it is bad; brought up in the pride of Roman citizenship, they nevertheless know that Rome is doomed; patricians by birth, they are intensely democratic.

The Bad Romans drink heavily, grab at pure girls, and do not believe in their gods. They too know that the Empire is on the skids, though they do not know that it will take another five hundred years to kill it, and we sometimes wonder if the author knows it, either.

Like Dumas in his attack and his ability to implicate us in the sweep of great events, Mr. Douglas is also like Dumas in his inability to create lifelike characters. His young Romans call their father "the pater" (producing an oddly English Victorian effect), but otherwise they are as flat as characters in a television serial. They are often elaborately colloquial. "Take it easy," a Roman girl of patrician birth may say to a slave, and to her brother: "You're pretty dumb." Lucia, sister to the hero Marcellus, is fifteen, and has attracted the gummy eye of a Bad Roman; the author takes great pains to let us know that she is a girl of many moods, for she never deigns simply to speak, but drawls, snaps, shouts, and even barks; she does everything, in fact, except convince. Marcellus himself is a stick. The Apostles, when they appear, are like actors in a bad pageant, bearded and wigged and sadly under-rehearsed. Even Peter, called The Big Fisherman in an attempt to give him individuality, comes to nothing. Mr. Douglas may have felt an understandable and creditable reluctance to put any strongly personal thoughts into the mouths of historical persons whom he revered, but the upshot is that his great personages seem strangely bereft.

Lack of convincing characters does not harm the book as much as might be supposed, for behind these waxwork dummies is Mr. Douglas's conception of Jesus, which, if sentimental, is powerful and deeply felt. This conception manifests itself by some passages of description, put in the mouths of the Apostles, but chiefly through the Robe itself, which is the garment discarded by Christ on Golgotha and won by Marcellus in a game of dice. The Robe is magical; the unworthy are awed by it, and Marcellus is for a time driven almost to madness by it; the worthy derive a supernatural strength from it; it is a touchstone of virtue, for only the good can hold it. Narrative power of a considerable order comes to Mr. Douglas's aid when he writes of the Robe. He cannot write about romance, and his love scenes are chilled by puritanism; the Dumas in him can maneuver a girl into a boy's costume, but the Lutheran parson does not then know what to do with her. He cannot conceive of a type of young manhood superior to an American basketball hero, or of mature manhood which does not suggest an inferior character actor in a Hollywood Bible movie. He makes his characters despise slavery, though he uses at least one slave in the old tradition of the Comic Valet, making him relinquish his chance of freedom to stay with his master. But he does know how to manage his great moments with the Robe, and it gives power to his book which commands respect from the honest critic, and may awaken the envy of many a more sophisticated and thoughtful author. In what is most vital to his book, the work is sometimes crude, but always strong.

Another View of Ancient Rome

COMPARE *The Robe* with Robert Graves's *King Jesus*, which appeared in 1946, and was reprinted in 1959, after being unavailable for years. Graves is among the finest historical novelists of our day, and there has never been so good a group of historical novelists as are writing at present. He will have nothing to do with the sentimental notion that people in the remote past were precisely like ourselves, except for superficial differences of dress and custom; he knows as well as any man living how different was the color of a Roman mind from anything we are acquainted with today. He will have nothing to do with cardboard characters or Hollywood fancy dress. In this book he presents us with the welter of religious belief and superstition in the Roman world of the first century A.D., and he makes real the tangle of doctrine and dispute which was the preoccupation of the Jewish world. A sense of the past rises from his pages which is the result not only of wide scholarship but also of original thought and deep reflection. More, the book is poetic in concept; what it says about the life of Jesus may be startling and repugnant to orthodoxy, but it is illuminating, also. We are held by the fact that the writer has dared to think originally and postulate daringly on a subject where original thought is almost impossible. We may reject what Graves presents as a reconstruction of the life of Jesus (though there are passages of such beauty that the most orthodox will let them go with regret), but we shall never accept twaddle about Jesus again; there is intellectual and moral and spiritual sinew in Graves's book which makes the best-seller seem vulgar and naïve, and a poetic splendor which awes, rather than flatters, the mind. It is not a book for those who like their religion to be snug. One might have hoped it was for the clerisy, but they failed it.

Pleasures of Identification

ALTHOUGH Graves's book awes us, it does not deny us one of the legitimate pleasures of novel-reading—a pleasure which

The Robe offers so amply on a very different level—the pleasure of identification. To discuss this pleasure adequately would require some space, and Dr. Morris Bishop has put it with so much wit and concision in verse that the best and most economical plan is to reproduce what he has to say here.

When, in my effervescent youth,
  I first read "David Copperfield,"
I felt the demonstrated truth
  That I had found my proper field.
As David, simple, gallant, proud,
  Affronted each catastrophe,
Involuntarily I vowed,
  "That's me!"

In Sherlock Holmes and Rastignac
  Much of myself was realized;
In Cyrano de Bergerac
  I found myself idealized.
Where dauntless hardihood defied
  The wrong in doughty derring-do,
I periodically cried,
  "That's me too!"

The lads of Bennett, Wells, and Co.
  Confronted many a thwarting thing,
But well-intentioned, fumbling, slow,
  They tried to do the sporting thing;
And some would nurse a carking shame,
  Hiding the smart from other men.
They often caused me to exclaim,
  "That's me again!"

The fiction of the present day
  I view with some dubiety;
The hero is a castaway,
  A misfit to society,
A drunkard or a mental case,
  A pervert or a debauchee.
I murmur with a sour grimace,
  "Where's Me?"

This pleasure of identification must never be undervalued, either by writer or reader. In youth, as Dr. Bishop says, we are especially prone to it. (The Dramatic Publishing Co. of Chicago, which specializes in plays for high-school groups, is well aware of this, and offers pieces in which young amateurs can be their favorite television stars; versions of *Our Miss Brooks, I Love Lucy, Meet Corliss Archer, December Bride,* and *Father Knows Best* are to be had from them. Simple stage plays based on popular movies are included: *Rebel without a Cause* (be James Dean) and *Gentlemen Prefer Blondes* (be Marilyn Monroe) are on the list, and so is *The Robe*, based on the film, not the book. Because identification on this level is frank and naïve, let us not suppose that it is, in origin, different from what boys and girls with more literary discrimination practice when they read the books of their choice.)

Not that this pleasure is confined to those under twenty. I once knew a group of undergraduates whose pleasure it was to assume, each for a day, the character and outlook of some favorite character in Proust, maintaining the pose until some other enthusiast identified them. I could never see that it did them anything but good, sharpening their wits and very often improving their manners. Hero worship has value in relation to the hero chosen, and I would rather know people who read in order to add something to their emotional or intellectual store than for the crabbed pleasure of tearing books to pieces. To be always in the coldly critical vein is to diminish one's own pleasure and perhaps to do oneself permanent harm. Arnold Bennett and Aldous Huxley, for instance, are two writers who have of late years been much buffeted by the younger critics and the undergraduates who follow their lead; such criticism is only safe if we bear in mind how much sheer talent it takes to rise to the level of either of these writers, and how much enjoyment they have given to people who are by no means undiscriminating fools.

Where Are You?

THE PLEASURE of identification is likely to change its character, however, as the reader acquires years and experience. He no longer wants to be the hero, or the villain, or the genius in every book he reads. He may become interested in the many novels of our time which have neither a hero, nor an antihero, but a collection of characters more or less baffled and defeated by life, with whom nobody in his senses would wish to be associated for long. Yet his pleasure in reading is great. What is he doing? He is identifying himself with the author.

This is not new, of course. The successful reader of Henry James, for instance, has long enjoyed, legitimately and admirably, sharing the sensibility and insight of the master. Readers of Dostoevski or Thomas Mann are projecting themselves imaginatively into the characters of those writers, rather than into the men and women they write about. In *King Jesus* we share the speculative scope, the poetic sweep, and the far-ranging scholarship of Graves, and in that way we penetrate his book. If we want to act one part, rather than all the parts and the role of interpreter as well, we shall find more pleasure in *The Robe*.

Identification with the author is not new, but never before have so many novels called upon this power and requited it so miserably as at present. Among people who care about sophistication, it is understood that it is unsophisticated to want to play hero; the modish reader is he who wants to play author, partaking of the creator's character. But the authors, while they seem to invite this sort of response, appear also to resent it, and they make the identification gritty and unrewarding. As Roy Fuller says:

> The treason of the clerks is when
> They make a fetish of the pen,
> Forget that art has duties to—
> As well as to the "I"—the "You,"
> And that its source must always be
> What presses most, most constantly.

If the author cannot find it in his heart to welcome his reader, he should at least refrain from rebuffing, snubbing, and bamboozling the wretch. He must not retreat into complexities of feeling so personal and incommunicable that the reader feels like somebody in the presence of a man having a fit, and who stands powerless to help or comprehend, yet forbidden by decency to go. This is artistic bullying of a kind that literature has never needed before, and which it stands to gain nothing from now.

Charms of Romantic Despair

YET WE MUST beware of finding fault with the younger modern novelists merely because they write of "what presses most." The clerisy are under an obligation to try to understand, and to try to discover why what presses most is so often a form of philosophical and moral defeatism; it is not nihilism, which is very much more difficult to achieve than is supposed by people who use the word loosely to mean the reverse of popular opinion; it is defeatism and despair. If this is what presses most with so many talented writers, why is it so?

Before we can arrive at any answer, however tentative, we must try to decide how much of this defeatism and despair is romantic posturing. Because historians of literature talk about and teach the Romantic movement as a revolt against the classicism loosely associated with the eighteenth century, we are sometimes blinded to the fact that it persists as the most widespread and still the most popular influence in American literature today. The reason is unflattering. Romanticism asserts the supremacy of individual feeling over discipline, learning, or thought. Anybody can feel, and if his feelings are powerful, his discipline bad, his learning small, and his thought trivial, who is to blame him for making his feeling the measure of all things?

The Romantic attitude is not a possession of individual writers; it is something which, on the North American continent at least, envelops the whole of society, coloring not only the present, but the popular idea of the past and the popular conception of the future. It is inevitably distorting to all ideas which are uncongenial to it, with the result that discipline is confused with harshness, learning is confused with personality development, and thought, if it inclines toward scepticism, is confused with cynicism. With continents, as with individuals, a preoccupation with feeling tends to isolate the feeler in his own warm, caressing bath of ill-examined sensation. Is it surprising if many of the writers who live in such an atmosphere write in a manner suitable to it? Only if they are exceptionally "inner-directed," to use the expression which Mr. Riesman contrasts with "other-directed," can they do otherwise. Not only must such a writer be inner-directed; he must also have been given, or have acquired for himself, an education and an attitude unusual in his surroundings.

The contrast to romanticism is, of course, classicism, which has its own diseases. Adopted by masses of people, it inevitably becomes a thing of schemes, of rigid rules, of infallible tests, and evokes a great deal of writing which is correct by the rules, but narrow and arid by every test of common sense. It is just as easy to be a classic fool as to be a romantic fool; intellectual abandonment to the prevailing tide is all that is wanted.

Yet in our romantic age an undercurrent of yearning for the classic approach is to be felt, and sometimes, as in the great welcome given to James Gould Cozzens's *By Love Possessed*, it declares itself loudly. The characters were shown in a framework which did no violence to the idea of order possessed by most readers. They were observed by the author with understanding and sympathy, but he did not seem to be wholly committed to them; their psychology was displayed to explain what they did, but not to excuse or justify their actions. The story was offered as a thing complete in itself, yet related to a vast and perhaps very different world surrounding it. Passion was shown to the reader, but he was invited to observe it and not to join the dance. The result was a degree of acclaim for the book which no one could have predicted; even that American equivalent of a Roman official triumph—the picture of the author on the cover of *Time*—was not withheld, and semidivine status was accorded to Mr. Cozzens for several months, by which time this small piece of classic rock appeared to have been subsumed in the romantic sludge. The response of critics in England was one of astonishment; far more than their usual resistance to a book which had been a great success in America was shown; they could not understand what all the fuss was about. The reason was that the attitude displayed by Mr. Cozzens is far more familiar in English fiction than in American; there is a tradition of classicism there which has never been entirely submerged, and, perhaps more important and significant for the writing of fiction, a classical restraint in the expression of romantic feeling.

The Yahoo Hero

In 1958 a sharp attack was launched on the romanticism of much popular American writing by Edmund Fuller, in *Man in Modern Fiction*; what gave this book more impact than much criticism along roughly similar lines was Mr. Fuller's intellectual Christianity and his Judaeo-Christian concept of Man as a being with freedom of choice, responsible to the God who created him. This is a classic point of view, and its application to a large body of fiction which is romantic in character produced some brisk and revealing criticism. Specifically, it revealed the sentimentality of the writers he attacked; sentimentality is among the commonest diseases of romanticism. Mr. Fuller's concept of Man is neither supported nor contradicted by the modern novelists whose work he examined; it is by-passed in favor of a notion (concept is too definite a word) of man as a derelict and irresponsible creature existing in a world where no moral values apply.

Mr. Fuller was not attacking such writers as Camus, whose idea of the absurdity of man's fate is conditioned by hope and courage; the true Existentialist asserts the greatness of man. Rather he is gunning for a body of American novelists of whom James Jones and Norman Mailer are but two, who have exalted what he calls "the Yahoo-hero"—a coarse-fibered vulgarian, grotesque in his thinking, and immature in his attitude toward life, who lives for the kicks he can get out of it. He particularly attacks the sentimental attitude which their creators take toward characters who are demonstrably criminal, representing them as victims of a society much worse than they; this leads to the sentimentality which exalts the genial rapist, and finds in the keeper of a bawdy house a philosopher and perhaps a saint. This squalid outlook is the shadow side of the general sentimentality of our time. It is possible to applaud what Mr. Fuller has said without agreeing in every detail. For myself, I think that the writers he attacks write as they do in fullest sincerity. Several of them are men of undoubted literary gifts and they are writing of "what presses most." Are they immature in intellect? If so, they call to a corresponding immaturity in a large body of readers. Their chief defect seems to be that they are desperately badly educated; potentially powerful intelligences have been given nothing to feed on, and they operate in a society where most people are as deprived as themselves. They and their readers have intellectual and spiritual rickets. This will undoubtedly appear to many readers to be intellectual snobbery, which is as unsympathetic and out-of-fashion in North American literary circles as Mr. Fuller's religious conviction. But well-educated people could not think or write so sentimentally. Sentimentalism is the philosophy of boobs.

The Echo in the Cave

REGRETTABLY, it is perfectly possible to be an effective writer and a boob as well; writers are not, by definition, intellectual or even specially literate. But in past ages and in other lands, the boob writer has found it hard to impose upon a public in which a clerisy was aware of his deficiency. Writers do not have to be mature in their attitudes if there is a majority of immature readers upon whom they can impose, and plenty of self-doubting intellectuals who are prepared to accept as a genius any man who asserts loudly that life is a swindle, and God and morality are fakes. Such gutless twaddle finds an echo in the great cave of emptiness and self-pity which so many people carry in their hearts. But because it echoes gloomily within us, need it be truth?

Belief in God and a good education are not enough to produce a good novel; only talent can do that, and where talent exists, it may produce the novel without either of the other aids. Belief in the Devil could provide some writing of interest, but the Devil is as unfashionable now as his Almighty Father. To be out of fashion, of course, is not to be any less potent. The sentimental pseudo realism against which Mr. Fuller inveighs so ably is the Devil's gluepot, sweetened to catch some very foolish flies. It bears no relation to realism as it is practiced by, for instance, Frank O'Connor. The true realist is he who believes in both God and the Devil, and is prepared to attempt, with humility, to sort out some corner of the extraordinary tangle of their works which is our world. He cannot rely on his feelings alone; he must use his intellect. But at present the American novel suffers from the insularity and bigotry of the determined romantic, who asserts the despair and disintegration of man as dogmatically as the doctrine of Pollyanna was ever asserted by the Glad Girl.

> Though critics may bow to art, and I am its own true
> lover,
> It is not art, but heart, which wins the wide world over.

Thus Ella Wheeler Wilcox. How truly, and yet how paradoxically, she sings of the fate of the modern American novel.

Heart—not the high heart or the stout heart, but rather the heart bowed down by weight of woe—is in control, and Head is nowhere at all. Neither writer nor reader thinks highly of Head. Do not despise Mrs. Wilcox. She was a happy creature, and happiness often gives an effect of shallowness. Yet her hope was no more shallow than is the despair of the creators of the Yahoo hero; both moods seem to be the outcome of minds ill-adapted to the accommodation of more than one strong idea.

Will it long be thus? Are we to look forward to another decade or more of novels dealing with such romantic delights as rape, homosexuality, Lesbianism, incest, and the furies of fighting men? Must we face more writing in which *frottage, cunnilinctus, fellatio,* and the other classically named specialities of the bawdy house are rendered in terms of prose? How long will the novelist go on—in the words used by Byron against Keats—"viciously soliciting his own imagination"? Modern poets, at their best, have for some time abandoned this wallowing, but that is no reason to assume that the novelists will follow their example. The poets, after all, count their readers by scores, the novelists by thousands, and they fill different needs.

More Confusion to Come

IF THE NOVEL should change within the coming decade, however, I do not think that it will change in a way which the people who are always hoping for a return to the past will like. The direction of its extravagance may alter, and the tone and vocabulary of the writing may alter, but the extravagance will persist, and may seem even more outrageous to the timid. It may well be another fifty years before we have any clear idea what is happening in the world of letters.

We must never forget that the world of letters is but one part, and by no means a dominant part, of the very much larger world. The chaos of that world, political, economic, moral, and ideological, is plainly apparent. Is it a purposeful chaos? Such a question is, at least in part, ridiculous, for it is always our custom, when we reconsider the past, to attribute purpose to it. After all, has it not resulted in ourselves? And what nobler purpose could any welter of events, however seemingly chaotic and costly, have than that? We may be sure that the world in 2020 will find purpose in our present chaos. But what do we know and what can we deduce as we journey toward that time?

When I said that the world of letters was not dominant, I did not mean to imply therefore that it was insignificant. Like all art, it reflects what is and foreshadows what is to be; it does not influence events directly or obviously. The confusion which bewilders so many people who look at literature as something separate from the rest of life is apparent in the plastic arts, and in music, as well. It is apparent in religion, and Arnold Toynbee has told us that advances and clarifications are in progress in the religions we know, and will manifest themselves strikingly. The vast body of the devout, of course, do not read Toynbee, and the time is not propitious for him to roam the world in a goatskin, prophesying. But can we read what he says without some powerful intimation that we are listening to a prophet as authentic as any?

Outcries against modern painting and sculpture are heard everywhere, and every sort of explanation has been offered for its vagaries. It is subjective; it sometimes arouses feelings of dread; it seems to mirror chaos. Not possessing the clarity of foresight given to the characters in *The Robe*, we are unable to say with certainty that this chaos portends the disintegration of our present civilization, but we have our fears. The intensely disturbing quality which so many people find in this art cannot be dismissed simply as annoyance that painters have foresworn simple representation. These pictures, these images, these contorted forms speak directly of things which lie below the level of consciousness, and in those who are afraid of what lies there—afraid, that is to say, of all but a small part of what comprises their minds—such revelation gives rise to sensations so disturbing that they can only meet them with indignation and rejection. But unless these painters and sculptors are wry jokers, engaged in a vast plot to hoodwink the world—unless, that is to say, they are something that their kind have never been before in the history of art—they are performing their usual mighty task of giving form to what lies deep in the time in which they live. Is it chaos and disintegration or the unfamiliar face of the future which confronts us in these works? Do they show us the future as it matures in the womb of the present?

In literature such evidences of chaos are not so easy to identify, though in the work of Samuel Beckett, already alluded to, chaos and disintegration are directly presented, and it may be that in this, Beckett is ahead of his time. We need not suppose that the macabre world of his plays and novels is a literal presentation of the world of the future, any more than the novels of Sade were a literal prediction of the romantic world of the nineteenth century. But the attitude from which Beckett's works are written—an attitude in which all that is conventional is rejected, and all values turned upside-down—may be prophetic. We may see much more writing akin to his within the next twenty years, and as he has derived from Joyce, so may others derive from him. The failure of literature to offer anything upon which we can fasten, finding in it a reflection of what is deepest in our time, is partly owing to the nature of literature itself; it has become a form of entertainment during a period when the plastic arts have moved out of that category. It has become commercial as it never was before, with a resultant obscuring of its true purposes. And it is true also that literature rests upon a foundation of general acceptance, and is dependent on the civilization in which it is produced, as painting and sculpture are not; the painter may find a sympathetic buyer for his single picture, but the writer must find at least a few hundred buyers for his book, or his career is at an end. The popular nature of literature has led it to reflect the chaos of our time—the chaos which lies beneath the surface—but in a muddied fashion, because the writer does not want his reader to suspect what he himself only half knows.

A Millenary Parallel

THESE ARE gloomy reflections, and hard-headed readers may think them hare-brained. Let me at once provide them with further evidence of hare-brainedness. We are approaching a millennium; the year 2000 draws on apace. The last time mankind had this experience a chaos comparable to our own was observable in many parts of the world; monsters and portents were reported from all quarters of the globe. We need not believe in these monsters and portents as actualities any more than we need believe the reports of flying saucers today; what is significant is that men yielded to an inner compulsion to fancy such things, and in this sense they were artistic creations rooted in fear much as are the pictures and images which we have been discussing. Journeys to Jerusalem were undertaken, for it was amply clear to the best minds of the time that Christ was going to reappear there when the millennium was completed, and conduct the Last Judgment, preparatory to the end of the world. We have our own dread of the world coming to an end, though the nearest thing we have yet produced to compare with a Last Judgment is a series of Summit Meetings. Such reflections as these, in the words of Dr. C. G. Jung, "come perilously close to those turbid fantasies which becloud the minds of world-improvers and other interpreters of 'signs and portents.' " I advance them not as a millenarian, but simply as one who thinks that historical parallels should neither be exaggerated nor ignored. I refer the curious to Dr. Jung's remarkable little book on *Flying Saucers*, and also to his *The Undiscovered Self.*

This book was not undertaken to explain the world—only to make some comment on literature as it has developed during the past century. But to divorce literature wholly from the world in which it is produced is absurd; it is, indeed, to deny that literature is anything more than a form of entertainment which may, in the hands of finical writers and critics, be lifted to the status of a minor art. But there is nothing minor about it, and when it truly mirrors any part of the soul of the time, it is revelatory and prophetic as nothing else can be in quite the same way.

Is it revelatory and prophetic now? Some of it unquestionably is so, but the task of sifting valid prophecy and revelation from the mass of what is meant only for entertainment, from what is timid, what is purblind, what confuses ignorant romanticism with clear-eyed disillusion, what fears chaos and can discern no hope in it—this is work for which few of our literary critics are fitted, and we must turn to a Toynbee or a Jung for a hint at the answer we seek. The best among our writers are doing their accustomed work of mirroring what is deep in the spirit of our time; if chaos appears in those mirrors, we must have faith that in the future, as always in the past, that chaos will slowly reveal itself as a new aspect of order. And so great is the change in the direction that civilization is taking that we cannot reasonably expect this new order to be welcome or familiar to everyone; the world is full of people whose notion of a satisfactory future is, in fact, a return to an idealized past.

It is for the clerisy to show themselves more alert, more courageous, and better prepared, so that when the first shafts of the dawn appear in our present night, they will know them for what they are.

Epilogue

My book shall end as it began—with a call to the clerisy to take themselves more seriously as readers. Yet I have repeatedly said in these pages that they should not attempt to assert themselves as a group, or claim attention by concerted action. Why? Is this a paradox? It is not. This is an age of groups, clubs, associations, and whatnot; most members of the clerisy belong to enough of these already. It is within the groups to which they already belong that they can best assert the values of the humanist—curiosity, the free mind, belief in good taste, and belief in the human race. The advocates of these values must be everywhere. In the end, it is upon the quality of individuals that all group movements depend; let the clerisy make it their task to leaven the groups, taking to them all they have acquired in their hours of literary solitude. For them, in a time when the individual has lost significance (despite loud assertions to the contrary), an informed, rational, and intellectually adventurous individuality must take precedence over all else. In their seeming disunion lies their real strength.

An Informal Bibliographical Note

Any bibliographical information from my hand must necessarily be informal, for I have never been an adept at the exact, scientific description of books. Indeed, one of the shameful moments of my university life was when, on a bibliography examination, *viva voce* before Oxford's archivist, I was so foolish as to describe a book as "chunky," when I should have called it a "thick octavo." When next I presented myself for that examination, I knew better, but my heart was never in bibliography. What follows is some information about the books mentioned in *A Voice from the Attic* which are not easily come by, or which may not be familiar to booksellers. I can promise no more.

In Chapter One, *The Fine Art of Reading* by Lord David Cecil was published in England by Constable in 1957. The passage quoted from Sir Thomas Browne may be found in his *Christian Morals*, Part One, section 2, and I particularly recommend this splendid, baroque book to those who believe that morality is necessarily austere. If anyone should be curious about Dr. Blimber, he appears in Dickens's *Dombey and Son*, and Mr. Curdle is to be found in Chapter xxiv of

Nicholas Nickleby. The poem by Ben Jonson, "It is not growing like a tree," is the first verse of his *Ode to Sir Lucius Cary and Sir H. Morison*; Addison's "The Vision of Mirzah" is in number 159 of *The Spectator*; Thomas Campbell (1777–1844) is still remembered for "Hohenlinden," "Mariners of England," and "The Battle of the Baltic"; he is of curious interest to American scholars because of his long poem, written in 1809, called "Gertrude of Wyoming"—meaning the Wyoming Valley in Pennsylvania. The passage on "panegyric and praise" comes from Samuel Foote's comedy *The Patron*, where it is spoken by Mr. Puff. Those who wish to read all of what Sir Nathaniel says in *Love's Labour's Lost* will find the speech in Act IV, scene 2.

In Chapter Two, Samuel Smiles's *Self-Help* is mentioned as being published in 1859, and there were many subsequent editions; the latest was a centenary edition, published in London by John Murray, with an introductory essay by Professor Asa Briggs, who discusses the book sympathetically. Arnold Bennett's *How to Live on Twenty-four Hours a Day* has gone through several editions since 1908; if you wish to learn how Bennett practiced what he preached, read his *Journals;* in full they run to over a million words, but an excellent condensation, made by Frank Swinnerton, is number 999 in Penguin Books. *The Art of Thinking* by Ernest Dimnet passed through several editions, and a particularly convenient one is that which Jonathan Cape included in the Travellers' Library in 1931. The poem "As a white candle . . ." which is quoted, is called "The Old Woman," by Joseph Campbell. *Social Class and Mental Illness* by A. B. Hollingshead and F. C. Redlich was published by John Wiley and Sons, New York, in 1958. Of the three books on self-analysis mentioned, *Experiment in Depth* by P. W. Martin (Routledge and Kegan Paul, London, 1945) and *Self-Analysis* by Karen Horney (W. W. Norton, New York, 1942) are not hard to find, but

A Practical Method of Self-Analysis by E. Pickworth Farrow is more elusive; George Allen and Unwin, London, published it in 1942, and International Universities Press, New York, in 1948; a good second-hand book dealer can find a copy, given time. *The Anatomy of Melancholy* by Robert Burton, frequently referred to, is to be found in many editions, but there is much to be said for that of Holbrook Jackson in Everyman's Library (Dent) because it translates the Latin passages. It was re-published in Vintage Books in 1977.

Few of the books in Chapter Three offer any difficulties. Ovid's *Ars amatoria* has frequently been translated. Havelock Ellis's *Studies in the Psychology of Sex* is available in the Random House two-volume edition of 1936, and Van de Velde's *Ideal Marriage* (1928) and *A Marriage Manual* by Drs. Abraham and Hannah Stone (1936) can be bought anywhere. Professor Fowler's *Science of Life* is not so easily found. He appears to have published it himself in 1870; my copy was published by the Physical Culture Publishing Co. New York. *Man's Strength and Woman's Beauty* by Dr. P. H. Chevasse was published in the United States by Jones Brothers and Co. of Cincinnati, Philadelphia, and Chicago in 1880. Krafft-Ebing's *Psychopathia Sexualis* was published in English by Rebman of London and New York in 1899, translated by the publisher.

First editions of the books mentioned in Chapter Four will be found in large libraries; second-hand booksellers sometimes offer copies. *Valentine Vox* ran through many editions, but the first, with sixty illustrations by T. Onwhyn, was published by Routledge in 1844; it is not easy to find in good condition. Nor is *Sylvester Sound*; I have not been able to get a first edition, and have had to be content with the book in Routledge's Sixpenny Series, without pictures. *The Curtain Lectures of Mrs. Caudle* was first published in 1846 (after appearing serially in *Punch*) by Bradbury and Agnew; it is finely illustrated by Charles Keene. Bradbury and Agnew also brought out *Mr. Sponge's Sporting Tour* in 1852; the illustrations by John Leech are part of its charm, and if you are buying a copy, be sure you get one in which not only the colored plates, but also the charmingly drawn initial letters and tailpieces are included. *The Commissioner* by G. P. R. James is hard to find; it was published in Dublin in 1843 by Curry, and has twenty-seven fine illustrations by Phiz (Hablot Knight Browne, 1815–82). *The Greatest Plague of Life* by the Mayhew brothers is valued for its illustrations by George Cruikshank; David Bogue published it in 1847, and though it may take some time, it can be found both in the first edition and in the six original monthly parts. Modern books which provide a background for this sort of reading are *Mayhew's London, London's Underworld*, and *Mayhew's Characters* edited by Peter Quennell and published in London by William Kimber in 1950–1; they contain illustrations from Mayhew's original work. If you are curious to know what sort of song Job Caudle sang at the party when his wife was away—indeed, what songs the Victorians sang during convivial evenings of all kinds—you will find the subject pleasantly explored in *Victorian Song, or from Dive to Drawing Room* by Maurice B. Willson Disher, published by Phoenix House, London, 1955.

Nineteenth-century plays, in their earliest editions, are not easily come by, for they were fragile and were usually bought, not for reading, but for use in the theater, where they were given hard wear. A good modern collection is *Nineteenth Century Plays* edited by George Rowell and published by the Oxford University Press in its World's Classics series, number 533; *Black Ey'd Susan* is in it, and also *The Bells*. For American plays of the same period, *S.R.O.* edited by Bennett Cerf and Van H. Cartmell, published by Doubleday Doran in 1944, is very useful. There is also, of course, the twenty-volume series of *America's Lost Plays* produced by Princeton University Press, and there is a single volume extract from this vast compilation, called *Favorite American Plays of the Nineteenth Century*, also by Princeton. The *Dramatic Works* of Sheridan Knowles were published in London in 1856, by Routledge, in two volumes. Wills's *Charles I* was published, somewhat more durably than most plays, by Blackwood in 1873, and may still be found. Clement Scott's *Drawing-Room Plays and Parlour Pantomimes* was brought out in 1870 by Stanley Rivers and Co., a firm which described itself as "publishers of Scientific Amusements and Pastimes of Society"; it is now rare. William Winter's three volumes of *Shakespeare on the Stage* were published by Moffat Yard and Co. in 1911, 1915, and 1916 respectively. A. C. Sprague's useful books, *Shakespeare and the Actors* and *Shakespearean Players and Performances*, were produced by the Harvard University Press in 1944 and 1953. The anthology called *The English Dramatic Critics* by James Agate now appears in the Hill and Wang paperback series called Dramabooks. Anyone who is curious to read *Guy Domville*—a play which has been disproportionately condemned—will find it in *The Complete Plays of Henry James* edited by Leon Edel and printed in London by Rupert Hart-Davis in 1949.

Old jestbooks are as hard to find as old plays; they were literally worn out, and the copies which have been spared to us are usually much thumbed. *Nugae Venales*, in the 1686 edition, is very rare, and if you should imagine you see it advertised in a bookseller's catalogue, look carefully to be sure that it is not, in fact, the Latin jestbook of the same name which appeared in 1689. My *Nugae Venales* has several MS pages of stupefying jokes (probably from the eighteenth century, if we may judge by the handwriting) which have been added by some thrifty owner. The original *Joe Miller* is not very rare; the first edition contains seventy pages and 247 jokes, and was published by T. Read, Dogwell Court, White Fryars. I cannot date *Puniana*, but it was expanded and republished by John Camden Hotten in 1873; it is not easy to find; writing of it, the *Saturday Review* said: "We should suggest that, to a dull person desirous to get credit with the young holiday people, it would be a good policy to invest in the book, and dole it out by installments"; it contained "nearly 3,000 of the best riddles and 10,000 most outrageous Puns"; probably the young holiday people wore out most of the copies. *Cole's Fun Doctor*, in two volumes, is usually much worn when found; my copies were published by McClelland and Goodchild of Toronto, in 1913, but the original editions date from the 'nineties. Daniel George's books are all easily available and are all published by Jonathan Cape, London. Sigmund Freud's *Wit and Its Relation to the Unconscious* was published by Moffat Yard in New York, and Kegan Paul in London, the translator being A. A. Brill. Osbert Sitwell's *Before the Bombardment* was published by Duckworth, London, in 1926, and has since been reprinted; for a time it was available in the Penguin Books, number 162.

For obvious reasons, the books of dubious character which are mentioned in Chapter Seven do not lend themselves to bibliographical identification. To people who did not read Latin, Richard de Bury's *Philobiblon* was unknown until 1888, when E. C. Thomas produced a fine translation which was, however, printed in a small edition; in 1902 it was given wide circulation in a series called The King's Classics, edited by Israel Gollancz. The history of *The Gregynog Press* by Thomas Jones was published by the Oxford Press in 1954. *Fanny Hill* is now published in a neat edition with an introduction by Peter Quennell by Putnam; early editions can be very expensive. Crébillon's *Le Sofa* is readily available, and in 1951 the Folio Society of London brought out a new and excellent translation by Bonamy Dobrée. *The Awful Disclo-*

sures of Maria Monk is now published by the Camden Publishing Co. of Islington, in London; the pictures are the same crude cuts that adorned the early American editions, and seem to have been made for use with some other book. Mark Twain's *Fireside Conversation* can be found in a variety of reprints, without too much difficulty. *A History of the Rod in All Countries* by the Reverend William Cooper B.A. appeared about 1873, but is hard to date accurately; the publisher was John Camden Hotten; the *Daily Telegraph* declared the book to be "very readable," containing "much matter for reflection, and not a little amusement"; what would it say today? My copy, a bookplate tells me, used to be in the library of the Society of the Sacred Mission, a Church of England monastery at Kelham in Nottinghamshire. For reflection, one wonders, or amusement?

The books mentioned in Chapter Eight are all comparatively easy to find, but it may spare you some searching to know that George Gissing's *New Grub Street* can be had in the Oxford Press's World's Classics, number 566, and that *Writers At Work* was published by Viking Press in 1958. Dr. Edmund Bergler's *The Writer and Psychoanalysis* was published by Brunner, New York, in 1954. *The Heart of Jade* by Salvador de Madariaga was brought out by Creative Age, New York, in 1944; Harcourt Brace published *The Root and the Flower* in one volume in 1947; the two works of Alejo Carpentier were published by Knopf; Mervyn Peake's *Titus Groan* books were all published in London by Eyre and Spottiswood, the first volume having been published in the United States by Reynal and Hitchcock.

The books mentioned as best-sellers in this chapter are so identified in Alice Payne Hackett's *Sixty Years of Best Sellers 1895–1955*, published by R. R. Bowker Company, N.Y., 1956. There a best-seller is defined as a book which has sold over a million copies. The books mentioned which appeared before 1895 are vouched for by Miss Hackett as having attained this sale, though in some cases their success was not immediate.

The poem by Dr. Morris Bishop which is quoted is from his collection, *A Bowl of Bishop*, published by Dial, New York, in 1954; I am grateful to the late Dr. Bishop for his permission to quote it.

Index

FOR THE BEST IN PAPERBACKS, LOOK FOR THE 

In every corner of the world, on every subject under the sun, Penguin represents quality and variety—the very best in publishing today.

For complete information about books available from Penguin—including Pelicans, Puffins, Peregrines, and Penguin Classics—and how to order them, write to us at the appropriate address below. Please note that for copyright reasons the selection of books varies from country to country.

In the United Kingdom: For a complete list of books available from Penguin in the U.K., please write to *Dept E.P., Penguin Books Ltd, Harmondsworth, Middlesex, UB7 0DA.*

In the United States: For a complete list of books available from Penguin in the U.S., please write to *Dept BA, Penguin*, Box 120, Bergenfield, New Jersey 07621-0120.

In Canada: For a complete list of books available from Penguin in Canada, please write to *Penguin Books Ltd, 2801 John Street, Markham, Ontario L3R 1B4.*

In Australia: For a complete list of books available from Penguin in Australia, please write to the *Marketing Department, Penguin Books Ltd, P.O. Box 257, Ringwood, Victoria 3134.*

In New Zealand: For a complete list of books available from Penguin in New Zealand, please write to the *Marketing Department, Penguin Books (NZ) Ltd, Private Bag, Takapuna, Auckland 9.*

In India: For a complete list of books available from Penguin, please write to *Penguin Overseas Ltd, 706 Eros Apartments, 56 Nehru Place, New Delhi, 110019.*

In Holland: For a complete list of books available from Penguin in Holland, please write to *Penguin Books Nederland B.V., Postbus 195, NL-1380AD Weesp, Netherlands.*

In Germany: For a complete list of books available from Penguin, please write to *Penguin Books Ltd, Friedrichstrasse 10-12, D-6000 Frankfurt Main I, Federal Republic of Germany.*

In Spain: For a complete list of books available from Penguin in Spain, please write to *Longman, Penguin España, Calle San Nicolas 15, E-28013 Madrid, Spain.*

In Japan: For a complete list of books available from Penguin in Japan, please write to *Longman Penguin Japan Co Ltd, Yamaguchi Building, 2-12-9 Kanda Jimbocho, Chiyoda-Ku, Tokyo 101, Japan.*